Veteran Activism and the Global War on Terror

Veteran Activism and the Global War on Terror

Post-9/11 Narratives of Dissent and American War Literature

M. C. Armstrong

BLOOMSBURY ACADEMIC
NEW YORK • LONDON • OXFORD • NEW DELHI • SYDNEY

BLOOMSBURY ACADEMIC
Bloomsbury Publishing Inc, 1359 Broadway, New York, NY 10018, USA
Bloomsbury Publishing Plc, 50 Bedford Square, London, WC1B 3DP, UK
Bloomsbury Publishing Ireland, 29 Earlsfort Terrace, Dublin 2, D02 AY28, Ireland

BLOOMSBURY, BLOOMSBURY ACADEMIC and the Diana logo are
trademarks of Bloomsbury Publishing Plc

First published in the United States of America 2024
This paperback edition published 2026

Copyright © M. C. Armstrong, 2024

For legal purposes the Acknowledgments on p. vi constitute an
extension of this copyright page.

Cover design: Eleanor Rose
Cover image: The younger brother of Mohamedou Ould Slahi, Yahdih Ould Slahi poses with a copy of Mohamedou's prison memoir 'Guantanamo Diary' open to show pages that were redacted by the US government in London on January 20, 2015. Photo © Ben Stansall / AFP / Getty Images

All rights reserved. No part of this publication may be: i) reproduced or transmitted in any form, electronic or mechanical, including photocopying, recording or by means of any information storage or retrieval system without prior permission in writing from the publishers; or ii) used or reproduced in any way for the training, development or operation of artificial intelligence (AI) technologies, including generative AI technologies. The rights holders expressly reserve this publication from the text and data mining exception as per Article 4(3) of the Digital Single Market Directive (EU) 2019/790.

Bloomsbury Publishing Inc does not have any control over, or responsibility for, any third-party websites referred to or in this book. All internet addresses given in this book were correct at the time of going to press. The author and publisher regret any inconvenience caused if addresses have changed or sites have ceased to exist, but can accept no responsibility for any such changes.

Library of Congress Cataloging-in-Publication Data
Names: Armstrong, M. C., author.
Title: Veteran activism and the global war on terror : post-9/11 narratives of dissent and American war literature / M. C. Armstrong.
Description: New York : Bloomsbury Academic, 2024. |
Includes bibliographical references and index.
Identifiers: LCCN 2024006164 (print) | LCCN 2024006165 (ebook) |
ISBN 9798765112861 (hardback) | ISBN 9798765112854 (paperback) |
ISBN 9798765112878 (ebook) | ISBN 9798765112885 (pdf)
Subjects: LCSH: Veterans' writings, American–History and criticism. |
War on Terrorism, 2001–2009, in literature. | Dissenters in literature. |
American literature–21st century–History and criticism.
Classification: LCC PS153.V48 A76 2024 (print) | LCC PS153.V48 (ebook) |
DDC 810.9/3581–dc23/eng/20240508
LC record available at https://lccn.loc.gov/2024006164
LC ebook record available at https://lccn.loc.gov/2024006165

ISBN:	HB:	979-8-7651-1286-1
	PB:	979-8-7651-1285-4
	ePDF:	979-8-7651-1288-5
	eBook:	979-8-7651-1287-8

Typeset by Integra Software Services Pvt. Ltd.

For product safety related questions contact productsafety@bloomsbury.com.

To find out more about our authors and books visit www.bloomsbury.com
and sign up for our newsletters.

Contents

Acknowledgments		vi
I	The Challengers—Fearless Speech from the Forever War	1
	1. Parrhesia and the Conceptual Apparatus of Outspokenness: From Rhetoric and Politics to Aesthetic Analysis	3
	2. The Map of the Territories: Argument Structure	25
II	Disidentity Politics	31
	1. More than Ground Zero: Mall Warriors and Patriotic Correctness	35
	2. Geographies of Value: Klay's *Redeployment*	49
	3. Truth in Digital Space: Snowden's *Permanent Record*	60
III	The FOB and Beyond: Patriotism at the Limit	77
	1. Democracy in No Man's Land: Elliot Ackerman's "The Fourth War"	82
	2. Empathic Unsettlement: Ackerman's *Green on Blue*	92
	3. The Sheepdog: Transgender and Trans-space in Beck's *Warrior Princess*	103
IV	Extraordinary Renditions	117
	1. Staging Dissensus	118
	2. Stay Deviant: Powers's *The Yellow Birds*	127
	3. Camp No: Hickman's *Murder at Camp Delta*	139
V	Conclusion—Ethics, Style, Space: The Soldier-Writer Subculture	153
Notes		164
Bibliography		177
Index		180

Acknowledgments

In March of 2008, I traveled to Iraq as a freelance journalist to embed with Joint Special Operations Forces. Fifteen years later, I find myself completing the project that began on the banks of the Euphrates River with that first immersion in America's military community. There's no way to adequately thank all of the people who made this journey possible, but I will be forever indebted to Christian Moraru for his guidance of this work during my time in the doctoral program at the University of North Carolina at Greensboro. Christian's scholarship, kindness, and patience have been a compass all these years. Many thanks to Anthony Cuda, Stephen Yarborough, and Nancy Myers for their advocacy and careful attention to early drafts of this book during my time at UNCG. Thanks to MaxieJane Frazier, a veteran of the Air Force Academy and an excellent writer and editor, for her nuanced critiques of these chapters. Additionally, there is no way this book is born without the courageous voices in the military writing community who have given so generously of their time to help me see this world as more than a monolith. Adrian Bonenberger, Randy Brown, James Burns, Caleb Cage, Tracy Crow, Mary Doyle, Erik Edstrom, Amalie Flynn, Colin Halloran, Bettina Hindes, Peter Molin, Cat Parnell, Brian Turner, Andria Williams, and the late George Kovach of *Consequence Magazine* were all instrumental in challenging my assumptions, expanding my reading list, and inspiring this book.

In the same vein, I would like to thank all of the writers included in this book, but Joseph Hickman, in particular, for taking the time to visit my classroom at Duke University when I was teaching in the Talent Identification Program. If I had not seen so many young people respond with such enthusiasm to the words and deeds of Hickman, I do not think I would have ever undertaken this project. Joe is a profile in courage.

Additionally, thanks are certainly due to Hali Han and Haaris Naqvi of Bloomsbury. My deepest gratitude to you both for supporting this study and the voices of these brave writers who have risked so much.

Finally, I would like to thank Kurt Muhler, Steven Van Newton, Chris Porter, and my father, all of whom served and all of whom, many years ago, took the time to tell me their stories.

I love you all.

I

The Challengers—Fearless Speech from the Forever War

This book offers a literary and cultural analysis of American veteran-activists after the attacks of September 11, 2001. Their discourse, I contend throughout, challenges pivotal assumptions about allegiance, solidarity, national identity, and the political-emotional maps of responsibility as well as belonging that artists, activists, and citizens at large mentally draw up as they picture their affiliations with and duties to a community, territory, country, or state institution. Specifically, I read the works of these soldier-writers as the loci of a "dissenting" overhaul of such maps during the United States' Global War on Terror.

My study focuses not only on the book-length narratives such writers have composed but also on these authors' new media presence. One such writer is Edward Snowden, a military veteran. In his case, the interweaving of evolving digital discourse and hermetically sealed narrative is particularly instructive. Shortly after the attacks on 9/11 and prior to blowing the whistle on several secret domestic surveillance programs in the United States, Snowden chose to serve in his country's military. He enlisted in the United States Army on May 7, 2004. On January 18, 2018, eight months away from publishing his memoir, Snowden, while under asylum in Russia, tweeted that "65 senators just voted to expand an unconstitutional law permitting Trump to spy on communications with one leg in the US—without a warrant. For the next six years, any unencrypted internet request that even touches a US border will be 'ingested' (intercepted) and parsed by NSA."[1]

Here is a quintessentially contemporary rhetorical moment and "Ur-scene" of my project: a former American soldier performing digital activism against his government from Russia through a multinational corporation's constrained and multimodal interface. Using Twitter's (now X's) social media platform, Snowden is encouraging dissent against a state he once defended as an intelligence officer. While he is charged with espionage by his "homeland," Snowden is openly encouraging the citizens of his nation to resist their state, maintaining that S.139, the bill in question, represents "an unconstitutional law," and he makes this argument while under the care of a Russian government and intelligence service that were being investigated by the US government for the 2016 election interference. His tweet is a unique species of rhetoric, both textual and visual. It contains within it an embedded tweet from the Electronic Frontier Foundation, which submits that "[t]he bill, S.139, is a disaster for our constitutional rights" and goes on to declare that "EFF vehemently opposes the passage of it. It allows our government to spy on its own citizens without justification."[2] Thus, living in Russia, this former North Carolina resident, US citizen, contractor, soldier, and soon-to-be author, is pleading alongside and literally on top of an international nonprofit that advocates for digital rights located in San Francisco, California. Location-wise, then, Snowden is a political subject who, one could claim, is "all over the map." But the rhetorical and geographical complexity of his circumstances does not change the fact that, politically speaking, he is still a citizen of a particular nation, the United States. Thus, as long as Snowden avoids trial and maintains his position online, he operates at and ultimately represents a new frontier of identity, a whole new species of political subject. Now it's important to mention the novelty of his position is not just a matter of physical location. W.E.B. Du Bois and James Baldwin, just to name a few, spoke up against the American government while in self-imposed exile in Ghana and France, respectively. But Du Bois and Baldwin, whose citizenship status, as Black, was also unique, were not veterans, and they knew nothing of the Internet. In other words, Snowden's current whereabouts (Russia), coupled with the spatial target of his outspokenness (the United States), are not the sole element at odds with an official contemporary world mapping that has traditionally determined a nation-state's territorial jurisdiction as the geographical purview of political self-expression. From Russia and Twitter/X, Snowden, with his unique citizen status, voices opinions about "us" *over here*, whereas, from the United States and other places in the world, other veterans in this study express concerns about "others" *over there*, outside the United States. Inside and outside the national territory, these authors, with their unique citizen status, in turn deterritorialize critically mainstream understandings of duty, patriotism, and political identity. They problematize and reconstruct these notions, successively decoupling and recoupling them from and with the very national territory in relation to which such ideas and values have been forged and practiced throughout modernity. They stage a new species of dissent.

1. Parrhesia and the Conceptual Apparatus of Outspokenness: From Rhetoric and Politics to Aesthetic Analysis

Three concepts structure this book's argument about the contemporary rhetorical moment broadly and about the narratives of post-9/11 American soldier-writers more specifically: parrhesia, dissensus, and cosmopolitanism. Given the elasticity of these concepts in diverse areas of study, a few clarifications are in order. Stepping back and forth across continuously shifting frontiers, Snowden, to begin with, is surely not the only one participating in the de- and re-territorialization of subjectivity, agency, and responsibility and in the redrawing of his country's and the world's political and ethical maps. Torn between allegiances and between moral choices, and enabled by the fast-expanding Internet and social-media culture, this geopolitically fluid and legally complex kind of American identity is what this book seeks to identify. Specific to this identity is an evolving subculture of military "truth-tellers" to lift a term from Foucault and his lectures on "fearless speech" and "parrhesia." Parrhesia, with its long history tied to the story of the world's first democracy, is essential to addressing the current problems of leaking, whistleblowing, and the narrative activism of a warrior caste at war with its own history.

Appearing in literature for the first time in the works of Euripides, parrhesia, like most significant philosophical and rhetorical concepts, has evolved across centuries. In Eurpides's *Ion*, not unlike in the narratives of post-9/11 soldier-writers, location and dislocation are essential variables in the civic and literary enterprise of outspokenness. Basic to the idea of parrhesia, a term that occurs in the New Testament of the original Bible more than thirty times, has remained the Ancient Greek valuation of brave truth-telling or free ("fearless") speech.[3] Parrhesia refers to dutiful speaking out that places the citizen of a democracy at risk. Ancient Greece, generally, and Athens, specifically, are in fact where this term was born. Not only was Athens a city-state located between what many now call the East and the West, but it was, again, the mythical birthplace of democracy. In *Ion*, Euripides's narrative changes the traditional Athenian location of truth-telling from the oracle at Delphi to the city-state of Athens. Ion is a young man who lives at Delphi and does not know his lineage. He is unaware that he was fathered by the god Apollo. In his quest to understand the truth of his life, Ion must travel to Athens where his mother, Creusa, lives. His understanding of the truth comes not from a God outside of civilization but from human beings within the city-state. His struggle, however, pays off because it occasions an important insight:

> If I may express a prayer, may my mother be a woman of Athens / So that on my mother's side free speaking is my right. / An alien entering a city of pure blood, / though he be technically a citizen, / does not enjoy free speech—his lips are fettered.[4]

Here readers see the relationship between citizenry and truth-telling and the problem of speaking one's truth as fundamentally related to one's location and one's political status within that place and its polity. As the American soldier-writer, Phil Klay, argues in *The Citizen-Soldier: Moral Risk and the Modern Military*, a soldier's conception of citizenry is shaped by a sense of special responsibility to the places where he or she has served. Unlike many civilians and politicians living stateside, Klay writes, "it's impossible for the veteran to pretend he has clean hands."[5] Likewise, Ion's ability to perceive and speak the truth depends on his voyaging *beyond* the walls of his home at Delphi and into the contested realms of political speech he encounters in his motherland, Athens.

More than two thousand years after *Ion*, Foucault gave his series of lectures on Euripides, parrhesia, and the problems of truth-telling. *Fearless Speech*, the book that emerged out of those talks at the University of California, Berkeley, in 1983, provides useful critical context for understanding Euripides's work, but the location of Foucault's lectures, the United States, and his dislocation from his homeland, France, are also worth noting. France and America have offered the world two very different stories of revolution, terror, and democracy. Foucault's lectures, therefore, triangulate the struggles of the two countries with a third study in democracy: Athens. Building on Foucault's emphasis on location and his careful attention to the role different identities play in the human struggle for truth, I argue in this book for what I call a "disidentity politics." For Ion is only able to tell the truth when his false identity is revealed to him by his mother, Creusa. Creusa, who was raped by Apollo, is involved in a struggle quite different from her son's. As Foucault writes, she "will not use parrhesia to speak the truth about Athenian political life to the king, but rather to publicly accuse Apollo for his misdeeds."[6] Ion's struggle is bold, but Creusa's may be bolder, for she challenges the gods. Like Foucault and Snowden, Creusa and Ion offer students of democracy and truth-telling different paradigms for understanding the relationships among identity, truth, location, and authority. But unlike

Foucault, and much like Ion, Snowden himself reveals a new identity through his new location. If Ion's new location was Athens, then Snowden's is the Internet.

Let readers recall, too, that Snowden is neither the first American rebel nor the first American soldier to take a parrhesiac stand against his government and state apparatuses. Before the American Revolution was won, George Washington also represented such a politically and territorially "liminal" identity. Prior to their becoming America's "founding fathers," the leaders of the American Revolution were viewed as children by George III, a king who once famously said, "A traitor is everyone who does not agree with me."[7] To be an American, one might conclude in a similar vein, is to be, from the very beginning, part of an identity historically tied to parrhesia, dissent, and resistance to political authority. To be an American, whether one is a chained slave or a Virginia squire who writes of freedom while keeping slaves, is to live in that liminal zone between ideal and institution, nation and state, "here" and "there," and nation-state and other nations-states and their "others." Although there is some debate as to whether the most violent actions of the "founding fathers," like Samuel Adams and the Sons of Liberty, would now be constructed as acts of terrorism, it is safe to say that these men disidentified with the laws and allegiance assumptions passed or promoted by their government and argued that specific laws of England ran counter to "higher" laws and "commonsense." In light of such conflict, the "founding fathers" declared the laws of the crown null and void and subject to civil and not-so-civil disobedience. This parrhesiac dynamic becomes complicated as one moves through American history, particularly the Southern secession, the Civil War, and the Internet, but it is this pattern of rebellion based on a rhetoric of appeals to elusive codes that recurrently marks the American identity, broadly, and the identity of the post-9/11 soldier-writer community, specifically. When applied to this history of rebellion, parrhesia provides a sound rhetorical lens for grounding a contemporary community of citizens with deep concerns about the future of America's experiment with democracy, whether these individuals are located outside the US territory, like Snowden, or inside it, like Joseph Hickman, another veteran who has blown the whistle—this time on the death of three detainees at Guantánamo Bay.

Whereas Snowden's "brave speech" now issues from Russia after his refusal to obey the chain-of-command, Hickman, by contrast, followed his chain-of-command and remained behind in the American homeland to tell his story about the murders of Ali Abdullah Ahmed, Mani al-Utaybi, and Yasser al-Zahrani. There was once a secret detention center on the grounds of Guantánamo Bay,

America's most notorious international prison. Camp No, as the detention center was called by Hickman and other soldiers, was a facility about a mile and a half from the border of Cuba and about three hundred yards away from Camp America where Hickman manned the watchtower over the detainees. As Hickman writes in *Murder at Camp Delta*, "we would nickname the place Camp No—as in 'No, it's not there.'"[8] But this liminal facility did, in fact, exist and was revealed in 2013 to have been a secret CIA interrogation center focused on converting Global War on Terror detainees into double agents. The Central Intelligence Agency referred to the facility as "Penny Lane," outsourcing its nominal provenance to London, England, but I often think of this community of veteran-activists as "Camp No" because the place name subverts the double agency of the place's official purpose and speaks to the dissensual attitude of the soldiers whose stories shine a light of truth and reconciliation into the darkness of these ongoing wars.

The phrase "dissensual attitude of the soldiers" introduces reiterations of a term I intend to trouble in this work. Like "parrhesia," dissensus is a rhetorical mechanism of challenge, disruption, and disidentification with a polity, group, state agency, and so forth. At the same time, and most importantly, dissensus also entails, and can also *be*, an aesthetic—an aesthetic of dissent. Although, to be clear, participation in the staging of dissensus or disidentification with, say, a religion or polity, is not necessarily an act of atheism or treachery. On the contrary, dissensus may imply that what appears binary or monolithic to one appears riddled with complexity, tension, and division to another. What dissensus does is reveal that tension by staging a gap within conceptual categories. When artists and scholars seek to challenge contemporary assumptions and by the same token the inherited maps of affiliation and perception, readers are right to mirror skepticism with skepticism. But what if there is indeed a gap or a rot in the construction of those cherished conceptual categories without which the very drawing of those maps—of those pictures and limitations of our associations and self-identifications—would have been impossible in the first place? For example, the concept of nation implies both immaterial principle and material government, idea and institution. The nation is often laden with the implication of state. But, if so, must then loyalty to nation always equate with fealty to state? If the sovereign notion of the nation is usefully complicated by the claim that a nation's principles and actual actions may often be at odds in places like Guantánamo Bay, what other identity categories are marked by such schisms and who are the most qualified social groups to speak to and render sensible such divisions?

An American citizen who has been deployed all over the globe often possesses unique insights about the intersection of a territorially understood or "territorialized" nation, on one side, and "the world," on the other. Soldier-writers, like Hickman and Snowden, repurpose their privilege and their access to primary and classified materials to challenge their nation's mission and expand the territory of American patriotism. As the leak of *The Afghanistan Papers* demonstrates, many such "citizen-soldiers," as Klay labels them, have offered valuable dissenting opinions that were ignored within their chains of command, leading to tens of thousands of casualties, a global refugee crisis, and countless victims of torture. But, again, dissenting opinions are nothing new. The presence of a soldier's words in *The Senate Intelligence Committee Report on CIA Torture, The Afghanistan Papers,* or any number of other official primary national documents from the Forever War is not the focus of this book. In my project, the "dissensual" derives not just from the lay idea of dissent but also from Jacques Rancière's concept of dissensus as a stylistic mechanism that unifies the rhetorical and the aesthetic. Dissensus stages a break or a porous border and, thereby, seeks to alter "the distribution of the sensible" and complicate or collapse the binaries of personal/political, passive/active, and aesthetics/politics. I engage the complexities of Rancière's term in depth later on, but as an opening gambit, let me specify that dissensus, contrary to consensus, begins when artists "make the invisible visible, and make what was deemed to be the mere noise of suffering bodies heard as a discourse concerning the 'common' of the community."[9] Accordingly, my study maps the territory where, specifically, soldier-writers speak out and disidentify with a narrow, nation-state commons and its physical-symbolic space only to "redistribute," as Rancière would say, the latter so as to expand through this space of responsibility a care, and with it an ethical identity outside the comfort zone of kin, kind, and nation-state borders. Through this parrhesiac redistribution and dilation of tangible public space, these soldiers chart a new map of dissent and worldly involvement.

Rancière's theory of dissensus helps readers apprehend this emerging map. Foundational to my work is, then, a close reading of soldier-writer narratives alongside an engagement with Rancière, particularly *Dissensus: Politics and Aesthetics* and *The Lost Thread: The Democracy of Modern Fiction*, as these two texts share the dominant concern of the American soldier-writers: the democratization of literature in the face of authoritarianism masquerading as democracy. Furthermore, *Dissensus*, first published in 2010, latches onto the same geopolitical conflict as the context for its concern: the Global War on

Terror. Again and again, in *Dissensus*, Rancière returns to America's invasion and occupation of Iraq in light of the 9/11 attacks. Two decades have now passed since those attacks and the beginning of that war. In *Dissensus*, Rancière challenges the reader to witness, in the inception of the Iraq War, the problem of "consensus." One cannot fully fathom Rancière's political-aesthetic and his concept of dissensus without first appreciating what he states as an elementary problem: how in the West, broadly, and in America, specifically, "politics proper has been replaced by consensus."[10] Without any real debate and inquiry from Congress, the administration of George W. Bush led America to war with a country that did not attack the United States. Rather than challenge the Bush administration through the democratic processes available to them, America's citizenry accepted the Bush argument that the terrorists hated America for its "freedom" or, as Rancière paraphrases, "they hate us because freedom is our very way of life."[11] Rancière argues that a politics based on "way of life" is no politics at all, at least not in the traditional sense. This mode of politics as sensible style or "way of life" translates into a culture war fought on the fronts of religion, ethnicity, and identity more broadly. The problem of consensus is the problem of politics without a representation of the true voices of the people, without the dissenting "freedoms" that clash in a state truly marked by "freedom." Far from the ideal community of democratic citizens animated by conflict and dissenting voices, Rancière's consensus is, instead, descriptive of the America that, in the wake of 9/11, traded animated citizenship for naive consumerism or worse. Consensus, rather than democracy, describes a public bullied into the Global War on Terror. Consensus marks a shift from democracy to something else, a move Rancière essentially deems a shift from politics to ethics and aesthetics. If this is, indeed, the new game, he claims, perhaps one needs to learn how to play it, and by "play it" Rancière means inverting its processes. "Consensus," Rancière writes, "is the form by which politics is transformed into the police."[12] Dissensus, in turn, takes this new theater of the state with its media commodities and stages an aesthetic process that repurposes the policing and the divisive identity politics.

Dissensus, like parrhesia, addresses the crisis of a democracy in the midst of a charade. What is the relationship between politics and theater? What is a democracy without outspokenness or free speech? What is a democracy without dissent and what does one mean by dissent other than simple discrete acts of "yes" and "no" in response to government policies? The propaganda of the consensual state must be met, Rancière submits, with the political-aesthetic of the demos staged in the sensible space of the new public spheres. In *The Lost Thread: The*

Democracy of Modern Fiction, Rancière deepens his argument for such a staging as an inversion of police-states in which the demos utilize both propaganda and art to overthrow the enterprise of politics. As Steven Corcoran writes in the introduction to *The Lost Thread*, Rancière's theory of dissensus represents "nothing less than a revolution in the ontology of fiction."[13] The revolutionary practices of dissensus, *The Lost Thread* makes clear, did not begin with the attacks of 9/11. What makes Rancière's argument about the birth of modern or democratic fiction so compelling is the way in which he roots his theory in the works of writers like Joseph Conrad, Gustave Flaubert, and Virginia Woolf. Here in the modernists and the precursors of modernism, readers see the "new fiction" that continues to seed and evolve the historicity of the present. Fundamental to this seeding is an "excess" body of sensory materials, a narrative environment that has been flooded with disruptive empathy and democratized and populated by seemingly "superfluous" details: names, places, and things external to insular and chronological plots. These excesses unsettle the Aristotelian pleasures of hermetically sealed stories and linear cause and effect narratives mapped more by time than space. The truth effects of these sensory glints from the "outside" subvert the aesthetic ideal of the walled-in narrative imaginary and offer, in its place, a new spatiality, a porous interactive operating system in which the boundary between "inside" and "outside" breaks down. "*The Lost Thread*," Corcoran claims, "turns precisely on the singular ways in which the new fiction reinscribes this outside—of things and people encountered in the randomness of life within itself."[14] The map of resistance readers witness in the narratives of the American soldier-writer *community* is, indeed, coded with this particular excess of the *trans-communal*, of the outside, of the broader world's "things and people." Their fiction is constantly ontologized by leaks from their history and their histories are constantly problematized by the conceits of their stories. Thus, just as Rancière's theory expands space and blurs the line between politics and aesthetics, so do the narratives of soldier-writers like Snowden and Hickman trouble the divides between narrative and rhetoric as well as nation and state.

To be sure, the theories of Rancière and the narratives of a small cadre of American writers are not the only rhetorics resisting and testing the old borders. This map of challenged boundaries would certainly be incomplete if it excluded the territories of the Internet. That is to say, the kinds of spaces I am talking about are not just theoretical but are also material in a traditional (geophysical) *and* digital sense. The American experiment with democracy has been, to say the least, troubled by globalization and the digital revolution. The same "worlding" forces that gave birth to the First World War and its aesthetic twin, modernism, continue to impact contemporary writers, the contemporary understanding of the planet, and the reader's sense of a shared humanity. The electronic frontier, the rise of the Internet, and the birth of what Fred Turner calls "cyberculture" are surely part of the central context for understanding this new cosmopolitan figure.

Admittedly, referring to these soldier-writers as "cosmopolitans" risks creating confusion. As is well known, such a charged identity term has been favored by Fascist and Communist dictators like Hitler and Stalin, for whom it was a slur. The frequently misunderstood ideas implicit within cosmopolitanism, in the words of scholar Martha Nussbaum, challenge "the limits of our patriotism," but it is precisely this ethical provocation to narrow concepts of patriotism and citizenship that interest me.[15] Between the old concepts of national identity and the more recent "politics of difference," a new kind of cosmopolite has emerged of late that challenges both. Cosmopolitan identity, as Nussbaum points out, is not incompatible with partiality to nation or the valuation of diversity. Furthermore, cosmopolitan discourse is grounded, like parrhesia, in the works of the ancient Greeks and their experiment with democracy. Early cosmopolites, like Diogenes the Cynic, believed in an identity based not so much on nation or province but on "more universal aspirations and concerns."[16] In keeping with the etymological root of the word, Diogenes, when asked where he came from, famously replied, "I am a citizen of the world." Likewise, the soldier-writers of this study do not position their identity as opposed to any one nation or as a function of single nations, races, religions, or genders. They build their ethos instead by challenging such concepts across transnational spaces and in the name of distant others and "more universal aspirations and concerns."

By the same token, this book complicates the traditional and liberal discourse of cosmopolitanism. There is a powerful irony in some of the core critiques of contemporary cosmopolitan theory. Francis Fukuyama is famous for extolling the virtues of globalization and free-market capitalism, as well as for his prediction that the fall of the Berlin Wall would lead to "the end of history." In *The End of History and The Last Man*, Fukuyama makes the argument that culture and economics can be separated, a position he quickly modifies in subsequent works. But before the folly of his most famous claims became apparent in the epoch that followed after 9/11, Fukuyama was still at the forefront of defending globalization as an economic model while, at the same time, disdainfully attacking the premise that nations and individuals should evolve a code of responsibility to the distant others they encounter in this new globalized economic system. In 1997, writing in *Foreign Affairs*, Fukuyama eviscerates Nussbaum's argument for a new cosmopolitanism in her book, *For Love of Country: Debating the Limits of Patriotism*. As he writes, "cosmopolitanism has no emotional appeal to anyone except a small group of intellectuals like the author herself, and perhaps a stratum of CEOs of multinationals for whom she presumably has little sympathy." A member of the policy elite himself, Fukuyama dismisses cosmopolitanism as a theory whose only appeal is to a tiny cadre of intellectuals. But there is nothing inherently wrong with "a small group of intellectuals" offering new ideas. And intellectuals offering skepticism about the opinions of a minority report within the world of intellectuals is common practice in American history. Still, Fukuyama is not without a point. The charge of elitism and class bias, albeit from a man employed by the RAND corporation, is not without value. As long as cosmopolitanism remains nothing more than "a small group of intellectuals" and a small "stratum of CEOs of multinationals," its impact will be, proportionally, small. Until something like a working-class or "grass-roots" cosmopolitanism emerges, the ideas of cosmopolitans will be easily dismissed by the gatekeepers of nationalism and globalism alike. However, the post-9/11 soldier-writer is one of the harbingers of a new type of cosmopolitanism.

Much the same as whistleblowers such as Snowden, who are often attacked on the grounds of identity rather than the quality of their arguments or of the data they disclose, cosmopolitans have often been assaulted in a very particular identity territory: the grounds of class. Thus, a "popular" cosmopolitanism represents a significant intervention in cosmopolitan discourse. But even if American soldier-writers do constitute a new kind of cosmopolite, such an identity status does not leave them immune from criticism. For instance, is the post-9/11 soldier-writer who is now embedded as an advisor in the bunkers of Ukraine virtuous simply for the sake of an ostensible transnational concern? And how is such a figure viewed by writers from the countries he or she once occupied? Hassan Blasim, the acclaimed Iraqi author of *The Corpse Exhibition* and other works of fiction, addressed this issue when he was recently asked about including American soldiers in his stories of the Iraq war. He revealed that he "deliberately ignored" American soldiers in his work, claiming that their narratives were part of a capitalist profit machine. "America occupied Iraq," Blasim said. "Then oil companies came to profit, then Hollywood made heroes of the war and it too profited." For Blasim, American soldier-writers are not so much critics as "stars" that were "created in the realms of politics, war, arts, and literature."¹⁷ Thus, even if I do confer, say, a working-class status upon the American soldier, the echo of Fukuyama's questions about cosmopolitanism and class still remains when the conversation turns to the soldier as soldier-writer. The industrial labors of the soldiers have turned into the intellectual commodity productions of writers and some, like Blasim, view such work as indistinct from the entertainments produced by the "stars" of Hollywood.

Hasty as their generalizations may be, there is more than a kernel of truth in the criticisms of Fukuyama and Blasim. Cosmopolites of the sort scrutinized here—"combat cosmopolites," as I sometimes call them—present a host of problems, just as any identity category does. Let it be clearly stated: no identity category is sacred. Post-9/11 soldier-writers are not saviors, and these veteran-activists are certainly not a class of individuals free from ethical indictments on the grounds of participation in occupation, appropriation, exploitation, imperialism, torture, ecological destruction, or surveillance capitalism. Pioneering as their rhetoric and rhetorical identities may be, many of these individuals were also the pioneers of the assassin drone, cyberwarfare, and the psychological operations that traumatized innocent civilians across nations. But rather than condemn all American soldiers to the dehumanized role of demon and all Iraqis or Afghans to the parallel dehumanized role of angel, this book seeks to explore more challenging territory and to investigate the problems of empathy, ethics, and truth-telling in this complicated conversation where cosmopolites from all countries are compelled to consider the role of the other in the fight for a more humane, just, and inevitably shared future.

On this account, the works of Nussbaum and other cosmopolitanism scholars like her are instrumental to this pursuit of new, less "high-brow," martial cosmopolitanism. Nussbaum's essay, "Patriotism and Cosmopolitanism," and the book that emerged out of that work, *For Love of Country*, supply a rhetorical framework for reimagining cosmopolitanism as a way of thinking that is not necessarily opposed to patriotism or love of America's revolutionary principles. Incidentally but notably enough, Joshua Cohen, Nussbaum's co-author in *For Love of Country*, was also one of the editors for *Permanent Record*, Snowden's 2019 memoir. In the repurposing of the rhetoric of the frontier in *Permanent Record*, readers will find a bridge between Nussbaum's argument and Snowden's, a deep valuation of the transnational experience framed as a means for extending abroad, to others elsewhere, American values like liberty, democracy, and free speech.

Nussbaum's mission in *For Love of Country* is educational. Written prior to 9/11 and America's destabilization of the Middle East, her book imagines a pedagogical future in which American students recognize a special responsibility to distant others. Rooting her argument in the philosophy of the ancient Greeks, Nussbaum writes that the Stoics "insist that the vivid imagining of the different is an essential task of education."[18] While I agree with Nussbaum's thesis that a "vivid imagining of the different" can lead to various recognitions of universal aspirations, I see more than an educational mission here. In Nussbaum's critique, I read an opening for conversation about narrative ethics and the politics of aesthetics in a vein similar to Christian Moraru who, in his 2011 book *Cosmodernism*, builds on Nussbaum's argument for a new cosmopolitanism. Recognizing that ideas evolve and are rarely discrete artifacts trapped in one time and one place, Moraru synthesizes current notions of cosmopolitanism with the evolving discourse on modernism and postmodernism to suggest a new contemporary aesthetic, which he dubs *cosmodernism*. Moraru maps his aesthetic in the new cultural territory unfolded worldwide after the fall of the Berlin Wall, the digital revolution, and the "cosmopolitan studies boom" of the late 1990s. Like Nussbaum, he finds useful precedent for the new cosmopolitanism in ancient Greece, framing the Eurocentric flavor of globalization in terms of its Hellenic predecessors. He draws on the works of Kwame Anthony Appiah, Emily Apter, Rebecca Walkowitz, as well as Nussbaum and others, and he notes cosmopolitanism's imperial and evolutionary heritage. Moraru calls nuanced attention to the diversity within the discursive "boom." He suggests that readers investigate "cosmopolitanism*s* instead of cosmopolitanism."[19] Arguing for a new aesthetic that he locates in the patterns of post-1989 American narratives, Moraru finds, in Nussbaum's work, a vital part of the pattern. If America's revolutionary ideals are still relevant but simultaneously calcified by a history of imperialism, classism, and racism, how can an American patriotism be "decoupled from the national"?[20] How does a writer utilize American rhetoric—namely the very rhetoric of Americanness—to challenge the control of American interests over the planet and global narratives?

Questioning the US commitment to democracy and free speech, writers like Snowden and Hickman seem ideal case studies of patriotism pushed to its limits. From their respective locations in Russia and Guantánamo Bay, Snowden and Hickman beg readers to address the outspokenness of Americans from territories where silence and patriotism are synonymous, and freedom of expression is far from encouraged. The two authors present the reader with a martial cosmopolitan identity that was still nascent during the cosmopolitan boom of the 1990s. The American citizens who have been compelled to travel around the world in the Global War on Terror are not the same elites of international finance and luxury tourism that populate the late twentieth-century critiques of cosmopolitanism. I argue that this community of post-9/11 soldier-writers represents a new social group marked by compulsory violence, compulsory labor, and compulsory travel, but also, and most significantly, by a choice to speak out against military missions and on behalf of those others they were assigned to pacify, civilize, democratize, torture, and kill. Therefore, this "martial cosmopolitanism" or "combat cosmopolitanism" is not so much a function of wartime experience but of the personal decision to write boldly about the war experience and the encounter with the other on the new frontiers of world conflict.

The conceptual triad of parrhesia, dissensus, and cosmopolitanism is at play precisely in the disruptive spaces of these new frontiers. Such frontiers, once crossed by the writers' spatial reimaginings into other geopolitical and cultural terrains, redefine political allegiance, citizenship, and the act of terror by profoundly complicating all sense of national jurisdiction and obligation. Alongside Christianity's call for a law beyond Caesar's, and Enlightenment principles such as liberty, equality, and justice, one of the most important factors in forging the rhetoric of what it means to be an American is the evolving concept of the frontier and the social practices associated with it in the digital environments of the post-9/11 era. In *The Frontier in American History*, the historian Frederick Jackson Turner contends that "American social development has been continually beginning over again on the frontier. This perennial rebirth, this fluidity of American life, this expansion westward with its new opportunities, its continuous touch with the simplicity of primitive society furnish the forces dominating the American character."[21] Turner's antiquated and sentimental notion of the frontier has evolved into a complicated arche-concept that has been repurposed in diverse realms of discourse, and that evolution has certainly been catalyzed by the communities without place one finds on the Internet. The specific "community without place"—or without a single place, rather—I seek to map in this study is the post-9/11 cosmopolitan community of dissensual soldier-writers. Otherwise, it goes without saying that to assume the position of a cosmopolitan truth-teller from the Global War on Terror, the American writer must decide how to situate himself or herself on political, legal, and moral maps, what rules to follow and what rules to break depending on his or her notions of sovereignty, individual responsibility, legality, and so forth. For *the veteran-activist*, however, these rules are both aesthetic and real, and by real I mean legal and sometimes questionably so insofar as the Global War on Terror is a war without limit in time and space while still imposing rigorous boundaries on the terrain of its subjects. To operate in this geopolitical context inevitably leads to challenging these very limits and the conceptual, ethical-political maps they enforce, which is, in certain cases, equivalent to breaking the law of nation-state X while abiding by the law and possibly furthering the agenda of nation-state Y or transnational organization Z. Thus, to map this "forever war," the stakes are high nationally and internationally. My project, then, is a study of a contentious and troubled map drawn by a new community whose aesthetic I describe and analyze throughout as rhetorically parrhesiac, politically dissensual, and ethically cosmopolitan.

Ultimately, this is the story of the American soldier-writer challenging an old code in order to describe not just a new code but also the uncounted people and places where the old codes have been abandoned. However, this inquiry into codes and categories is not the story of every tweet, poem, play, and novel to have emerged out of these wars. Nor does my book tell the story of American dissent dating back to Daniel Ellsberg, John Brown, Aaron Burr, or George Washington. What I undertake, instead, is a study of the dissensual narratives of American soldier-writers post-9/11. My goal here is to bring to the fore fictional and nonfictional accounts by the men, women, and transgender individuals who have lived and fought on the conceptual and territorial frontiers of this war. Elliot Ackerman, Kristin Beck, Hickman, Klay, Kevin Powers, and Snowden all have two things in common: they served in the US Military, and they have stepped away from that service to tell their stories, sometimes with the government's permission and sometimes in such direct dissent that their stories have put their lives at risk. These veteran-activists write from a diversity of perspectives. Their discourse occasionally takes the traditional form of a novel or a short story. In the case of Beck and Snowden, it is a memoir but also a speech framed by the new rhetorical forms of the electronic frontier: the tweet and the YouTube video, the multiplicity of media indicative of the multitudinous message. Each of these soldiers has a unique story to tell, but a common thread runs throughout. Although a number of books could be written, and already have been written, about the new surveillance state, unlawful detention, torture, the corporatization of the military, and the demolition of American civil liberties, this book is not focused on any of these particular issues. The common thrust of this rhetoric and these narratives—and also a major focus here—is a concern that American principles, broadly, and the ideal of democracy, specifically, are in crisis and that awakening to this crisis has something to do with a new kind of subjectivity. My argument is that there is a new imaginary that scholars and writers are creating as we question and disidentify with traditional, national-geographical, and legal narratives. Indeed, the post-9/11 veteran-activist displays a way of envisioning and narrating the world, its spaces, and socioethical codes, that is profoundly cosmopolitan. The driving force behind this worldview is, to reemphasize, a parrhesiac rhetoric of free and dissensual speech. Referring to an ancient Greek concept of "fearless speech" that is incumbent upon a particular class of citizen within a democracy, parrhesia privileges not only fearless self-expression but also narrative, or storytelling, a mode of argumentation specific to the experiences of the speaker. One of the great appeals of literature is the way in which it approaches complex, historical, legal, and moral discourses from the intimate domain of the individual human psyche.

To give just a quick example, in "Psychological Operations," a story from *Redeployment*, his National Book Award-winning short story collection, Klay assumes the identity of Waguih, a veteran who is a Coptic Christian and is mistaken for a Muslim by Zara, herself a Muslim African-American woman at the US college Waguih attends after his most recent deployment to Iraq. "Psychological Operations" follows a conversation that dissolves in a classroom, fails in the formal mediation attempted by the university administration, and then gains strange traction in the detailed environment of a private moment that leads the reader back to Iraq. To anticipate the more extensive analysis of the story in this book's opening segment, I will note here that "Psychological Operations" reveals a "perverse" (Klay's words) but elegant snapshot of the outspoken and the dissensual as I define them in my book. "How could you kill your own people?" Zara asks Waguih, whom she initially mistakes for a Muslim. Waguih replies: "They're not my people." Zara, still under certain assumptions about Waguih due to his name and skin color, replies: "We're all one people."[22] Waguih gets into trouble at this point, as he bristles at Zara's pseudocosmopolitan presumptuousness. He makes a remark that Zara construes to be a threat to her life. He says to her, "I can kill Muslims as much as I like … Shit, in my religion, that's how you help an angel get its wings."[23] Common parlance might call this offensive comment a defense mechanism, a performance of brashness and stereotypical military-masculine bluster used to conceal a deeper vulnerability, but there is more going on here. As Klay writes:

There's a perversity in me that, when I talk to conservatives, makes me want to bash the war and, when I talk to liberals, defend it. I'd lived through the Bush administration fucking up on a colossal scale, but I'd also gotten a good look at the sort of state Zarqawi wanted to establish, and talking with anybody who thought they had a clear view of Iraq tended to make me want to rub shit in their eyes.[24]

A veteran of the United States Marine Corps, Klay is now a public writer. His character, Waguih, draws from the martial cosmopolitanism of his own past while at the same time expanding the haunt of this ethos. In short, fictional identity's fluidity, this identity's constitution and reconstitution in relation to others across spaces and political territories, is the purview of this book. Waguih's liminal status here, caught between the state of Klay, his avatar Waguih, Zarqawi, Bush, the Black of the Muslim, and the Black of the Coptic Christian, provides a clear example of the specific disidentification I read as a deep pattern in the rhetoric of American soldier-writers returning from the fight against world terrorism, shining light not just on the war that has led American soldiers to dissent but also on the new identities, the new rhetoric, and the new politics these authors' fictional and nonfictional dissensus suggests for our future. Yet again, this identity remaking occurs as people, notions, and values cross and are carried over spatially concrete, geographical expanses and cultural-material environments. Consider, for instance, how the sensory domain of Klay's story alters the "distribution" of such "sensible" continuum. As is well known, fundamental to Rancière's idea about democracy in literature is the reshuffling of the physical space of the story's world and the ensuing complication of plots. Rancière demonstrates how the dilation and unsettling of said world can suspend the linear, cause-effect logic and destroy "the hierarchical model subjecting parts to the whole and dividing humanity between an elite of active beings and a multitude of passive ones."[25] Zara and Waguih do not resolve their dispute in the institutional enclosures of the campus. The gap between this man and this woman is not bridged through the narration of formal logical processes, although these processes are part of the story. Instead, the story proceeds into increasingly informal territory where a bridge is built in the detailed moments of a private conversation.

Thus, the text tracks the spatial course of dissent. In the same vein, it is worth noting here that the key to dissensus, according to Rancière, is not in ideological proclamation but in texture, or the "blended fabric of perceptions and thoughts, of sensations and acts."²⁶ It is not in what authors say so much as it is in how they say and imagine it. This concept of dissensual style is bound to

> the new music of indistinction between the ordinary and the extraordinary, which seizes within the same tonality the lives of servants in the countryside and those of great ladies of the capital, the music expressing the capacity of anyone at all to experience any form of sensible experience at all.²⁷

This democratic texture is found in a story that does not choose to privilege the elite and ostensibly logical environment of the academy *or*, later, the informal conversation between Zara and Waguih that transpires over a hookah filled with "shisha." Far from prescribing a radical erasure of one identity or environment in the name of the other, Rancière's democratic aesthetic, instead, suggests there is a great ethical rupture to be achieved through the staging of decoupling and recoupling, an acumen in the placement of certain names in certain places. However, to simply deploy the names Zara and Waguih at an American higher-education institution in Massachusetts is not enough. Dissensus is not just affirmative action for racially coded language or carefully crafted backstory peppered with nods to the East. These contexts and names disrupt the place—Amherst College—of Klay's short story, but dissensus, at its pinnacle, is more than this. Where the reader truly begins to encounter dissensus is in its topology, in the spatial fabric of a text that decenters the regime change war in Iraq by situating it in a diversity of locations.

The story of the Iraq War's haunt is told in a classroom, an administrator's office, and then a porch of a rental property where a man and a woman smoke "shisha" and the woman arrives "ten minutes late" for this informal conversation. The man then asks the woman, after she finally does arrive, if she wants "rose- or apple-flavored tobacco, and when she said rose, I told her apple was better and she rolled her eyes and we went with that."²⁸ This smoky casual moment of dilation on the porch with the hookah foreshadows the rupture I will explore in greater depth in Chapter II. But for the time being, let it be clear that these sensory details are more than just tokens evoked to further an ideological agenda. On nearly every level, Klay's narrative redeploys conventions and by doing so challenges the representational order. The presence of Zara and Waguih on the porch of a rental property in a moment shrouded with smoke signifies not a grounding in ideology or identity but a deliberate deferral of meaning, an immersion in a sensory environment designed to reveal the illusion of separation and the characters' shared humanity.

Removed from the elite and formal location of conflict resolution in the Dean's office, the two characters resort on the porch to an informal reckoning of their own, and the context is storytelling and smoke from shisha, the Egyptian name for a tobacco one smokes through a water pipe. "No ideas but in things," said the poet, William Carlos Williams, but for Rancière it is more like "no ideas but in a clash of things."[29] Dissensus is an aesthetic of dissent that operates as a redistribution of the sensible. In Klay's story, the Egyptian smoke deranges the American rental house and makes it the setting where Waguih departs from Massachusetts, returns to Basic Training, and then travels overseas, to Fallujah. The shisha smoke envelops two out-of-place students, an American veteran and a Muslim woman. Here, in "the bubble of America," the bubble bursts and whole worlds cross over.

In this informal setting, Waguih describes the Battle of Fallujah and also the very particular psychological operations or "propaganda" he literally employed there to kill a man named Laith al-Tawhid.[30] But prior to narrating the death of al-Tawhid, Waguih sets the stage. When he explains that part of the psychological warfare in Fallujah involved flushing insurgents out of mosques using aggressive American music like "Eminem and AC/DC and Metallica," Klay is alerting his reader to the sudden clash of rap and mosque, rock and prayer, death metal and death chant. Indeed, Waguih narrates a battle of music on the streets of Fallujah: "We'd have something going on all the time. And the muj would play shit, too. Prayers and songs. There was one that cracked me up. It was like, 'We fight under the slogan Allahu Akbar. We have a date with death, and we're going to get our heads chopped off.'"[31] The name Waguih's unit of Marines gave this clash of music was "Lalafallujah," a hybrid of the American festival (Lollapalooza) and the Iraqi place-name: Fallujah.[32] Waguih described the earsplitting hubbub as a "music festival from hell." However, as constituent details in a story within a story, the "Lala" and the "Fallujah" open a window into the workings of dissensus mechanisms. Dissensus, or the democracy of modern fiction, obtains, according to Rancière, in "sensible equality" or "coexisting sensible states."[33] This coexistence can take place on the level of the sentence or the paragraph, but it can also be located in a single word. "Lalafallujah" tears down the wall between the domain of the American rock festival where banners of counterculture fly and the domain of the American soldier, together with his or her distant adversary. The stateside hippie, the deployed soldier, and the occupied Iraqi all meet in this story, on this porch, and on this narrated street in this very particular juxtaposition of syllables.

For dissensus is also a linguistic mechanism. It is a psychological operation all its own. It is a transformation of the story's sensory state, a condition not of placelessness or senselessness but of one place leaking into another, one territory's sensory details migrating into the other. When Waguih comes home from Fallujah, Klay has him tell Zara of his mother making him "kosheri" (Egyptian street food) in Virginia and his father taking him out "for a real American meal. Outback Steakhouse!" The irony of an Egyptian American father wanting his son to enjoy a "real American meal" at a place whose brand depends on an Australian locale for its exotic appeal is all part of the picture of the text's deliberate spatial policy. Australia is here. Iraq is here. The other is here within "the bubble of America." The other is over there on the streets of Fallujah. There is no gap. There is no outside. In Chapter II, I will explore in greater depth the way Waguih challenges his father in the telling of the story of the murder of Laith al-Tawhid and the subtle ways in which Klay describes a keen awareness not only of language as a weapons system but also of how and why the adversarial other's death "over there" must be afforded the same dignity as kith and kind "over here." Klay's Waguih, with his outspokenness and martially cosmopolitan take on war propaganda, provides readers a good contrasting foundation for understanding dissensus as a kind of anti-propaganda. A dissensual narrative, like Klay's, challenges the sensory partitions of the old fictions or what one might call "national literature." "Psychological Operations" begins with two entrenched identities engaged in formal argumentative discourse and the politics of difference. But when Waguih and Zara finally leave the formal sensory environment of the classroom and the administrative office, the guard goes down and the reader is drawn into a world of "shisha" smoke and "Lalafallujah," "the music of indistinction." Two human beings from different backgrounds collide, through story, and as the story unwinds and the darkness falls, the characters begin to appreciate how little they understand about each other. Thus, "Psychological Operations" represents the failure of the representational order and addresses that failure by producing a useful confusion where unexpected names signify unexpected places and traditional identity categories are, thereby, revealed to be illusions. Under such a spell, Klay's characters speak out against each other and then, ultimately, speak disruptively with each other as human beings in a final dilated moment that is profoundly dissensual in that it allegorizes spatially "the sensible fabric within which the 'illusions' are produced."[34] In the end, Zara and Waguih do not marry, make love, or even kiss, but these two identities, through this disruptive sensory state, become characters aware of a shared but contrarian essence. They detach and bond. They become cognizant, in the words of the philosopher Emmanuel Levinas, that "the other is in no way another myself."[35] Klay's story, therefore, showcases the power of the conceptual triad by spotlighting a spatial aesthetic integrating parrhesiac rhetoric, dissensual politics, and cosmopolitan ethics.

Klay, Hickman, Snowden, and other soldier-writers demonstrate the disruptive act of a very particular class of citizens speaking truth to power. These writers explicitly challenge the established symbolic order via an imaginary of spatial redistributions that actually allow for and reinforce ethical and political redefinitions. Instrumental to the study of this complex effort is, then, my engagement not only with recent scholarship on the conceptual triad deployed above, parrhesia, dissensus, and cosmopolitanism but also with how their interplay inside and outside the works of soldier-writers might prompt significant change at the level of political subjectivity and action. In the philosopher and sociologist Geoffroy de Lagasnerie's *The Art of Revolt*, Lagasnerie describes a new kind of political subject emerging in the post-9/11 world. Like me, Lagasnerie sees Snowden (as well as Julian Assange and Chelsea Manning) as representative of this new identity. Essential to this book is, then, an argument for expanding the parrhesiac parameters of Lagasnerie's work and extending the elements of his characterization of three "truth-tellers" (Assange, Snowden, and Manning) to the American veteran-activists of this study. Lagasnerie argues, through the context of the Global War on Terror and the stories of Snowden, Assange, and Manning that the world is in the midst of something new, and that it is time to look forward. Therefore, the most dangerous thing the world can do in this transitional moment is seek refuge in old broken forms and calcified jargon. Virginia Woolf argued after the First World War that "we can best help you to prevent war by not repeating your words and following your methods but by finding new words and creating new methods."[36] Likewise, Lagasnerie maintains that the entire "political scene is being displaced and a new form of political engagement is emerging" and that it is the job of the scholar not to use old names like "whistleblower," "civil disobedience," and "coward" to describe the revolution of our time.[37] This aesthetic of dissent and its corollary disruptions of contemporary commonsense is the conceptual territory of this book.

Not unlike a great deal of scholarship on parrhesia, Lagasnerie's study emphasizes the role of truth and "truth-tellers" in a democracy. An aesthetic of dissent suggests a constantly evolutionary relationship with language and power. Instead of classifying Snowden, Assange, and Manning as "whistleblowers," and thereby locating them in an extremely circumscribed discourse, Lagasnerie chooses to highlight the declassifying nature of these individuals and to refer to them more broadly as truth-tellers, a term Foucault, specifically, highlights in his study of parrhesia. "The task," Lagasnerie writes,

> is to prove as radical in terms of theory as they have been in terms of politics. To display intellectual loyalty to Snowden, Assange, and Manning, one must offer a theory commensurate with the heights their concrete engagements have attained.[38]

Unlike James Clapper, John Kerry, Barack Obama, Donald Trump, Joe Biden, and others who have sought to minimize and caricature figures like Snowden due to their flight from the state, Lagasnerie says it is precisely in this mode of flight, refusal, and anonymity that we see the code for a new kind of revolution organized not just around public collectives (think marching in the street) but also around private individuals. Lagasnerie's truth-teller is in many ways the negative or the double of the unclassified "terrorist" or "detainee" from the Global War on Terror: the bare and precarious individual who never receives trial at a place like Guantánamo Bay. The truth-teller reveals the state's claim to democracy as a farce by staging the gaps, by revealing the state's built-in exceptions, its secret unaccountable and, therefore, undemocratic programs and people. Whereas the civil disobedient from the twentieth century asks the state to return to democratic order, the truth-teller calls for democracy now, as if for the first time. "Subjects who engage in civil disobedience," Lagasnerie asserts,

> do not seek to escape sanction. They recognize its legitimacy and allow themselves to be punished. Engaging in civil disobedience means considering oneself subject to punishment by the very state that maintains Guantánamo Bay and invaded Iraq.[39]

There is also a "meta" dimension to Lagasnerie's intervention. His identity matters. His ethos supplements his logos and vice versa. Lagasnerie, a Frenchman, is a professor at the Ecole Nationale Superieure d'Arts in Paris. *The Art of Revolt*, published by Stanford University Press, represents a kind of international collaboration that is not at all unique to the world of scholarship. Where would science's best theories be without scientists collaborating across national borders? Where would evolutions in computing be without the open-source sharing of information that defies proprietary identity markers like Russian, American, Chinese, or Indian? Such questions are remedial in the realms of scholarship but become transgressive when applied to the old national models of politics. And so, as the world wrestles with the implications of the current binary moment in which politics and computing find themselves increasingly bound together, readers must ask themselves a far less remedial question: what kind of world do they wish to build for future generations? Do readers wish to continue with the secret prisons, the partitioning of the indigenous, and the other markers of "The Forever War?" What Lagasnerie confronts readers with, if they are still capable of deep reading in this post-truth age, is a fundamental choice: Do they choose to identify with the nation or the state? In an increasingly binary conversation about identity politics, Lagasnerie urges the reader to consider the actions of three individuals who have disidentified with the state structures of the twentieth century. He begs readers to consider the new kinds of identities the Internet fosters and "the relationship between the Internet and the predisposition to flight, or 'treason.'"[40] Lagasnerie is indeed as bold in his theory as Snowden, Assange, and Manning have been in their actions against the state. But I propose to complicate Lagasnerie's argument by showing how the conceptual apparatus described above, once deployed, alerts us to ways in which post-9/11 soldier-writers engage in a range of "respatialization" games so as to incorporate various territories of remoteness and otherness into the geo-ethical continuum of care and duty traditionally reserved to the spaces of home, homeland, and kin.

Like Lagasnerie, Rancière too comes from France. This book's cross-pollination of French theorists and American soldier-writers is intentional. The structuring principle of my study is the platitudinal secret to success in real estate: location, location, location. Or, *dis*location, rather; dislocation and relocation; the transnational expansion of our ideas and feelings about justice, freedom, duty, and responsibility. Just as the early American revolutionaries were dependent on international aid from French revolutionaries like Lafayette, so do the American soldier-writers of the twenty-first century find allies from abroad to help frame the dissensual nature of their project. Shortly after the 9/11 attacks, Rancière retired from teaching, but he did not retire from writing. Much of his work on "dissensus," in fact, developed in response to the conditions of the post-9/11 rhetorical landscape. Like Lagasnerie, Rancière sees something novel in the Global War on Terror. Dissensus, for Rancière, is understood as the opposite of consensus, and just as it is a polar part of this binary, it also troubles a number of binaries that shape conventional understanding of the Global War on Terror: friend and foe, public and private, aesthetics and politics. Dissensus is not just people saying "no" to war. There is a logic to dissensus, and it has to do with a democratic subject staging dissent with a unique aesthetic that challenges the undemocratic speech situation that calls itself democratic. This refusal or dissensus dramatizes inequality and leads to "counting the uncounted" and leveling a "fractured speech situation" through "aesthetic rupture" and what Matheson Russell describes as "the law of theatre disrupting the theatre of law."[41] In short, dissensus breaks with formal argumentative discourse and embodies, as I show, through literary protocols, the artist's fundamentally contrarian argument that the proper forms and terms no longer work.

This elemental dissatisfaction with the "idea of the proper" is not unique to some rarefied artists but is instead the latent property of the artist within everyone. When citizens gather in public locations and demonstrate against the status quo of what has become proper or consensual, they are only dissensual to the extent that, like an artist, they refrain from proposing a proper solution, a new social form such as Marxism or Fascism. In other words, art dies as it bodies forth into a political setup and ontologizes ideologically. Art becomes politics as its vision calcifies into the ideological. A rhetorical map pointing toward an American solution or a French solution or a Russian solution or any other kind of national or ideological solution is not the territory of Rancière's concept of dissensus. It is in the troubled legend of the frontier, the limit and liminal, the unnamed space of the future and its possibilities, that the dissensual—the artistic—achieves and constantly undermines power. The parrhesiac and cosmopolitan rhetoric of the post-9/11 veteran-activists locates their challenge to sovereign notions in the same theater as their aggressor-nation's Global War on Terror: the world.

Rancière challenges writers to stage the gray, that gap between nation and world, aesthetics and politics: "When art is no more than art, it vanishes. When the content of thought is transparent to itself and when no matter resists it, this success means the end of art."[42] The art of these soldiers is, thus, more than just art. Likewise, their narratives are not easily dismissed as simply political acts. Dissensual politics, like modernist aesthetics, depend on this fundamental contrarian variable of the resistant, a social reality perpetually at war with itself. This is the self constantly disidentifying with the collective pressure toward category, stereotype, and certitude, the stable identity. The soldier-writers I am interested in are the ones who inhabit this liminal territory that is not national or international, stated civilization or unstated wilderness, but, instead, those spaces between. What these writers map is a literature and a rhetoric that travels beyond nations to forward-operating positions or frontiers that challenge extant notions like nationalism and globalism with a sense that there is something better beyond, something yet unnamed, a new story yet to be told.

2. The Map of the Territories: Argument Structure

Besides this first chapter, which lays out the basic objectives and architecture of my book, my study consists of three additional chapters and a conclusion. In this introductory movement, this study has charted the terms, methodology, and specific modes of literary and cultural analysis I will deploy to frame what I take to be one of the most intriguing American literary movements of our time. The three forthcoming chapters—II: "Disidentity Politics"; III: "Beyond the FOB: The Limit of Patriotism"; and IV: "Extraordinary Renditions"—supply a close reading of fiction and non-fiction that explore the porous borders of the Global War on Terror as it manifests in troubled conceptual and geographical territories that are at once American and "other." To conclude, this book's final segment, "Conclusion: Ethics, Style, Space: The Soldier-Writer Subculture," draws from the scholarship of Dick Hebdige, his study of British punks, and the concept of "signifying practices" as an evolutionary synthesis of the triad of parrhesia, cosmopolitanism, and dissensus when it comes to evaluating the creative processes of the soldier-writer community.

In Chapter II, part one, "More than Ground Zero: Mall Warriors and Patriotic Correctness," I conceptualize twenty-first-century America as a paradoxical hypermediated nation-state with permeable borders, troubled identity categories, and a globalized military-industrial economy that prosecutes a war without territorial limits while at the same time defending the sanctity of such limits "at home." After establishing my argument in part one, I turn to close readings of Klay's *Redeployment* and Snowden's *Permanent Record* in parts two and three. *Redeployment* travels all over the world, but it is Klay's construction of the homeland in this collection that interests me and makes his titular conceit so powerful. Just as soldiers are brought home from the Global War on Terror only to be sent to new theaters, so does Klay redeploy the rhetoric of this war in novel theaters like the American university. By decentering the events of 9/11 as the axis of this war, Klay, like Snowden in *Permanent Record*, invites his audience to consider a more nuanced vision of American identities as they interact with actors and forces from abroad. Both Klay and Snowden demonstrate cosmopolitan aspirations, a desire to tell the truth in the face of threat and deception, and a dissensual awareness of how troubled their truth-telling undertaking might be because it involves the ethical consideration of others elsewhere that evolves as one moves from fiction to non-fiction. Snowden's memoir, constructed in a more linear and chronological fashion than

Klay's fragmentary collection, I note, offers its fragmentations and dissensuality in its own way by emphasizing, through theme and subtle shifts in point of view, the most revolutionary challenge to spatiality and national identity from our time: the Internet. The Internet, for a young Snowden, is home. Though raised in the recognizable national geographies of North Carolina and Northern Virginia, Snowden's America is not the America of his parents or grandparents. The global "common frontier" of the early Internet is both the playground for Snowden as a child and the theater of war when he decides to enlist after the attacks on 9/11.[43] Essential to my argument, therefore, is Snowden's construction of the "hyperobject" of the Internet as both home and war space for a young man growing up in contemporary America. Here and throughout my project, the key is the focus on the cultural and spatial dynamic of positioning, namely on how soldier-writers "wield" space and location to place, displace, and sometimes replace older, familiar and, indeed, familial—home-bound—notions of duty, care, respect, and humanity.

Theorists like Bertrand Westphal orient my assertion that writers like Klay and Snowden are remapping the world's sense of the American war narrative. Westphal's attention to the "spatial turn" and the evolving relationship between literature, history, and geography provides a critical framework for highlighting the mobile and transdisciplinary environments showcased in this book.[44] Klay's dissensual vision of America and Snowden's desire to explore the new "common frontier" of the Internet challenges the reader to see ostensibly static state places as dynamic geospaces and to reimagine the relationship between representation and reality. Their spatially supple texts trouble the idea of national literature and, thus, dovetail into my introduction to Chapter III, part one, where I investigate the American military discourse of identity and space-bound identity for those soldiers located abroad but confined to forward operating bases (FOBs). The "fobbit," like Tolkien's "hobbit," is a fearful and fortified character, a liminal soldier who never leaves the borders of his base or "the wire." This pejorative mocks the American homeland "office space" quality of base life and stands in stark contrast to the locations and narratives of soldiers like Ackerman and Beck who take readers beyond the wire and the domain of the fobbit. However, just as Snowden and Klay's ostensibly domestic narratives challenge stable definitions of American identities, so do Ackerman and Beck reveal fractures in American identities as their characters operate on the frontlines of the Global War on Terror. Part one of Chapter III, "Democracy in No Man's Land: Elliot Ackerman's 'The Fourth War,'" provides the reader with a close reading of Ackerman's essay, "The Fourth War," and sets up the argument to come in parts two and three where I explore the relationship between geography and ethics and the expanded patriotism on display in the fiction of Ackerman and the memoir of Beck. Ackerman's novel, *Green on Blue*, and Beck's memoir, *Warrior Princess: A U.S. Navy SEAL'S Journey to Coming Out Transgender*, both take readers beyond the FOB and into the narratives of "special forces" and the problems of brave and risky speech in the Global War on Terror. Ackerman, unlike many soldier-writers from his generation, risks assuming the identity of an Afghan soldier. Ackerman's character, Aziz, works with American "special forces." The multidimensionality of Aziz is quite likely a function of Ackerman's martial cosmopolitanism, his exposure to distant others. Likewise, Aziz's parrhesia or "fearless speech" is partially a function of this same reinvented and dissensual identity. Aziz has been exposed to Americans and repurposes American rhetorical codes in subversive fashion. Like Beck who argues directly and forcefully against monolithic American constructions of warriorhood and gender, so does Aziz's "fearless speech" both challenge and embody distinctly American codes and, therefore, problematize both these codes and seemingly stable notions of America and truth-telling.

The penultimate section of the book, Chapter IV, intentionally disrupts the all-white and all-American identity regime of this book and investigates the narratives of a Guantánamo Bay detainee and two soldier-writers whose works reveal locations where soldiers and "combatants" face consequences for violating the penal codes of the Global War on Terror. In part one, "Staging Dissensus," I argue for the dissensual inclusion of Mohamedou Ould Slahi's *Guantánamo Diary* as the form-meets-content context for the two soldier-writer texts that follow in part two: Powers's *The Yellow Birds* and part three with Hickman's *Murder at Camp Delta*. By binding Slahi's staging of dissensus with Powers and Hickman, the reader will witness dissensus both described and performed and, thereby, better understand the parameters of this project as well as the contentious geography of Guantánamo Bay. Thus, in part two, with this context in mind, I give a close reading of *The Yellow Birds*, followed, in part three, by an analysis of *Murder at Camp Delta* that synthesizes the strands from parts one and two and evolves an argument about the relationship between the dissensual, spatial imagination, and truth-telling. The problem of parrhesia, as Foucault insists, breaks down to four questions, which are pertinent here: "who is able to tell the truth, about what, with what consequences, and with what relation to power?"[45] Thus, my interest in Powers's novel and Hickman's whistleblowing account of three suicides/murders that took place at Guantánamo Bay is not to evaluate whether their accounts of the Iraq War or a secret detention facility are true, but how their fictional and nonfictional narratives, together, reveal the problem of truth-telling in the new mobile environment of a veteran-activist community where victims of their wars, like Slahi, are never far away. Like Klay, Snowden, Ackerman, and Beck, Powers and Hickman have been all over the world, but not as tourists, migrants, or entrepreneurs. The particular compulsory cosmopolitanism these veterans exhibit is unique, and their truth-telling is rooted in particular locations that inform the genres they deploy, the stories they tell, and the ethically subversive ways in which they tell them.

Finally, in Chapter V, the conclusion's synthesizing territory is the room where writing and editing take place. In this last section, "Conclusion: Ethics, Style, Space: The Soldier-Writer Subculture," I attempt to bring this conversation into the contemporary moment of the writing workshop and the Ukraine War and reveal here and there the difficulty of making monolithic claims about patriotism, the military, and its diverse community of identities and signifying practices. These veteran-activists are real people, many of whom live under threat of "gag orders." All of their narratives and histories, when considered together, lead us to a profoundly contemporary confrontation with the problem of what Foucault calls the "analytics of truth." With so many soldier-writers bound by the echelons of classification that come with rank and the non-disclosure agreements that attend their deployments, how can scholars say anything reliable about the fragments of the Forever War they struggle to map as the Security State now pushes on to its next theater of war? Though this study engages Diogenes the Cynic, this is not a cynical book that retreats into nihilism and this is certainly not a book that is interested in serving a lie, which is even worse than a resort to nihilism. To be sure, trauma, redaction, and threat of punishment, to say nothing of heuristic factors, make "the truth" a challenge. However, the challenge, or the process, is part of the story and part of the truth. Although the narratives of this book do offer tantalizing historicized glimpses into the cartography of a heavily redacted map of American wars, the story here is just as much a contention with the techniques and new space of storytelling as it is with the problem of truth-telling. Rather than choose meta over meat, the conclusion, much like the rest of this book, attempts to dissensually disrupt such binaries. By grounding this conclusion in the territory of the theory of Dick Hebdige and *Subculture*, his study of British Punks, I offer a third path. If the conceptual triad of parrhesia, martial cosmopolitanism, and dissensus ultimately leads the critic to disrupt the stale conceptual categories of contemporary common sense, Hebdige's discussion of style offers future critics a tenable path forward in establishing an "analytics of truth" for the signifying practices of American soldier-writers.

The dissensual code of the American soldier-writer, like the code of the American soldier, is fundamentally deferential to principle and community. Just as the national soldier places "service above self," so does the soldier-writer repurpose this national training toward a more expansive cosmopolitan sodality of truth-tellers and truth-telling. As Sebastian Junger writes,

> Today's veterans often come home to find that, although they're willing to die for their country, they're not sure how to live for it. It's hard to know how to live for a country that regularly tears itself apart along every possible ethnic and demographic boundary.[46]

Junger highlights what this book explores in-depth: American soldiers are trained to disidentify with traditional identity categories. Such conditioning is part of who they are. "In combat," Junger writes, "soldiers all but ignore differences of race, religion, and politics within their platoon. It's no wonder many of them get so depressed when they come home."[47] Many soldiers do, of course, get depressed. Unfortunately, many commit suicide. But a growing number of veteran-activists in the post-9/11 era have begun to form communities organized around the ethically subversive principles of art. In unprecedented numbers, they have formed writing communities via social media platforms. The soldier-writers of this study have repurposed the authority of their experiences in the name of the future. They write with each other in encrypted spaces and in small rooms. They write and share work on X, TikTok, and Facebook. And like so many literary voices before them, they write with a certain kind of reader in mind, a fellow prodigal who wishes to see beyond the towers and walls of home.

II

Disidentity Politics

In this first portion of my argument, I frame contemporary America as a hypermediated nation-state with porous borders and problematic identity categories that have been transformed by the Internet, the attacks of 9/11, and the citizenry's resultant engagement in a war without territorial limits. After a brief engagement with Phil Klay's essay, "The Warrior at the Mall," in part one, I turn to close readings of Klay's *Redeployment* and Snowden's *Permanent Record* in parts two and three. Klay's conceptualization of the contemporary American homeland in his essay and his resistance to divisive identitarian discourse in his fiction gives rise to the title of this chapter: "Disidentity Politics." In *Redeployment*, Klay repurposes the rhetoric of the Forever War and reveals a rhetorical battleground here at home. Through a defamiliarization of these overseas conflicts, Klay, like Snowden in *Permanent Record*, challenges readers to test fundamental assumptions of American identity. These soldier-writers demonstrate an innovative martial cosmopolitanism, a hunger to reveal the truth of their generation's war, and, simultaneously, a sophisticated awareness of how difficult truth-telling can be as one moves from context to context and genre to genre. In light of this difficulty, throughout my argument I offer the reader context, which is to say artifactual evidence that this community of soldier-writers is real, their discursive presence online is real, and the ongoing conflicts overseas that trouble their storytelling remain real to this day, which is to say, these wars and their life and death consequences are not hypotheticals or abstractions. The context I offer, like the context offered by the authors themselves, serves to continually remind readers that the Forever War is not just a catchy conceit. Throughout this argument, my focus is on how these American veteran-activists trouble space and often displace old assumptions about geography, nation, and ethics in order to expand the reader's notions of patriotism and humanity. But for this ethical remapping to take place, it strikes me as imperative that the reader appreciate the very real locations and ethical dilemmas that inform these narratives. The fact that Klay has a demonstrable network of soldier-writers he supports online speaks to the new media presence of this community. The fact that Snowden writes to his audience from Russia is noteworthy, to say the least.

One such member of Klay's network is Matt Gallagher. Gallagher is not one of the primary authors in this study, but his work opens a window into the discourse on the community of soldier-writers. Gallagher joined the ROTC at Wake Forest University the week before 9/11. In 2005, he commissioned into the US Army as a second lieutenant and served in the 2nd Brigade, 25th Infantry Division in Saba al-Bor, a village northwest of Baghdad. As of 2023, this soldier-writer (author of *Youngblood*, *Kaboom*, *Empire City* and coeditor of *Fire and Forget*) could be located in Lviv, Ukraine, advising a civilian defense force there, and on Twitter/X. Among his Twitter/X followers one recognizes two of the authors from this study: Klay and Ackerman. In the new digital space of this twenty-first-century community of American soldier-writers, one occasionally witnesses Gallagher and his comrades argue about politics, aesthetics, the Internet, and literature. There are a number of features that haunt Gallagher's ethos as one studies his profile on Twitter/X's multinational interface, but perhaps nothing says more about his conception of the soldier-writer than the quote from Grace Paley he once featured in his bio: "It's not that you set out to oppose authority. In the act of writing, you simply do."[1] Literature defamiliarizes and transgresses. It challenges. It includes through exclusion.

If there is an impermeable "personal" territory for the American writer, the post-9/11 veteran-activist invades, occupies, and transforms that space by publicly writing about his or her experiences in the Global War on Terror. As Paul Giles argues in *The Global Remapping of American Literature*, 9/11 forever altered the American notion of the homeland. "9/11," Giles writes, "has become for the United States the most visible and haunting symbol of the permeability of the country's borders, its new vulnerability to outside elements."[2] What marks the literature of the post-9/11 soldier-writer is an orientation that is unusually sensitive to this new "permeability." The parrhesiac, dissensual, and cosmopolitan pattern I read in this community's public writing strikes me as indicative of imaginations that are at least liminally aware that readers are now in a new world where the concept of discrete spaces and, in particular, the old ideas of home and abroad no longer work. Whether readers travel with these soldiers to secret detention facilities in Guantánamo Bay, the tribal regions of East Afghanistan, or a website opened in a home office in Northern Virginia, the haunt of this new post-9/11 ethos remains. "To turn a home into a 'homeland' is, by definition," according to Giles, "to move from a zone in which domestic comforts and protection could be taken for granted to one in which they had to be guarded anxiously and self-consciously."[3] For Giles, "the very phrase 'homeland security' could be seen as a contradiction in terms, since it rhetorically evokes the very insecurity it seeks to assuage."[4] It's not that Gallagher and his post-9/11 peers set out to challenge our notion of identity and the American "homeland." But as former soldiers embarking on a literary journey in the digital age, they have all ineluctably noticed the new reality of their war as it permeates the mall and the airport, the home and the home office, to say nothing of the new theater of war in Ukraine. In other words, the Global War on Terror did not simply invade, occupy, torture, and liberate Iraq and Afghanistan. It also invaded, occupied, tortured, and, in a sense, liberated the United States as it brought all these spaces together in the private and public spatial imaginary.

One cannot talk about this new contemporary space without approaching its digital component or what scholar John McClure calls the "jungle-like techno-tangles."[5] Now living stateside, Gallagher and Klay regularly retweet/repost each other. These soldier-writers do not make a habit of amplifying Snowden who, as of this date, still resides in Russia. To be clear, this book is not arguing that Ackerman, Beck, Hickman, Klay, Powers, and Snowden share a singular activist or anti-war disposition or a particular partisan politics. What they do share is what I call a disidentity politics. This term, coined in response to "identity politics," serves as an ethically subversive lens into the remapping I read as operative in the digital rhetoric and published narratives of the veteran-activist community. If the pre-9/11 American homeland was a geographical territory, a literary marketplace, and a digital-rhetorical space, one has to engage with the legend of this once dominant map and its ostensibly stable identity categories. Just as a census maps a nation via race, religion, age, and gender, so do the writers of this study speak out against the accepted stability of these categories. Writing about Gallagher and Klay, Caleb Cage, in *War Narratives*, claims that fiction gives these veterans "the room they need to write harsh and foreign truths about the wars that are seldom presented elsewhere."[6] Foreign truths indeed. The "room" Klay and Snowden inhabit is a new space where the "jungle-like techno-tangles" intersect with the desert and the office. The space they shape is an evolutionary and ouroboric space where the America that invades has simultaneously been invaded. This novel American room is, in a certain sense, a continuum of the ever-evolving map of an America that has been expanding its territory and merging its identity categories since the Revolution, but this new room is marked by a new global media that splits and tangles the senses, blurs the personal and political, and defies the dominant narratives of identity politics. What is the Global War on Terror? Is this a race war, a religious war, a cyber war, or a class war? Something there is in the American mind that wants a wall and a bullet point, a host of easy answers and identitarian partitions. But the new literary discourse of the Global War on Terror undermines what E. Ann Kaplan calls the "empty empathy" Americans tend to find online or on TV when seeking to understand this conflict. Kaplan, in *Trauma Culture: The Politics of Terror and Loss in Media and Literature*, warns readers that media representations of the Global War on Terror tend to focus on individual American soldiers "rather than on the larger issues to do with the reason for war on Iraq, its global impact, its effect on America's political alliances worldwide, and especially its devastating impact on Iraqi women, children, and innocent civilians."[7] For Kaplan, like this author, the media coverage of Iraq, specifically, and the Global War on Terror, broadly, fails to challenge this "empty empathy" with difficult questions like, why are so many of the heavily marketed American-built girls schools in Afghanistan empty, what are we to make of the absence of white prisoners at Guantánamo Bay, and why are we still in Iraq and Syria?

Current debates about the efficacy of identity politics suggest a great contemporary schism over the role of representation in our new hypermediated reality, as well as over the enlightenment notion of individuality and individual rights. As Wendy McElroy writes, "Identity politics is a sharp departure from the traditionally American ideal that rights are universal, not particular."[8] Identity politics, in many cases, draws admirable attention to the gap between the American ideal of universal rights and the historical reality of white supremacy and the discrimination and marginalization of particular individuals. But in its fundamentally literary push for particularization, the granulation of identity rhetoric can alienate. And so, in what appears to be a dialectical shift *within* identity politics, readers seem to be witnessing a new spatial imaginary, a unifying schism that echoes the impetus for disruption in Rancière's dissensus, what one might call a new mode of identification. To conduct a study of writing almost exclusively produced by soldiers might seem, on the one hand, a tribute to Kaplan's "empty empathy," but it is this seemingly monolithic community's contention with the stability of its own identity that compels this work.

1. More than Ground Zero: Mall Warriors and Patriotic Correctness

So how does it work? What does it mean to remap the American homeland? If, as Giles argues, "geographical consciousness" has always entered "subliminally into American cultural narratives," how has the relationship between geography and imagination changed in the digital era? If, as the Greeks argue, the parrhesiac individual speaks with four qualities—frankness, criticism, danger, and duty—how might a frank critique of an American website or an American mall endanger our concept of duty and dissensually compel us to construct a new one in light of the soldier-writer's cosmopolitan worldview? Prior to a close reading of Klay and Snowden's first books, I would like to consider Klay's description of America in his 2018 essay, "The Warrior at the Mall," and then examine an interview between Snowden and the songwriter and activist John Perry Barlow. Both of these documents help to frame the new space this book seeks to map and the role parrhesia, dissensus, and cosmopolitanism play in that cartography. Parrhesiac accountability is rooted in the concept of outspokenness or frankness. Jonathan Simon argues that frankness is not merely a synonym for honesty, but instead refers to "a truth" that "will be painful to hear" and a truth "that is anchored in the experiences of the speaker herself, and if it is effective, it directly touches the self of the interlocutor, whether that be a sovereign-like figure or a democratic assembly."[9] Frank criticism, therefore, is a power relation, a challenge up the chain of command. Klay's description of "The Warrior at the Mall" is indeed a destabilization of the homeland for the way it challenges the all-encompassing American cult of the soldier, an identity category to which Klay belongs. Whereas a good portion of Snowden's argument lives on the digital frontier (as we shall see in the interview and his memoir), Klay's essay brings the war home to the homeland, the new agora. Before entering the territory of his collection and Snowden's memoir, I would like to use Snowden's interview and Klay's essay to question, in a straightforward public-facing mode, fundamental assumptions about American borders; then, as we step into Klay's fiction, my analysis will chart the new imaginative regime and the way it operates through the coordinates of time and space.

In "The Warrior at the Mall," Klay stands in the space of what has been for millennia the uncontestable zone of the public square. Regardless of what one might claim about the public or private nature of the new digital square or sphere, the American mall bears a resemblance to the Athenian agora or the

Iraqi souk. Grounding his narrative in the rhetoric of George Washington, Klay's essay reminds soldiers that contemporary contempt for American civilians runs counter to the principles of the founding fathers. "The other," in the life of the American soldier, has increasingly been constructed as not just the dark enemy abroad, but the domestic citizen no longer worthy of the name. These two identity categories place the soldier in a seemingly liminal position, alienated in a perilous space, a no man's land between enemies both inside and outside national borders. At first glance, in the geography of "the mall," the American citizen is on one side of the divide as a mere consumer and the soldier is on the other as a soldier, an identity category, like others, that Klay argues is now "sacred." Through personal testimony, grounded in his service and his contemporary status as a civilian, Klay's essay transcends this binary and challenges American readers to reinvert this code and to see anew the American homeland and the sanctity of citizenship. He begins "The Warrior at the Mall" with a derisive "well-worn phrase" from his time in Iraq: "We're at war while America is at the mall."[10] Here is the divide for the post-9/11 nation that no longer requires national service and where consumerist values trump the democratic values of civic duty and service. Klay repeats the phrase like a chorus, simulating its indoctrinating rhythm. For an active-duty soldier in his twenties, Klay writes, "it sounded right. Just enough truth mixed with self-aggrandizement." "Back home," he continues, "was shopping malls and strip clubs. Over here was death and violence and hope and despair. Back home was fast food and high-fructose corn syrup … We were at war, they were at the mall." In this rhetorical moment, the problem of the American homeland and America's ethical map is laid bare. The "Us versus Them" binary that characterizes the Cold War and the Global War on Terror has been inverted to such a degree that the American soldier now sees his adversary as the American consumer while, abroad, the map of the war expands into Africa. After the deaths of four American soldiers in Niger and the disdainful responses of the Trump administration to challenges over the incident (which Klay sees as a "continuation of an Obama administration policy"), Klay steps forward and amplifies the civilian call for explaining why America is deploying special operations forces "to 149 countries."[11] As the Global War on Terror grows both larger and more invisible in contemporary American discourse, Klay challenges the reader to not accept this invisibility and to not acquiesce to the "neat, partisan parables" America is constantly asked to accept as sufficient context for "the Forever Wars." He quotes a "former member of the Special Forces" who, in response to the deaths in Niger, wrote, "We did what we did so that you can be free to naively judge us, complain about the manner in which we kept you safe," and "just all around live your worthless sponge lives." Klay acknowledges the popularity of this contemptuous rebuke, and writes, that it "can be comforting to reverse the feelings of hopelessness and futility that come with fighting seemingly interminable, strategically dubious wars by enforcing a hierarchy of citizenship that puts the veteran and those close to him on top, and everyone else far, far below." But this veteran is not here in the public sphere to reinforce the hierarchy that Americans maintain by obeying the code of "patriotic correctness," a term Klay defines as an "odd form of political correctness" that bathes the soldier in divine light and, thereby, protects the soldier from the humanizing consequences of critique. In other words, Klay does not sanctify the identity category of the soldier. Instead, he questions his own authority and relocates that authority in its original source: the demos. "If," Klay writes, "I have authority to speak about our military policy it's because I'm a citizen responsible for participating in self-governance, not because I belonged to a warrior caste." And so we come full circle.

The disidentification pattern readers find in the soldier-writer community is not simply a nihilism, a negation, or even an imaginative olive branch to a distant other once encountered on a distant battlefield. Disidentification, as theorized by José Esteban Muñoz, is a performative minoritarian practice as a means of both survival and subversion. In other words, it's a way for the marginalized to camouflage transgression. "The Warrior at the Mall" challenges the reader to reimagine the life and death stakes of the sacred soldier identity as his or her own territory. Klay uses his military ethos—his national authority—to testify against this very authority that endangers the founding fathers' ideals of citizenship and democracy. Klay understands the power of this ethos and, thus, acknowledges that "pushing a military angle as a wedge makes a certain kind of sense." But it is this very *certain* kind of sense that the veteran-activists of this study subvert when they disidentify. A singular, monolithic linear brand of space and sense is not the territory of cosmopolitanism or dissensus or, more generally, good writing. The ethics of the dissensual (where politics and aesthetics merge) confronts the partitions that blind one party to another, one interest to another, one nation to another, and one individual to another. Rooted in the negative categories of modernist theory, the dissensual writer challenges even his or her own neatly constructed worlds and finds fragment and fracture. So it is with Klay in "The Warrior at the Mall." As a soldier who is now a civilian, Klay approaches the territory of the American mall and the rhetoric of "patriotic correctness" with two identities at his disposal. Rather than double-down on soldier, he challenges "the practice of a fraudulent form of American patriotism, where 'soldiers' are 'sacred,'" reframes the identity category as "warrior" and argues on behalf of what was once the "other"—the civilian. Grounding his views in the language of his country's original revolutionary leader, Washington, Klay writes:

> [O]ur peacetime institutions are not justified by how they intermittently intersect with national security concerns—it's the other way around. Our military is justified only by the civic life and values it exists to defend. This is why George Washington, in his Farewell Orders to the Continental Army, told his troops to "carry with them into civil society the most conciliating dispositions" and "prove themselves not less virtuous and useful as citizens than they have been persevering and victorious as soldiers."

If Klay is one of the representative voices of the soldier-writer community, I would argue that his status is a function of his willingness to complicate his status. In other words, many of the comforting assumptions about war, media, service, subjectivity, and the American homeland are no longer stable in the hypermediated terrains of the Global War on Terror. Thus, Klay repurposes his training as both soldier and writer and practices the warrior code of sacrifice on the level of the line and in the narrative spaces of forward operating bases as well as American universities and bazaars. His duty is to something more than a single battle or a single band of brothers or a single religion or a single flag. His narrative ethics trump his allegiance to "patriotic correctness." His fearless speech is not suicidal, but it risks a great deal in the name of the "other." The public commitments he makes in his writings suggest his duty is not to a Caesar or an ecclesia but to the demos. His sense of duty, as a soldier-writer, is to the "other," both at home and abroad. Therefore, it seems only right that this "soldier" dissensually defies one of the core identity categories of contemporary discourse—soldier—and replaces it with a title transported from the Middle English (werrieor) who adopted it from the old Northern French (guerreior), a term colloquially used to describe the adversary American soldiers vanquished on the old western frontiers: the warrior.

Those frontiers have changed dramatically over the course of history. America's post-9/11 borders did not simply open overnight. This new public space, and this new literary community, is not simply a function of the Internet's birth. The "permeability" Giles explores took root in the post-Second World War environment of emerging technologies and respondent art but also in the frontier rhetoric one can trace back to America's inception. Stewart Brand, like Phil Klay, is a veteran, an author, and one of the pioneers of this space.

Brand enlisted in the Army in 1960 just after graduating from Stanford University. Although qualified as a paratrooper, Brand never entered into combat. Trained as a photographer, he began repurposing the skills he learned in the military as soon as his two-year commission elapsed. He participated in protests of the Vietnam War. He found work photographing a Native American reservation in Oregon in 1963. He became friends with Ken Kesey, author of *One Flew Over the Cuckoo's Nest*, and joined Kesey's band of "Merry Pranksters" in their mission to unsettle the mind of America, the speaker-studded day-glo bus they drove all over the country during the 1964 election season a startling convergence of politics and aesthetics. "At government expense," Brand once said, "I was trained in leadership and small-unit management."[12] Also trained in biology at Stanford, what Brand began to discover in the 1960s was that the classified operating systems of the national military might be repurposed toward transparent and transnational ends. Then, in 1966, Brand conjured an original countercultural idea. In an interview he gave in 2001, he recalled:

> One afternoon, probably in March in 1966, dropping a little LSD, I went up onto the roof and sat shivering in a blanket sort of looking and thinking ... And so I'm watching the buildings, looking out at San Francisco, thinking of Buckminster Fuller's notion that people think of the earth's resources as unlimited because they think of the earth as flat. I'm looking at San Francisco from 300 feet and 200 micrograms up and thinking I can see from here that the earth is curved. I had the idea that the higher you go the more you can see earth as round. There were no public photographs of the whole earth at that time, despite the fact that we were in the space program for about ten years. I started scheming within the trip. How can I make this photograph happen? Because I have now persuaded myself that it will change everything if we have this photograph looking at the Earth from space.[13]

Shortly after President John F. Kennedy (another soldier-writer) asked the American people to imagine space as "the new frontier," Brand suggested a visual reversal of "the space race," the competitive national program to beat the Soviets and conquer space. Brand dedicated his life to the exigence of the planetary vision, the idea of the image of the planet invading the planet or, rather, a mediated image of the planet populating the planet with an awareness of itself and our basic unity—our shared humanity. Perhaps no intellectual in our time has contributed more to the notion and realization of planetary consciousness than Brand. In 1966, before the birth of discourse about "worlding," "geospatialiny," "geocriticism," and "planetary," this young entrepreneur handed out hundreds of buttons that said, "Why Haven't We Seen a Photograph of the Whole Earth Yet?" A few years later, after the Apollo 8 finally captured that vision of home, Brand published the first of a series of DIY (Do It Yourself) manuals called *The Whole Earth Catalog*. *The Whole Earth Catalog*, like the Internet, possessed no single author. According to Steve Jobs, it was "sort of like Google in book form." It was a book that served as a doorway to cutting-edge transdisciplinary thought about technology and ecology. Brand's eco-masterpiece was also a spatial template for the Internet insofar as it was a decentered operating system based on the premise that small-scale technologies and personal computing could change the world. In 1971, *The Last Whole Earth Catalog* won the National Book Award. In *From Counterculture to Cyberculture: Stewart Brand, the Whole Earth Network, and the Rise of Digital Utopianism*, Fred Turner places Brand in the center of this decentering movement that continues to transform America's relationship with space, computing, the planet, and how we tell our stories. Framing Brand as a "comprehensive designer" with one foot in the world of the military-industrial complex and the other in the emergent countercultural scene in Silicon Valley, Turner argues that Brand's *Whole Earth Catalog* prefigured the Internet and "became the single most visible publication in which the technological and intellectual output of industry and high science met the Eastern religion, acid mysticism, and communal social theory of the back-to-the-land movement. It also became the home and emblem of a new, geographically distributed community."[14] Before literary critics like Giles, Moraru, Rancière, and Westphal mapped the new geographies of American and global literary space, Brand was walking the streets in real time challenging the media to invite the image of the planet into the American home. By repurposing the cybernetic technologies developed by America's post-Second World War military industrial complex, Turner suggests that Brand laid the foundation for the Internet ideal of a disembodied community—a community without place— where the planet—the whole earth—begins to replace the nation as the guiding symbolic habitat of humanity.

What truly distinguishes the soldier-writers of the post 9/11 world is their reimagination of narrative space and their participation in this evolving community without place. The soldiers of the Global War on Terror may have enlisted in a national enterprise on a global scale, but when these same soldiers became writers a great number of them discovered, in one way or another, that they were now like the Apollo 8 and Brand, their national identities suddenly unsettled by a global gaze. Central to understanding this decentering and denationalizing imperative is the paradoxical and distinctly American rhetoric of the frontier as it plays out on the electronic frontier.

Like Brand, Snowden enlisted in the Army but grew wary of his generation's war. Like Brand, Snowden repurposed the tools he discovered. In 2013, with the help of a community of journalists and intellectuals he discovered online, Snowden revealed that the US government was conducting an unwarranted global surveillance program that extended into the homes, phones, and computers of its own citizens. The gaze of the Global War on Terror, it turns out, panned both outward and inward. Like the writers of this study, the war that shaped them invited Americans into a mission that defied national borders. To be sure, Snowden's actions call into question what it means to be an American as well as what spaces can still be properly territorialized as national. Snowden's core argument—that his parrhesiac actions were justified insofar as they privileged the nation over the state—demonstrates not only a brash revolutionary individualism consistent with the early American identity but also a reflection of an emergent identity of "pioneers" that has been growing for decades on the World Wide Web, a strand of cosmopolitan thought that runs counter to the narrow nationalist sentiments currently sweeping the world. Like many of the other soldier-writers in this project, Snowden deploys a number of narrative strategies to disidentify with official state policy in the name of an evolving transnational ideal. But Snowden's conception of the contemporary American homeland as increasingly digital, combined with his digital rhetoric and current geographical coordinate (Moscow), transports the reader into a more radical conception of space than his peers. While asylumed in Russia, Snowden conducts the vast bulk of his communication through the same multinational medium that deplatformed America's forty-fifth commander-in-chief, Donald Trump: Twitter/X. Both men, haunted by their Russian connections, herald different visions of nationalism and communicate constantly in the new public sphere of the Internet, each in their own way encouraging America to turn the page on what some call "the new Cold War." John Updike once asked, "Without the Cold War, what's the point of being American?"[15] Snowden and Trump's Russian connections in the twenty-first century defamiliarize Updike's question and raise the possibility of the new political space contentiously haunted by the old. Is America's only path forward a retreat into the old Cold War binary? Whereas Trump, prior to his deplatforming, promoted a nostalgic and narrow national vision from

Twitter, Snowden seems to understand the ironies implicit in these mediums of communication. Rather than encouraging a retreat from the planetary mind or the complications of early globalization, Snowden regularly argues that this new media space and this nascent digital community must evolve further. Snowden, in community with Barlow (author of "A Declaration of the Independence of Cyberspace" and a friend of Brand's), makes a compelling case for reimagining the American homeland and for repurposing the rhetoric of American aspirations toward a transcendent—transnational—enterprise: a World Wide Web guided by a code and thirteen tenets known as the International Principles on the Application of Human Rights to Communication Surveillance.[16] By briefly exploring the site of Barlow and Snowden's conversation, readers will see how real and representational spaces—foreign and domestic, private and public—are beginning to collide across national borders, remapping ideas about liberty, free speech, democracy, and what it means to be an American. As with Klay's warrior at the mall, Snowden's conversation with Barlow reveals the language of America's frontier past ethically subverting the discourse of its national present and, thereby, transforming the contemporary sense of a homeland.

As a coordinate on the map of this study, the conversation between Snowden and Barlow, like the novels, short story collections, and memoirs included here, begs unpacking and serious cultural analysis. If tweets and YouTube videos are to exist alongside these other more academically accepted genres of expression, it behooves the writer to make a case for their inclusion and to introduce the reader to their novel features. At the very least, the scholar should discuss these features and locate them in time and space. But historicization is complicated by the new geography. Time and place, in the new digital space, are even more entangled than they were before. When, on June 5, 2014, Snowden sat down with Barlow for a conversation about the future of cyberspace, one could be intellectually lazy and simply state the setting of the event as the setting asserted on the YouTube channel: New York City. However, to be more precise, this veteran sat down with a computer screen in Russia and interfaced with Barlow who sat with a live audience at New York University as part of the Personal Democracy Forum. If multimodality is important in assessing argument, and I think it is, it is perhaps also important to note the distorted visual dynamics of the conversation. Snowden's head, in the video, is about twenty times the size of life on the NYU movie screen and presides over the crowd with Barlow's mug captioned in the corner, about a tenth the size of Snowden's. This conversational convergence of faces and voices was transmitted to the live New York audience and then later uploaded to YouTube where it can still be watched and commented on today. "It's a pity you can't see the audience," Barlow says at the beginning of the conversation. "They're as happy as they would be if you were here."[17] And so, with this first appropriative claim, begins the public dialogue of a soldier-writer and a counterculture icon, two men loosely bound together through the organization Barlow co-founded, the Electronic Frontier Foundation (EFF).

Before burrowing deeper into the spatial dimensions of this transgressively American moment, consider Barlow and Snowden's unique roles in the history of the elusive, nonlocal, ungraspable "hyperobject," that is, the Internet. Barlow once wrote that Snowden "has done more to protect the individual civil liberties of those in America than any other single person."[18] Wherever one stands on Snowden's actions, one cannot refute that their impact would have been impossible without the Internet, a space Barlow and Snowden both helped to shape. Snowden's argument in their exchange is complex, more than occasionally technical in its language, but the general thrust of his conversation with Barlow should be graspable to any American audience with a high school education. Snowden leaked sensitive government surveillance documents "because," he argues, "you know, we fought a war to have protections and to have rights like our constitution, like our fourth amendment, that says not only can you not search our communications without a warrant, but you can't seize them in the first place."[19] By delivering this argument to Barlow, the Personal Democracy Forum and the mass media audience of YouTube, Snowden builds a bridge between not just Moscow and New York (his Russian location and Barlow's American location) but also between the rhetoric of the Internet, the American Revolution, and the rhetoric of the landscape that revolution inherited: the frontier.

The argument Barlow made throughout his second career (his first was as a lyricist for the Grateful Dead) is that cyberspace is the new frontier, the extension of that specifically American wilderness Frederick Jackson Turner claimed was officially closed by 1890. Like his friend, Brand, Barlow recognized that the secret computer systems the American military developed after the Second World War could be repurposed to the task of transparency and transnationalism and, therefore, consequently, the Internet could be used to change the way Americans imagine their home and their office. But what should Americans call this new space? Is it a mall? Is it a web? Is it a net? Shortly after 9/11, in an interview with *The American Spectator* titled "Cyberspace Cowboy," Barlow scoffed at Al Gore's characterization of the Internet as the "Information Superhighway." "Al Gore not only didn't invent the Internet, he doesn't understand it," Barlow argued. "The Internet is a self-generative organism, powered by the desire of people to communicate and connect. Gore's metaphor turns the Net into a massive centrally administered and planned government project, which it isn't."[20] Later in the interview, Barlow elaborates on his vision for the Net as something like a transnational utopia crossed with the original frontier: "If you can create an environment where anybody anywhere can say whatever they please, and nobody can stop them, then you have essentially solved the problem of tyranny," he said. And then:

> My family were frontier people from the time they hit these shores in the 1600s until they ran slam, bang, up against the end of it in Wyoming at the turn of the last century. I spent my youth in Pinedale, Wyoming—the only county seat in America without a traffic light—thinking I had been cheated out of a frontier until I found that another one was forming. On the Net you literally never can or will run out of space. And every time it changes in some fundamental way then the whole thing becomes a frontier all over again.[21]

Barlow, who launched the EFF with Mitch Kapor, the founder of Lotus, and wrote "the doc forwarded 'round the world'" (*A Declaration of the Independence of Cyberspace*), thus set the metaphorical table for a new generation of "pioneers," figures like Snowden.[22] So, if the Internet is the new frontier, it is, at least ideally, a frontier that shares two fundamental characteristics with Frederick Jackson Turner's concept. One, a frontier can, even if briefly, decentralize capital (redistribute wealth) and, thus, liberate the voices of those outside the old aristocratic orders. It is in this chain of consequence, of freedom in market leading to (or from) freedom of speech, that we arrive at the second characteristic of the frontier both Barlow and Turner describe: the freedom of citizens to govern themselves, the flourishing of true democracy. "From the beginning of the settlement of America," Turner writes, "the frontier regions have exercised a steady influence toward democracy. In Virginia, to take an example, it can be traced as early as the period of Bacon's Rebellion."[23] These claims are far from uncontested territory, but I would like to add a third attribute. The electronic frontier not only transforms our relationship to capital and governance, but it also destabilizes our relationship with narrative space, the stories readers and viewers see and hear, the stories writers tell. Far from a highway, the Net Barlow framed and Snowden exposed reveals a world within the world, a new space inside the borders of the American homeland.

In Barlow's early conception of this new frontier, the state effectively disappears. When asked by *The American Spectator* if the state has any utility at all like "Defense?" or "Police?" Barlow responds with: "Defense against what? Other nation states? We've seen where that leads. The nation state had its apotheosis in Auschwitz and the gulag and Hiroshima. I'm not going to mourn its passage."[24] It is here in the conflation of "nation" and "state" as "nation state" that Snowden will intervene in Barlow's rhetoric and offer a third path, a choice beyond the binary of nation state versus wild frontier expressed as a question: "Are we protecting the nation or are we protecting the state?" Snowden's question cuts to the uprooting root of the dilemma. Snowden's parrhesia extends to the interlocutor ostensibly on his side, thousands of miles away. Snowden suggests there is a powerful difference between the "nation" and the "state," and in this challenge to the linguistic packaging of reality, Snowden sets forth a model of critique that is more than just utopian.

"Utopia," in its original Greek construction, means "no" (ou) "place" (topos).[25] To call the Internet, generally, and the soldier-writer community, specifically, a community without place is to inhabit the paradox of digital utopianism. Is there a place that's not a place? Geocritics like Westphal beg readers to imagine this page itself—printed or screened—as a site of encounter, a place for you and me, a social space where "referential space" and the narrative text mesh and twine.[26] Although Barlow's early language is indeed utopian in both senses of the word (eu/ou, good/no), it is certainly too reductive to argue that he simply possessed an immature idea of the Internet's potential until Snowden suddenly arrived as a kind of Moscow Moses to codify his impulses in 2014. Between the time of the interview with *The American Spectator* and his conversation with Snowden, Barlow was evolving toward a more nuanced perspective on "the electronic frontier," an evolution leading to what Brian Doherty, years before Snowden, called "John Barlow 2.0." By 2004 Barlow claimed that he no longer found it responsible to simply ignore or turn away from the machinations of the state:

> I've gone back and forth with politics. I've been a Republican county chairman. I was one of Dick Cheney's campaign managers when he first ran for Congress. But generally speaking, I felt to engage in the political process was to sully oneself to such a degree that whatever came out wasn't worth the trouble put in. I thought it was better to focus on changing yourself and people around you, to not question authority so much as bypass it whenever possible. But by virtue of our abdication, a very authoritarian, assertive form of government has taken over. And oddly enough, it is doing so in the guise of libertarianism to a certain extent.[27]

Barlow, forever the contrarian, bristles at the fake libertarianism that has co-opted the free space of the early Net. The frontier is dead, but the frontier lives inside as a permanent protean promise. As Langston Hughes once wrote, "O, yes, / I say it plain, / America never was America / To me, / But I swear this oath— / America will be!" Like so many before him, and like the soldier-writers of this book, the space Barlow proposes is neither nostalgic nor cynical. It is a new intersectional space of agitation between such poles, not a space ideologically committed to one or the other. By the time of his conversation with Snowden in New York/Russia/the Internet, the intelligence disaster that led to the hundreds of thousands of deaths in America's war with Iraq (and the destabilization of Syria, Libya, Egypt, and others) was apparent, as was the aggressive growth of that same government's surveillance network at home, its desire to dominate the Net. As a result of these events and others, like the consolidation of media resources by multinational corporations, Barlow's notion of the frontier had changed by 2014 into a concept of a liminal territory, a still wild space "where anybody anywhere can say whatever they please, and nobody can stop them," but simultaneously a zone in need of protection if not regulation. EFF's role, increasingly, became that of "the primary mediator on that border," that line between the laws of the state and the largely lawless terrain the individual finds on the Net, even if that individual is himself or herself seated in a chair grounded upon a floor built atop the rock and soil of the American homeland.

Like the computer user seated in America and interfacing with an American in Russia, Snowden's notion of American crisis possesses the markers of both America and a frontier beyond. The new space of the Internet, developed by the American military, has now traveled beyond America's borders and now those beyond America's borders circulate back into America's new space. "It's important to remember," Snowden says, "that this is not just an American problem. This is a global problem."[28] While seated in Russia and speaking to an audience in New York City, site of the old World Trade Center and the new One World Trade Center, with Google's multi-national corporate logo stamped in the top-left corner of the screen and Barlow of the Electronic Frontier Foundation chuckling and grimacing in the bottom right, Snowden's plurimodal dialogue with the Personal Democracy Forum—with the world—with YouTube—demands granular and skeptical attention. Every time Snowden speaks to the world, it is, by virtue of his exiled status, in this dialogical mode, whether his interlocutor is the journalist, Glenn Greenwald; the comedian, John Oliver; the podcast host, Joe Rogan; or the cyberlibertarian activist, Barlow. In other words, whether he is near Ground Zero with Barlow, in Moscow with Oliver, or on a podcast aired from Los Angeles with Rogan, the world constantly receives Snowden as one part Snowden and one part "other," which is to say, the audience receives him as a dissensual two, not a one. Like the very term, "soldier-writer" or "veteran-activist," Snowden is a dialectical Internet construct, a double-helix of individual and trans/sub statal institutions whose representatives have elected to spotlight and, thereby, complicate his voice. This carefully orchestrated media strategy serves to support, on a structural level, the argument Snowden makes about the need for international standards and international cooperation.

Barlow, as Snowden's interlocutor in this instance, sets the table for the veteran-activist by emphasizing how American principles should be repurposed toward international ends. "I think a point that you and I and others of our ilk need to make, increasingly frequently, is that in the unique case of the United States, national security means the security of our founding principles."[29] Barlow and Snowden both suggest their argument is not targeted at just the people within the "vaporous" borders of the American homeland. Based as they are in the "founding documents we still profess to believe in," their principles may well have an American revolutionary flavor, but they are being actively repurposed toward a transnational end. If Snowden and Barlow are right—and it is certainly not this book's job to judge whether they are—but if they are, what are the ramifications for accepting their claims about a nation and a cyberspace community increasingly at odds with the American state? Is there something about this new space that calls for new rules and a new subjectivity, a new code for a new kind of truth-teller? Is there something about cyberspace that fundamentally demands exception from the increasingly classified codes of the American state? If so, how does this new narrative and rhetorical space—this new media sphere—change the way we view the American experiment with democracy and the state and all the non-state actors attempting to shape its future? Is it too simple or riddlesome to suggest that cyberspace might be a place where the occupied can occasionally occupy the occupier?

Marshall McLuhan, in *Understanding Media*, predicted the parrhesiac property of the new media space and the revolutionary qualities Barlow and

Snowden elaborate. McLuhan argues that twentieth-century America was in the middle of a "revolution in expression" and that the revolution had a great deal to do with the evolution of the text from a secure and tightly controlled "monastic" script to a "typographical" text with potential for reproduction, alteration, and global distribution. "Typography," McLuhan writes, "created a medium in which it was possible to speak out loud and bold to the world itself," and that this revolution in boldness would only be exponentially amplified by the new electronic media. McLuhan was right, and Snowden is the parrhesiac proof.[30] As Giles states, 9/11 transformed America's relationship to the state and the nation's sense of border, security, and homeland. Thus, how do readers map the legal, ethical, political, and aesthetic lines—as well as the electronic frontiers—of the American future? How do readers and writers conceptualize an American homeland when the space of nearly every home has been invaded and occupied by the webbed worlds of the Internet? As audiences begin to approach the fiction of Klay and the memoir of Snowden, it is important to be mindful of what is novel about their contexts: the Global War on Terror, the Internet, and the new spatial ethos derived from these contexts. Klay's collection defamiliarizes the reader's America in subtle but striking ways. His stories are often haunted by the Net and the migrations of information we find there between America and Iraq, but the Net is more a peripheral narrative attribute in the space Klay creates. Snowden, on the other hand, comes from the world of computing and embodies its dissensual ethos more than perhaps any other figure from his generation. However, his narrative gifts are not simply a function of empathy. Simulative reasoning, to lift a term from computational theory, involves "reasoning about another agent's reasoning," what an earlier generation might have loosely called "imagination." Simulative reasoning "is not unique to mass media persuasion," Douglas Walton writes, "[b]ut here"—on the Internet—"it has special features, because the respondent is not a single individual but a mass audience composed of many individuals who may think differently about any issue or problem."[31] Walton's work updates and evolves McLuhan, demonstrating the way the new media changes not just rhetorical dynamics but our very concepts of space and imagination. Like Barlow, Westphal, and Giles, Walton sees something new afoot. In contemporary America, the "mass audience" is not just the national newspaper readership of the twentieth century. This audience is now a space where "anybody anywhere can say whatever they please, and nobody can stop them," a host of terrifying exceptions aside.

2. Geographies of Value: Klay's *Redeployment*

To be sure, it is the scholar's job to problematize and complicate even the most seemingly stable categories of discourse and identity. But then even the category of "identity" itself deserves complication. In his review of Klay's collection in *The New York Times*, Dexter Filkins pairs *Redeployment* with Tim O'Brien's *The Things They Carried* for the way the two texts cumulatively estrange the reader from the soldier's national identity. Like O'Brien's depiction of the Vietnam War and the way it "splintered the psyches of the men who fought it," *Redeployment*, Filkins argues, "grapples with a different war but aims for a similar effect: showing us the myriad human manifestations that result from the collision of young, heavily armed Americans with a fractured and deeply foreign country that very few of them even remotely understand."[32] Like Filkins, I read Klay's work as participating in a tradition. But Klay evolves that tradition. Like so much great modern literature, *Redeployment* succeeds because it changes the rules of engagement, the ways in which character, author, and reader read each other. "Psychological Operations," the story I would like to focus on, takes place in a setting where the discourse about identity politics is uniquely dense and contested: the university. Unlike many soldier stories, Klay's project does not seek geopolitical or ideological shelter in the compartmentalized code of the platoon in the midst of battle. Instead, in his collection, Klay splinters the sensible space of the psyche (or authorial identity) and, thereby, confronts the complexity of identity, teasing out the loose threads that tie this soldier-writer's soldier-characters to an ethical code that, stretching beyond platoon and the state, effectuates a dissensual narrative spatialization that pushes and tests traditional American values beyond US boundaries.

"Psychological Operations" compels the reader into troubled territory, subtle meta-fictional terrain. Like many other stories in this collection, Klay's protagonist is indeed located in the American homeland, but also, more specifically, Klay's character finds himself in and at a writerly site. *Redeployment* is full of stories about contested narratives. In "Unless It's A Sucking Chest Wound," there is an "adjutant" responsible for handling the multiplicitous genres of "the battalion's paperwork: casualty reports, correspondence awards, FITREPS, legal issues, et cetera."[33] In "Money as a Weapons System," Klay takes the metanarrative model further. He plays the part of Nathan, a Foreign Services Officer whose translator is "a short and pudgy Sunni Muslim" who is called "the Professor" because he was once a professor before "you came and destroyed this country."[34] "Money as a Weapons System" is a master class in the many hats a writer must wear in order to capture the complex intersectional world of the American military in its engagement with the Global War on Terror, and in it Nathan is an American civilian working for the military alongside an Iraqi who is also liminally attached to that same military but not enlisted. Both men require constant translation from the other and Klay's protagonist must repeatedly translate for the reader the rhetorical minefield of merely sending emails in which Nathan requests money for projects such as a women's health clinic and a beekeeping grant for Iraqi widows. However, the story's central tragicomic enterprise involves Nathan restraining himself in emails with an American executive named Gene Gabriel Goodwin who wants to transform Iraq and instigate "democracy" by funding an Iraqi baseball league. The baffling pattern one finds in this story and, more particularly, in "Psychological Operations" is a clash between a simple and more complex "democracy" as well as a clash between the soldier and the civilian, the American and the foreigner. These are not the pure narratives of the platoon as a cocoon in a foreign land. Many readers may wish for the clarity of good versus evil and the stable identity categories and ethnically sealed genres and avatars of war stories past, but in *Redeployment*, broadly, and "Psychological Operations," specifically, Klay demonstrates just how subversively porous and connected the world can be when viewed through the lens of the Global War on Terror.

Like many veteran-activists, Klay resists the monolithic characterization of the military, but perhaps no soldier from the War has better captured what Leo Marx called "the singular plasticity of the American situation" than this particular writer in this particular story.[35] "Psychological Operations" demonstrates for the reader of literature what American military psychological operations demonstrate for the state and its targets: language as a weapons system. In the case of the story, the reader is the target. "Psychological Operations" begins with an epigraph from Ahmed Abdel Mu'ti Hijazi: "I learned words from among the languages of the earth/to seduce foreign women at night/and to capture tears!"[36] This is a careful strategic gambit that sets the stage for the narrative of Waguih, a Coptic Christian with roots in Egypt; for Hijazi, the poet, is himself Egyptian. Dissonant connections and interlocking identities build the ethos of this story even before Klay's first words. As the poem suggests, this is a story about language and seduction, targeting an audience through a cosmopolitan aesthetic. The trick, however, is that the target may well be our notion of targeting, the problems that arise when one identifies—targets—a problem too carelessly. Like

The Arabian Nights, this is a story about stories as tools of seduction and means of survival. But instead of a woman telling stories to a man, in "Psychological Operations," it is a man desperately telling stories to a woman.

Waguih and Zara seem to misidentify each other from the beginning. "Everything about Zara Davies," Klay writes, "forced you to take sides."[37] The same could be said for the narrator. The Black woman and the male soldier seduce the reader into the tempting territories of identity politics, the binaries that increasingly seem to divide the nation. Masculinity and conservatism over here, diversity and feminism over there. Imperialism and colonialism over here, liberation and resistance over there. Set at Amherst College, the reader/target of "Psychological Operations" is perhaps tempted to enjoy the one-dimensional stereotypes Klay deploys to pillory the traditional students in the "Punishment, Politics, and Culture" class Waguih shares with Zara: "the guys in khakis and polos, the girls either in sweatshirts or in expensively tasteful but boring clothes."[38] Yes, what we have here early on in the story is a monolithic block of white privilege, a Black woman, and a Black male soldier. If only the story were so simple. If only there were such a thing as a sacred identity category that conferred upon the subject a divine eye.

Klay draws Waguih as an Egyptian-American who plays at the game of identity and division, a soldier who "tended to play the world-weary vet who'd seen something of life" and had "had some soul-scarring encounter with the Real: the harsh, unvarnished, violent world-as-it-actually-is, outside the bubble of America and academia."[39] Zara, on the other hand, "was running her own game. As a Black girl from Baltimore, she had a fair share of street cred," but as the daughter of a Johns Hopkins physics professor and a real estate attorney, she was "a million times more privileged than 90 percent of the white guys I served with in the Army."[40] What Klay stages here, through his Coptic Christian avatar, is the complicated face of a human being possessing a mask of the "sacred" identity category he describes in "The Warrior at the Mall." Klay may be the soldier-writer, but Waguih is the soldier. Both possess the ethos of lived experience and the way that plays out in a contemporary college classroom, but, consistent with his essay, Klay does not write to elevate that identity category. Through a simultaneously unstable but precise weaponization of language, Klay creates a democratic aesthetic space similar to the one Rancière describes where language "destroys the identities and hierarchies of the representational order."[41] For Rancière, such linguistic operations are revolutionary insofar as they detach "power from the agents who put it to work in order to make it its own power, the impersonal power of writing."[42] As described in the introduction, Klay's characters, Waguih and Zara, offend each other. They ostensibly find each other offensive. They debate. They challenge, befuddle, and complicate. They resist each other's putative identities. They are, in Mark Danielewski's words, "the democracy of two" proffered by the one, the author.[43] However, when Zara perceives Waguih threatening her life in a private verbal exchange, she goes public and calls for adjudication. She, thereby, for the reader, serves as a call for mediation and code complicated by Waguih's echo when he himself calls for official intervention due to Zara's insensitivity to his PTSD. Waguih seems disappointed in Zara when she breaks the intimacy of their private dialogue by lodging her formal complaint with the university. "I'd never picked her for another thin-skinned golden child," Klay writes, "walking through campus like Humpty Dumpty on a tightrope, waiting for a scandalous word to unsteady her balance and shatter her precious identity."[44] Precious identity indeed. Such aggressive language from a character is, of course, ironized by the author's biography and his careful attention to the effects of such "scandalous" words, the narration of the nuanced scenes that follow from the POV of a "37F, a specialist in Psychological Operations. If I couldn't PsyOps my way out of this," Waguih says in the midst of mediation, "I wasn't worth a damn."[45] And so we witness Waguih/Klay move from casting aspersions on "precious" words to showing how a single word—language—can change everything. This attention to language and consciousness, rather than expedited linear plot, is in keeping with the aesthetic of dissensual spatiality. Here and elsewhere, Klay's work constantly presents the reader with "terps," writers, and students, literary characters translating the other or the "enemy" for the military and the reader and negotiating plots of consciousness, relationship, and socialization. If the central question of neogeography and theorists like Foucault, Giles, Moraru, and Westphal is why things happen *where* they do, Klay's work interrogates this seemingly simple question by constantly locating the language and experiences of distant others not just inside America's national borders but inside the sacred identity category of the soldier himself.

Klay has, in many ways, become the spokesman for a generation of writers that may one day take their place next to the Beats and the Lost Generation as representatives of a zeitgeist. As soldier-writers and editors for a collection called *The Road Ahead*, Adrian Bonenberger and Brian Castner, in a dual-authored essay, argue that veterans of the Global War on Terror not only have "unprecedented technical skills" correspondent to our digital age, but "many are also steeped in war literature, readers already well-versed in the canon from

Hemingway to Herr."⁴⁶ The PsyOps specialist in "Psychological Operations" is not just telling a war story. This narrative is a dense piece of critifiction that evinces a range of cultural literacy. Klay's deft references to "Althusserian interpellation," identity politics, Egyptian poetry, and American military propaganda may be nothing but the sleight of hand one often finds in young fiction writers who are privileged enough to work with daring and erudite editors, but I don't think so. A dominant pattern in Klay's work is his play with narrative space and the ethos of the veteran. To be sure, this ethos is what derails Zara's mediation with Waguih. "Psychological Operations" is a story about a debate that can never find a proper place for resolution. Why do things happen where they do? Maybe the better question is, where can we cultivate a space where the truth can finally be told? "Psychological Operations" tracks a conversation between two students who cannot seem to escape their performative identities within the confines of the university classroom and continually show contempt for each other within this setting. Not only do they perform contempt and outrage, but they threaten each other, reproducing the very violence they claim to abhor. So, in order to resolve the threat, the story moves to a new setting, an administrative office. But when the university's "Special Assistant" confronts Waguih with Zara's charge of threat, Waguih responds with a half-truth: "I'm a crazy vet, right? But the only mention of violence came from her. When she accused me of murdering Muslims."⁴⁷ Klay then describes a room that has been transformed by a single fictive word, space and perception reorganized by language. "In a way," he writes, "I'd lied. She'd never used the word murder."⁴⁸ As the Iranian-American poet, Solmaz Sharif, writes in "Look": "Let it matter what we call a thing."⁴⁹ The writer of literature knows that stories—like lives and nations—are often kept together by the barest gossamer of language. The granular and global drama is language, and Klay demonstrates this by building complex and dissensual narrative environments and by drawing soldier-characters like Waguih, a new generation of veterans returning from war with meta-cognitive gifts and cosmopolitan subjectivities that profoundly complicate their notions of ethics and identity:

> "In the Army we had a saying," I said. "Perception is reality. In war, sometimes what matters isn't what's actually happening, but what people think is happening. The Southerners think Grant is winning Shiloh, so they break and run when he charges, and so he does, in fact, win. What you are doesn't always matter. After 9/11 my family got treated as potential terrorists. You get treated as you're seen. Perception is reality."⁵⁰

For Waguih, a Black Egyptian-American Coptic Christian, and for his author, Klay, a veteran, a writer, a Dartmouth graduate and a white American man, the line "What you are doesn't always matter" resonates in opposite directions, splitting the reader's senses dissensually. When Waguih responds to Zara's accusation of linguistic violence with an accusation (and act) of linguistic violence all his own, the university's "Special Assistant" is left dumbfounded in the face of two students doubling down on the ethos of their "precious identities"—two actors performing outrage—until Waguih simultaneously concedes and attacks by saying, "I understand why she said that," but then adds, "sometimes I can't sleep at night ... I see the dead ... I hear the explosions."[51] Again, the fiction within the fiction is noted as such by Klay: "That wasn't true. Most nights I slept like a drunken baby."[52] But the move—the fidelity to the monolithic identity—the stereotype of the traumatized veteran—it works. "Zara, whose face had held a lively anger moments before, looked surprised and, I think, saddened."[53] Both characters have now disrespected each other equally in their fictions of disrespect and false outrage, and both feel a sense of disappointment not just in each other, but in themselves for having leaned so heavily on a singular, reductive identity. It is only here after the drama of the publicly performed monolithic identity that the true drama of disidentification, relation, and ethical remapping becomes possible.

The liminal zone where this reorientation finally takes place is the printed or digital page, a domain of narrative consciousness articulating itself in the constructed exchanges of characters, reader and writer, and also what one might classically call a setting: the "porch" of an "apartment" and a "ratty couch" that "looked out at the street."[54] In other words, in reference to this latter category of setting, readers find themselves in a private dwelling looking out on the common shared space of "the street," that public strip of common land where travel takes place. After their public mediation with the "Special Assistant," Zara and Waguih agree to meet in this particular geography that is not inside the "apartment" but certainly not outside on the "street." They share a hookah on Waguih's porch. "Possession of a hookah is against the student honor code," Zara says to Waguih. To which Waguih responds: "I don't follow the student honor code."[55] And so, as mentioned in the introduction, the public war between two rigid identity blocks becomes a private attempt at reconciliation between two complex individuals consecrated with a very particular forbidden object (with Middle Eastern provenance), shrouded in smoke. Two sacred identities, after being unable to resolve their differences in public, meet in private and agree to violate a "code." Thus, within the parameters of a narrative, what might loosely be called a simulation of mediated discourse, public speech, or rhetoric, turns to narrative or storytelling or, more precisely, a meta-narrative. Waguih, with the smoke in his lungs, tries, in the space of this storyworld, to tell the real story of what he saw in the war, the dead he witnessed while performing his duties as a PsyOps specialist. Here, the linear action pauses and the narrative space dilates. "I didn't know how to start, which was unusual," Klay writes. This dilation and dialogic uncertainty is at the root of the dissensual aesthetic, and so is attention to geography and space.

Waguih, like the reader, needs grounding, a synonym often used for understanding. Understanding what, one might ask. What Waguih has in mind is a setting of spatial parameters—an "orientation" in the basic coordinates of fictional topography and toponymy. "I needed to ground myself," he says to the reader. "I began, as you do in the military, with geographic orientation. I told her about East Manhattan, which was a section of Fallujah north of Highway 10." Grounding, in this story, means revealing Iraqi place names imported from the very city name where the Global War on Terror began: New York. The dignity of care Klay's story presents to both the reader and Zara is a constant ritual of grounding in dissensual place names, locations that are both "here" and "there." In "Psychological Operations," Klay challenges the singular, monologic, racist, nationalist character that dominates the narratives of so many war stories past. He invites the "other" into the story and its space. From the minimalism and stoic silences of Hemingway's the First World War veterans to the private mystifications of O'Brien's Vietnam veterans, readers now witness an evolution: a veteran of the Global War on Terror telling his story through an Egyptian-American avatar telling a story to an African-American woman, but the storyteller within the storyteller is not sure how to tell the story, and this "hesitant accountability," as the critic of post-9/11 fiction Georgiana Banita calls it, is crucial.[56] Waguih's hesitation to account—his shrouded uncertainty—does not mean that Klay himself does not know what he is doing. What this soldier-writer achieves, in this moment of smoky private dialogue between Zara and Waguih, is a public story read in private by a reader who must contend with the way that both Zara and Waguih continually resist not just Waguih's story, but perhaps even storytelling itself.

A contrarian genetics marks the democratic aesthetic. Klay's narrative is agitated, hesitant, and shaky, resistant to linear time. It thereby complicates the ostensibly simple words of Diogenes: "I am a citizen of the world." The American soldier-writer does not disown his or her nation, but he or she is often at war with the authorities that territorialize that nation's story, drawing hard lines between the homeland and the theaters of war. "Each night," Klay describes Waguih narrating to Zara how "the mosques would blast the same messages over the *adhan* speakers: 'America is bringing in the Jews of Israel to steal Iraq's wealth and oil. Aid the holy warriors. Do not fear death. Protect Islam.'"[57] Dissensus does not privilege or erase invasion, occupation, or the occupier's propaganda and certitudes, but it places these forces in contentious relationships. An official state narrative is not censored, but instead its unwinding becomes part of the narrative. Klay is, thus, making a number of dissensual *narrative* moves here, and it is probably time to reemphasize that this is how, in Rancière and others, dissensus operates, namely through symbolism, literary language largely, and specifically narrative voice and perspective. Klay is using the tongue of the other, Arabic. His story is told in the liminal zone of an Egyptian-American man telling the story of Israeli threat to Iraqi wealth while his interlocutor is constructed as an African-American woman. "As PsyOps, I told her, part of our job was to counter those messages."[58] This "counter"—this contrarian political-aesthetic—is the point. Part of the acrobatics of "Psychological Operations" is in the way Klay builds a counter-narrative into nearly every strand of his narrative totality. "'Gunfire was a part of daily life,' I started—but that sounded too hard-guy."[59] The counter is both within and without, internalized by both the storyteller and the storyteller within the storyteller, as well as the storyteller's built-in audience: Zara. As Waguih describes a unit of Marines with one "little square bodied Marine" who had not yet killed an Iraqi, but then suddenly had, putting the unit at "a hundred percent," Zara interjects by saying "'And Marines think that's a good thing.'"[60] "'Of course,' I said, though I realized I was simplifying." Waguih's divided response shows the way a doubled dialogic narrative structure builds resistance into itself. This is the democracy of two, a dissensual aesthetic, the rigid identity disidentifying with itself in the name of the other.

Klay's story goes deeper and deeper into the shroud of literal and figurative smoke, the *shisha*. Waguih continues what, on the one hand, seems a seduction and, on the other, a kind of therapy, a working out of the stories he refuses to see as mere trauma. The poem that serves as the story's epigraph teases the prospect that Waguih, like Hijazi, might be doing nothing more than eliciting tears to "seduce foreign women at night," but Zara is not a foreigner. Zara and Waguih are both Americans. And Zara does not sleep with Waguih. What she does do is help him tell the story of "Lalafallujah," his account of using a propaganda of heavy metal, hip-hop, and pornographic profanity to counter the propaganda from the mosques. She helps him tell the story of America's Global War on Terror rhetoric by being both present and resistant: "She shook her head," Klay writes.

> "So how did you kill people?" she said.
> "The insults," I said. "And of everything we did, that got the most satisfying feedback. I mean, the muj would charge and we'd listen as the Marines mowed them down. Sergeant Hernandez called it 'Jedi mind trick shit.'"[61]

Perhaps, like Zara, the reader shakes his or her head but continues to engage with this story of "Lalafallujah" as Waguih homes in on the climax: the narrative of the murder of a particular Iraqi named Laith al-Tawhid. As we approach al-Tawhid's death, the American storyteller as Egyptian-American storyteller describes the way his American propaganda begins to work within the mind of an Iraqi man as an African-American woman who has taken to wearing traditional Islamic garb listens. "Laith al-Tawhid was no idiot," Klay describes Waguih describing. "He was a fundamentalist, not dumb. He wasn't going to come running because I called him names. But I knew how to get him. Women."[62] Here we begin to see identity politics deployed as the protean "Jedi mind-trick" that it can be, a tool appropriated and weaponized by all sides for all manner of content and outcome even as it is, here, the context of this story that takes place on the edge of the university. Which is to say, in the midst of a contemporary context where women are dramatically transforming the cultural conversation and literary marketplace, the reader finds himself or herself in a story in which a woman both enables and resists a cosmopolitan man as he tells his story of using women to bait a fundamentalist man (Laith al-Tawhid) into defending women. Disidentification and ethical remapping occur simultaneously in the story within the story—Waguih's account of his hand in the death of Laith al-Tawhid.

As "Psychological Operations" approaches its close, Zara is holding Waguih's hand. Seduction still seems possible. The reader, at least, is seduced into a confrontation with his or her desire for a traditional sex- and death-driven plot, the linear model of time versus the dissensual model of space. Will Zara and Waguih hook up in the end? Who will die and how in this war story Waguih shares with a woman who is holding his hand? When Zara asks Waguih what he finally said to draw Laith al-Tawhid to his death, Waguih says he told al-Tawhid "'we have your women,'" "'your wife and your daughters,'" and "'I told him we found them whoring themselves out to American soldiers, and we were bringing them to the office building,'" and Waguih/Klay goes on, adding, carefully, that he had also told this story to his (Waguih's) father, and both his father and Zara seemed profoundly uncomfortable at the fact that he, Waguih, had "screamed out, in the Iraqi Arabic I'd learned in my private time, that we'd fuck his daughters on the roof and put their mouths to the loudspeakers so he could hear their screams."[63] It is just before this point, on a porch (neither inside or outside), in a sensory environment of "shisha" and after the description of "Lalafallujah," that Zara "pressed her hand into mine," and in this pressing of flesh we, the reader, witness two characters joined in a state of sensory liminality, a subversive narrative space layered with past, present, and future, joined identities, life and death.[64] Just before Waguih describes the perverse tools he deployed to kill Laith al-Tawhid, Zara is with him.

But then descends the "meta" moment when Waguih describes the death. The story's space, far from being enslaved to time, again moves recursively. It expands, roots moving rhizomatically down as branches rise slowly up. Klay tells of Waguih describing to Zara how he told

> this to my dad in our living room in their house in Virginia. It's not the house I grew up in. They'd moved to a cheaper area once I was out of high school, and we're in this tiny little room with an icon of Saint Moses the Black, who was a thief and a slave, and Saint Mary of Egypt, who was a prostitute, and Matisse's stupid fish and that goddamn flag and the fake 9/11 steel coin.[65]

In the instant before he conveys to Zara the obscene context of Laith al-Tawhid's death, Waguih retreats into details that enlarge the storytelling space and complicate the audience's relationship to place. These meta moves send the reader back in time so that they, like Zara and Waguih, are joined to a multidimensional narrative fabric that is at once Iraq, Massachusetts, Virginia, and Egypt, a diversity of habitats surrounded by an array of objects that juxtapose Black Saints (both men and women) with idols of the fallen towers from New York City. Prior to confessing to a woman that he had desecrated women in order to kill an ostensible enemy, Waguih is positioned by Klay as bonded to Zara, New York City, Egypt, Moses, Mary, Massachusetts, Virginia, Iraq, and the artwork of Matisse, quite likely a reference to the artist's 1912 masterpiece, "The Goldfish." Like an impressionist who favors round brushed contours and blended colors over fidelity to sharp shapes and linearity, Klay's story conjoins the discrete, the individuals who have been divided from each other in public institutional settings. However, even as impressionists emphasize unity and movement, their characters cannot move like those in literature and, thus, the effect here is novel. After hearing of al-Tawhid's slaughter, Zara "pulled back her hand."⁶⁶ The physical bond breaks, but the yoke of the narrative remains. Waguih continues the onslaught, the war story within the war story. He rubs it in, taking a strange but recognizable confessor's relish in finally telling the truth. "'I stayed on those speakers for an hour,'" Klay writes.

> Telling him how when his daughters bent down to pray, we'd put our shoes on their heads and rape them in the ass. Rub our foreskins on their faces. A thousand dicks in your religion, I told him, and in forty minutes, a thousand American dicks in your daughters.⁶⁷

When Waguih explains that he has shared these details of a psychological operation because they "worked," the reader is invited to either reject or accept this explanation and its grounds of causality, functionality, and utility. Zara, for her part, rejects the smooth explanation. Causality—the illusion of linear consequence—is not the kind of story she wants. As Westphal writes of what he calls "the new realism," the call for "smooth space" presents readers and characters alike with problems which seem "either nostalgic or incantatory, because striations are virtually everywhere."⁶⁸ Virtually indeed. "Psychological Operations," whether read in the digital environment of an e-reader or in the traditional materiality of a bound book, is a simulation, a virtual reality, a narrative operating system. And it is a transgressive one that disassociates itself with the linear models of the past and self-consciously utilizes those linear expectations in the name of a new spatial map. When Waguih can clearly tell that Zara does not like the ending of his story, he admits, "My dad didn't either. He'd rather I shot them in the face. In his mind, that's so much nicer. So much more honorable. He'd have been proud of me, if I'd done that. You'd like me better, too." To which Zara responds: "I'd rather you hadn't done anything."⁶⁹ In the end, Zara resists Waguih's assumption about her reaction.

Does the reader share Zara's stated preference—a story where nothing happens—a man who has done nothing? Waguih, as his confession reaches its strange and recursive conclusion, believes he has won. Klay frames him as feeling that he has Zara trapped in anger and an uncomfortable truth. For a moment, Waguih believes his story—his repackaged propaganda—has sealed the deal. Klay seems to suggest that if Zara had reacted in anger, Waguih, strangely, would have been safe, his identity preserved. "No one can really cut you when they're angry," Klay writes. "It clouds their mind too much. Better to be like me in Fallujah, lying through your teeth and shouting hateful things with calm intelligence, every word calibrated for maximum harm."[70] But Zara does not ultimately respond to this privately told story of violence and unclouded calculation in the way Waguih expects, and so a different kind of cloud is presented to the mind, a cloud of unknowing. Zara is not drawn into sex, rage, or violence like al-Tawhid. "Zara's outburst didn't come," Klay writes. "She just stood there. And then some emotion I couldn't identify moved through her, and she didn't seem angry anymore. She stepped back and looked at me, considering. She reached up and adjusted her shawl."[71] Klay does not call the "shawl" a "hijab," just as he does not call the "warrior" a "veteran" or "soldier." Zara, with her shawl back on, puts a hand on Waguih's shoulder and after telling him, "I'm glad you can talk about it," walks off the porch and Waguih becomes aware that Zara "didn't quite belong here" and "neither did I."[72] This disidentification, rather than a narrative outcome of sex or death, leaves the reader in an ethically subversive narrative space. The deferral or refusal of seduction's endgame, the "petit-mort" of orgasm and the consensual certitude of sleep that follows, is not the rightful inheritance of the American soldier-writer's Global War on Terror narrative. Instead, both parties remain awake and "unsettled," half-hopeful that "we'll talk another time."[73] Sitting on a porch in America, these two characters of color, triangulated by a white soldier-writer, have traveled to Iraq together, an Iraq known as "East Manhattan" and "Lalafallujah." Their narrative has transported them—and the reader—to Outback Steakhouse and Virginia, an American state imbued with the language of virginity that populates the texts of Christianity and Islam. But in the present tense space of their story, these characters do not eat, and they do not have sex. However, they do transgress. They violate the codes of sacred identity categories just as Klay subverts the old linear codes of storytelling. Together, with the reader, they participate in a disidentity politics.

3. Truth in Digital Space: Snowden's *Permanent Record*

In his review of *Permanent Record*, Jonathan Lethem describes what he reads as the climax of Snowden's memoir: the moment "in which the whistleblower-in-the-making sees behind the curtain."[74] The "curtain," for Lethem, refers to the walls—firewalls, border walls, and bedroom walls—that used to divide not just Americans from Americans but this particular American intelligence officer—Snowden—from the private lives of people all over the world. With the advent of "XKEYSCORE, the NSA's ultimate tool of intimate electronic surveillance," "which Snowden aided in perfecting," intelligence officers can now break down the geographical distances that used to protect private lives and private property. This moment of seeing "behind the curtain," like Dorothy's privileged glimpse in *The Wizard of Oz*, has a mythical quality to it, which Lethem emphasizes. Snowden's story, for Lethem, exists in a tradition of narratives like Robert Sheckley's short story, "Is That What People Do?," in which the narrator happens upon a pair of magical binoculars that "have a fabulous capacity not only for seeing through walls, but also for diminishing the distance" between the main character and those on whom he spies. Snowden's memoir, like *The Wizard of Oz* and "Is That What People Do?" travels to forbidden places, unveils the world "behind the curtain," and by doing so reveals the ways in which the wizardry of new technologies enable a new digital tyranny and a new digital cartography, an ever-evolving map of new subjectivities co-evolving with this new geographical space.

Like all of the writers in this book, Snowden cultivates a novel spatial ethos. Like the others, essential parts of Snowden's story "take place" in settings walled off to most American citizens. Therefore, his memoir raises questions about the storyteller's role as a kind of pioneer or cartographer, a subjectivity whose exposure to new environments is transformative for reader and writer alike. The relationship between geography and literature can be expressed as the relationship between truth-telling and place or story and space, but a responsible scholar will acknowledge that these terms are not simply interchangeable. Thus, a study of veteran-activists and ethical remapping can either conflate them all, treat each discretely, or carefully demonstrate the conceptual overlap and liminal domains that attend this problem of where the story takes place and how the narrative space is constructed as a rhetorical geography all its own. In *Permanent Record*, Snowden goes to great pains to map his memoir along a chronological line. A distant overview of his narrative map would show a story traveling from birth in North Carolina to adolescence in Maryland, to early employment in Northern Virginia, to a deeper immersion in the global intelligence community in Switzerland and Japan, to the decisive moment of whistleblowing in Hawaii. *Permanent Record* concludes in Moscow, Russia, where Snowden now lives (and posts) in exile. However, if one were to zoom in on this ostensibly linear narrative course, like a web surfer using Google Maps to burrow down from a geo POV to a national POV to a backyard POV, one would notice discrepancies, moments of recursivity and a careful, self-conscious handling of that "hyperobject" Lethem refers to in his review, that operating system that destabilizes every statal place into a series of dissensual spaces: the Internet.[75] Snowden may have been born in Elizabeth City, North Carolina, on June 21, 1983, but he grew up in the spaces of the electronic frontier, and his memoir often ventures into those new webbed spaces as well as back in time to an earlier frontier and the American Revolution. Snowden came of age in a generation that remembered a world without the Internet, but the narrative avatar he constructs, prior to that avatar's decision to blow the whistle in Hawaii, was, as a young man, suddenly thrust into a geography where the webs of the Net were increasingly interlaced with daily life. In his own words, "the computer and I were inseparable."[76] With a subjectivity constructed in almost cyborgian terms, Snowden's individual identity, in this seemingly linear plot, is bound up with an exponentially increasing cast of characters from all over the world. This section will focus on Snowden's construction of himself, his valuation of "encryption" in this construction, and the way this "encryption" or *disidentity* facilitates his moment of transformation in the geographical place and literary space he names "paradise": Hawaii. Snowden's memoir democratizes Hawaii, transforming a discrete statal place into a deeply textured literary space teeming with a diversity of voices that defy the boundaries of the state in the name of the nation.

Hawaii, for many, is a place of vacation, certainly more tourism than terrorism. It is a marketed image of a geography at once American and other. Packaged as both "paradise" and America's fiftieth state, this chain of islands, once known as "the Sandwich Islands," is indeed sandwiched between the East and the West. First settled by Polynesians in the sixth century, first visited by white settlers in the late eighteenth century and then annexed by the United States in 1898, Hawaii's soft and soothing public image—its public relations avatar, if you will—is often wildly at odds with its history. Like Snowden himself, the narrative territory where his story dilates teems with complexity and contradiction, a bristling history. If Snowden's individual identity is webbed to the world of others online, the American homeland is also now bound to the liminal lands and inhabitants it has colonized. Like the former geographical frontier, the electronic one blurs the borders between nations and concepts like place and space, to say nothing of the boundary between subject and object. Like the biblical Eden, Hawaii and the Internet possess a certain pastoral quality. These shared spaces trouble simple histories and enable elusive identities and subjectivities. Building on the work of Lagasnerie, Westphal, Nussbaum, Max Kirchner, and others, this chapter argues that Snowden represents a novel (dis) identity. Lagasnerie argues that the Internet is a space of "dissolving traditional allegiances" that "gives the subject the ability to practice what one might call a chosen socialization." Implicit in such discourse and this study is the evolving problem of truth-telling in digital space and the way such digital truths alter the traditional lenses of geography.

Thus, discourse on geography and parrhesia needs to be established, but, as Kirchner notes in his 2014 paper on Snowden and parrhesia, "Evidence of the concepts of parrhesia and truth-telling in geography are still virtually non-existent and papers on speaking truth to power are sparse and dated. Yet truth-telling and parrhesia are inherently geographical due to the truth-teller's necessary interaction with others, as well as the practical understanding that the concept provides."[77] Kirchner reads in Snowden a parrhesiac voice that is involuntary. Far from the Freudian conception of the discrete individual whose truth-telling is an act of will, Kirchner sees Snowden's parrhesia as an "event" bound to a web of mediating processes. Although I take issue with Kirchner's specifically Deleuzian and Foucauldian analysis of Snowden which renders the whistleblower merely as "someone who is produced by the event," it is important to mention that Kirchner's study preceded the publication of Snowden's memoir.[78] If Kirchner robs Snowden of agency and frames the whistleblower as one "acting out of necessity, rather than as a rational being," perhaps the blame for this construction rests partially with time and the writer. Snowden tried to erase himself. He enlisted the help of journalists, Glenn Greenwald and Laura Poitras, and initially allowed them to contextualize the documents he dropped. Snowden waited more than five years before telling his truth. By the time *Permanent Record* was published, the soldier-writer had been given ample time to read other readers and writers. The voice of Snowden's memoir seems, at times, to be an exercise in Walton's "simulative reasoning," an intertextual experience of the discursive domains the author's truth-telling has shaped, as well as the hole it has left. In other words, Snowden seems to know his audience.

Furthermore, like Klay, Snowden appears to relish the perversity of his disidentity and its intrinsic bond to his previous vocation, what he calls "the perverse reward of a self-denying career."[79] But rather than yield to the discourse of others (like Kirchner, Lagasnerie, or Rancière) Snowden, like an artist, gives this disidentity a name all his own and connects that name to the new respatializing processes that are remapping this hyperconnected world readers/users create every time they write, speak, post, surf, or otherwise leave their mark in cyberspace. In *Permanent Record*, the specific name Snowden gives for dissensual subjectivity derives from a self-consciously anti-idiomatic nomenclature. "Though there are a score of more popular and surely more accurate psychological terms for this type of identity split," he writes, "I tend to think of it as *human encryption*. As in any process of encryption, the original material—your core identity—still exists, but only in a locked and scrambled form."[80] Note Snowden's construction of identity here acknowledges "process" but preserves individual, the "core identity," all the while delivering his definition of "human encryption" in a voice that vacillates from first to second person. The notion of "human encryption," delivered here in the narrative space of a memoir, offers readers a way of understanding why this study of veteran-activists chooses to web together novels, short story collections, memoirs, and digital public writing. Like James Phelan who argues that narrative is rhetoric by virtue of its encounter with a public space and the audience implicit therein, I see a number of porous borders in the intellectual maps that seek to divide fiction from non-fiction, particularly in the domain of memoir. When Snowden becomes "Snowden" on the page (and online), he is taking part in a scrambling "process" that dissolves "traditional allegiances" and dissensually recouples this American citizen with distant others.

When *Permanent Record* arrives in Hawaii, Snowden's map for this narrative territory is guided not just by the simple legend of time but by the more complex legend of America's "founding documents." If each chapter of his memoir serves as a notional cartography—a space of ideas—for the place of his story, Hawaii is an exceptional domain where America's colonial texts coincide with its post-colonial history of twenty-first-century mass surveillance and the impressions of a young spy who is beginning to experience epilepsy and doubts about the ethics of his government. The narrative rhythm changes in Hawaii and becomes more recursive, three parts rhetoric for every one part narrative. But before readers arrive in Hawaii, Snowden prepares them for this strategic location in his introduction. *Permanent Record* is clear, from the beginning, that history was shaped by this particular geography: "It was only in paradise that I was finally in a position to see how all my work fit together, meshing like the gears of a giant machine to form a system of global mass surveillance."[81] Note how Snowden, even here, does not use the official place name of the American state. Instead, he prepares readers for a mythical place. Readers travel around the world with Snowden in *Permanent Record* but then pause in "the tunnel" in "paradise" and experience, like Alice going down the rabbit hole to Wonderland, a portal in which their relationship to time and space (as well as rhetoric and narrative) changes. The reader's time in the space of "paradise" expands. They receive six chapters for this geographical Hawaii territory, rather than one. They see subtle shifts in POV and a narrative state suddenly unmoored from the land, a voice freed from scene and launched into polemic, as if the two could be one. Like the model of play Westsphal describes in the "fictional pragmatics" of Kendall Walton, Snowden's narrative knows no bounds. Walton bases his theory of writing on "child's play," where the player, in his or her land of "pure make-believe," gives the reader the "gift of bringing fictional territories into relation with those of the referential world."[82] Snowden's memoir, like Walton's child, brings rhetoric into a relationship with narrative, a yoking together of worlds that is anchored by Snowden's ethos as not just a soldier and intelligence analyst but as a gamer who repurposed those very gaming tools to create world simulations for his government. It all becomes one in "the tunnel" of "paradise." But what the soldier-writer seems most adamant about emphasizing here in this dilated moment of decision is that the decisive moment in America's final most Western state was not inevitable.

"Nearly three thousand people died on 9/11," Snowden writes earlier in the book, but "over one million people have been killed in the course of America's response."[83] After traveling with Snowden, the freelancer in Northern Virginia, pre-9/11, to Snowden the enlisted Army soldier in Georgia at Fort Benning's Sand Hill training grounds, post-9/11, and from there into the labyrinth of America's international IC (Intelligence Community), the reader reaches a cumulative awareness of American ideals, motives, and transgressions filtered through the lens of Snowden's perceptions and narrative spatializations. After a childhood online and more than ten years inside the IC during the heart of the Global War on Terror, Snowden's identity is inseparable from the distant others he reads about, observes, and tracks. Snowden is certainly not the first American to express reservations about his country's military-industrial complex or its growing tally of war crimes, but by the time we land in Hawaii, Snowden has arrived at an awareness that he is "the only one in the region who knew the CIA's architecture," and "the only one in a room with a sense not just of how one system functioned internally, but of how it functioned together with multiple systems— or didn't."[84] Snowden's "sense" of intelligence "architecture" is precisely to the point of this book's concern with mapping. The soldier-writer's novel spatial ethos is not simply a function of "boots on the ground," "lived experience," or some other platitudinal expression of the soldier's authority. The soldier-writer, distinct from the soldier, offers readers a glimpse inside the "disposition matrix" of the Global War on Terror, a privileged point of view that subverts this privilege in the name of a greater duty to a democratic ideal.

True democracy in fiction, Rancière argues, only arrives when sensory impressions from different categorical valences clash and juxtapose, leveling the "aesthetic regime." Snowden in Hawaii, like Gramsci's "organic intellectual," is a worker inseparable from his work, a subjectivity with ideas bound to place and station, a technician who resides in a matrix surrounded by a tropical landscape that he hopes will be "beneficial for my epilepsy, since lack of sleep was thought to be the leading trigger of the seizures."[85] Can readers separate these Dostoyevskian symptoms of epilepsy and sleeplessness from the social fabric of the Global War on Terror? Snowden is at his breaking point in Hawaii, but also trying not to break, hoping the new assignment in "paradise" will allow him, like a computer, to reboot. "[T]he move," he writes,

> eliminated the driving problem: the Tunnel was within bicycling distance of a number of communities in Kunia, the quiet heart of the island's dry, red interior. It was a pleasant, twenty-minute ride to work, through sugarcane fields in brilliant sunshine. With the mountains rising calm and high in the clear blue distance, the gloomy mood of the last few months lifted like the morning fog.[86]

Note, without thinking about the colonial history of those "sugarcane fields," the soothing quality of the prose, the simulated ride through "paradise." What is perhaps most arresting about *Permanent Record* is Snowden's vacillation between "show" and "tell," narrative and rhetoric, manifesto and landscape. The mystery of Snowden's voice and his "human encryption," particularly as we approach his whistleblowing moment, becomes one of a multitude of subtexts that scramble his singular identity and complicate the narrative space of these decisive chapters set in Hawaii.

Hawaii, the most Western state in the American union, is also, of course, the state closest to the East. The islands, to this day, perform a pastoral function, providing travelers and residents alike a space that troubles the geographical binary of East and West. Hawaii's proximity to Asia is what rendered America vulnerable to the attacks on Pearl Harbor in the Second World War when Hawaii was still a "territory." Before Hawaii was an American colony, however, it was a chain of independent nations or tribes. *Permanent Record* carefully handles these islands of history where the territories of colonialism, tourism, and terrorism blur. "If the map is a means of interaction between the real and imaginary," Westphal writes, "everything is subject to reading."[87] What does

Westphal mean by this, and how does his concept of a one-world narrative map apply to Snowden's reading of Hawaii? Focal in Westphal's "geocriticism" is an awareness of the subjective (the imagination) in everything and the ongoing evolution of postmodern literary techniques. Westphal tracks the development of "dissociating strategies" that decenter discrete places like American Hawaii and transform them into an "open work" where writer and reader coalesce, a Borgesian space where "all the places of the world, seen from every angle, coexist."[88] Snowden's dilated and nodal Hawaii, opened by the suspense of impending decision, is, again, a kind of rabbit hole, an East in the West, a West in the East, an American state constantly subverted by American history and American ideals, a statal geography continually mined for its precolonial rituals and myths, the stories of the past at war with the present. "One night during the summer I turned twenty-nine," Snowden writes, "Lindsay finally prevailed on me to go out with her to a luau." Why, the reader might ask (like Snowden himself), are we about to spend our precious page/screen time at this "cheesy touristy" trap? Trap indeed.

Snowden and his girlfriend (now wife) attend the luau. Rather than emphasize, over and over again, as so many scholars have, that Hawaii (Pearl Harbor) was the ground zero of the Second World War just as New York was for the Global War on Terror, Snowden takes the reader farther back in time to ground his choice. "Hawaiian culture is ancient," he is careful to state, "although its traditions are very much alive; the last thing I wanted to do was to disturb someone's sacred ritual. Finally, however, I capitulated. I'm very glad I did. What impressed me the most was not the luau itself."[89] What transfixes Snowden is not the song and dance or the "fire-twirling spectacle." Just as Snowden the writer refuses to bite on the bait of the nation-state as a stable intellectual construction, he here turns away from a "spectacle" that might be viewed as colonial kitsch and instead directs the reader's attention to "an old man who was holding court nearby in a little amphitheater down by the sea."[90] Snowden listens to the old man. With his "soft but nasal island voice," the old man tells his audience a story about "the twelve sacred islands of the gods" and three in particular: "Kane-huna-moku, Khiki, and Pali-uli." Like Klay importing Arabic into his prose, so does Snowden allow a Polynesian tongue to invade the space of his American tale. The presence of these Hawaiian names—Kane-huna-moku, Khiki, and Pali-uli—serves a multitude of aesthetic purposes. Beyond the musicality of the language and the narrative ethics of respecting the linguistic territory of one's subject, the utterance of these names highlights the history of a nation within a nation, a world within a world. Just as the Global War on Terror systematically dislocates indigenous people all over the globe, the narrative pattern I locate in the soldier-writer community is one of refusal and restoration, a desire to honor the nations the American state historically and contemporaneously displaces. The novel spatial ethos on display in this veteran-activist community is, in effect, an ethical remapping. Specific to the old man's story and its intersection with Snowden's unveiling of America's secrets are "the lucky gods who inhabited these islands" and "decided to keep them hidden, because they believed that a glimpse of their bounty would drive people mad. After considering numerous ingenious schemes by which these islands might be concealed … they finally decided to make them float in the air."[91] Like the very national security secrets so many Americans were hearing rumors about in "the cloud," the islands of Kane-huna-moku, Khiki, and Pali-uli, were "exotic preserves that a pantheon of self-important, self-appointed rulers were convinced had to be kept secret and hidden from humanity." Unlike the "soft" voice of the old man, one can almost hear the sharpness of Snowden's tongue in his excoriation of the "self-important, self-appointed rulers." As Snowden's hunt for these "islands" of secrets heats up in Hawaii, he continues to develop his paradoxical narrative argument that the stakes of his individual struggle against "self-appointed rulers" are the stakes of the American struggle: democracy.

Snowden is himself "self-appointed." He was not elected to blow the whistle on the NSA, and he does not view himself, in Kirchner's words, as "someone who is produced by the event." Rather, his literary avatar, like a Promethean figure who has stolen fire from the gods, is constructed as an individual banished to that liminal territory between god and man, autocracy and democracy, sea and land: "I was alone," Snowden writes, "one man hunched over a blank blue ocean, trying to find where this one speck of dry land, this one data point, belonged in relation to all the others."[92] The islands of America's secret history are increasingly not secret to Snowden, but as he approaches the moment where he decides to declassify the NSA's system of mass surveillance, he continually circles back to America's revolutionary past and the stories of distant others. Just as he retreats into Hawaiian mythology in the chapter titled "The Tunnel," Snowden recursively travels back in time to 1787 in the Hawaiian chapter titled "Whistleblowing," and manages here, in this narrative space, to yoke contemporary America and its founding secular documents to the holy days and sacred ideas of people from all over the planet, both past and present.

The moves Snowden makes in the Hawaii chapters are consistent with the planetary, "one-world" pattern writers like Westphal, Banita, Walton, and Moraru extol as the future of narrative. Every time the reader thinks he or she is about to arrive at the "decision point," to lift the titular term from George W. Bush's ghostwritten memoir, Snowden disappears down the rabbit hole of history, myth, and sensory impression. What is rather remarkable about the book is the sense that, like with great novels, the digressions are precisely the point. Why does Snowden constantly return to America's revolutionary history? Why does he begin the "Whistleblowing" chapter by describing his duty of managing the NSA's "group calendars"? Why do readers waste time in an anecdote about the former employee's tendency to make "sure the calendar always had reminders of all the holidays, and I mean all of them: not just the federal holidays, but Rosh Hashanah, al-Fitr, Eid al-Adha, Diwali."[93] Is it too radical to argue that the tally of these holiday names with their histories rooted in far-off places embodies a basic cosmopolitan awareness of world religions and the people who honor them? And if one can grant Snowden a baseline martial cosmopolitanism, by virtue of his service, travels and erudition, is it really going too far to suggest that he evinces a narrative strategy by juxtaposing these transliterations of holiday names with the secular American holiday that falls on "the seventeenth of September"? What is the name of that national holy day, why is Snowden giving it so much space, and why won't he just cut to the chase and the whistleblowing moment?

Instead of cutting to the chase, Snowden plays with space and invades America's Global War on Terror present with its revolutionary past. Constitution Day, or Citizenship Day, "commemorates the moment in 1787 when the delegates to the Constitutional Convention officially ratified, or signed, the document."[94] Although Snowden is careful to mention established holidays mapped by Middle Eastern provenance, like "Rosh Hashanah," "al-Fitr," and "Eid al-Adha," he is also careful in stating that his "favorite" holiday, Constitution Day, "is not a federal holiday, just a federal observance, meaning that Congress didn't think our country's founding document and the oldest national constitution still in use in the world were important enough to justify giving people a paid day off."[95] Snowden's dissensual self-positioning consistently negates and includes, expands and resists, dilates and targets, moving in paradoxical and usefully contrarian circles around the untested assumptions of contemporary common sense. The focus of Snowden's rhetorical targeting and his narrative recursivity is the state or what he often more precisely refers to as the "Intelligence Community." His spatial ethos, like the IC's global purview, is all over the map. Like the state, he reads the individual and the nation's interests everywhere. He is, in a way, the negative of his abandoned circumambient community. He is everywhere as he disidentifies with the state in the name of the nation, or "the public" or "the people," in a move that is both narratively and rhetorically democratic. He remaps the idea of American allegiance by expanding his argument into digital and international territory and by continually locating his critique of the state not in the identities of "founding fathers" so much as in America's founding principles and documents, like the Constitution. Snowden does not sanctify the slave-masters posing on America's dollars, but he does amplify their aspirational tenets and the tension that still exists between theory and practice. "The Intelligence Community," Snowden writes, "had always had an uncomfortable relationship with Constitution Day … since the IC was rarely interested in spending some of its own billions on promoting civil liberties through stapled paper."[96] Whether Snowden's acerbic observations about the "IC" are accurate or not is beside the point of this study; the dissensual pattern is not.

Observe the careful attention to the senses; the observable world. Snowden is not taking on the IC's relationship with the abstract principles of the Constitution but, rather, its day-to-day handling of holidays. Rather than couching a "manifesto" in the unrooted realms of the autodidact, *Permanent Record* socially situates the whistleblower's claims in the sensory environment of a liminal state (Hawaii) and an office space where the choices come down to staples and paper or no staples and no paper. Do government officials print the Constitution and hand it out to employees by the water cooler or do they not? If it is okay to honor religious holidays like "Rosh Hashanah," "al-Fitr," and "Eid al-Adha," then why, in a country ostensibly committed to the separation of church and state, do "we" not honor "our" secular bible? Snowden plays the gadfly here, revealing, like Klay in "Psychological Operations," an ethical "perversity," or what one might call a useful Socratic contrariness. "I liked reading the Constitution partially because its ideas are great, partially because its prose is good, but really because it freaked out my coworkers."[97] In this single hypotactic sentence is a mirror reflecting the qualities of *Permanent Record*. Snowden's story continues to freak out his former coworkers and fellow citizens, but less and less with each passing year. His critique has now become a part of contemporary common sense. I argue, however, that this evolution of contemporary "common sense" could not have taken place without appeals to the senses, a body of rhetoric rooted in narrative and the dissensual and fundamentally "social" environments of the Internet. When readers finally do arrive at the "act" of whistleblowing, it is indeed a sensory act bound to a web of other acts woven together in a narrative fabric that includes Hawaiian myths, Islamic holidays, Nintendo video games, Mary Shelley's *Frankenstein*, Barlow's "A Declaration of the Independence of Cyberspace," corporate calendars, drone assassinations, Facebook posts, the terrorist attacks of 9/11, and the more than one million people that "have been killed in the course of America's response." To say nothing of the Constitution. Nearly two decades after the f(act), Snowden's "response" to "America's response" to 9/11, far from a hasty assault on distant others, is a deeply hesitant and imagined story that breaks down the walls between Americans and those precarious unnamed strangers that have been rounded up, tortured, killed, erased, or otherwise appropriated by the official narratives of the state. Like so many cosmopolitans before him, Snowden's story is a profoundly lonely one.

In the essay she wrote on cosmopolitanism that led to the book she co-wrote with Joshua Cohen (Snowden's collaborator), Nussbaum addresses the alienation of thinkers like Snowden, the paradoxical sense of exile that comes from including so many "others" in your landscape. "Becoming a citizen of the world is often a lonely business," she writes, seven years before 9/11. "It is, in effect, as Diogenes said, a kind of exile—from the comfort of local truths, from the warm nestling feeling of patriotism, from the absorbing drama of pride in one's self and one's own."[98] Seven years before 9/11 and one year before the first web browser (Netscape) went public, Nussbaum describes the "nestling feeling of patriotism" that would allure so many after the attacks on Washington and New York City. Like Klay, Nussbaum recognizes the danger of American values that evaporate on the other side of American borders. Snowden was not immune to that "nestling feeling" and, in fact, confesses to organizing his life around it by enlisting in the military. Like so many other whistleblowers who have served the US government, this soldier-writer's eventual exile was, to some extent, a function of an initial "nestling." What *Permanent Record* urges readers to imagine, however, is a recoupling after the decoupling, a new kind of nestling akin to the species Nussbaum describes, a new kind of American patriotism unbound to "vaporous" borders and "the comfort of local truths." For Snowden, Nussbaum, and, perhaps, their shared ghostwriter, Cohen, this new kind of thinking does not abandon America but instead expands America beyond its traditional constructions. "If one begins life as a child who loves and trusts its parents," Nussbaum suggests, "it is tempting to want to reconstruct citizenship along the same lines, finding in an idealized image of a nation a surrogate parent who will do one's thinking for one."⁹⁹ But if readers are not to obey the dictates of their parents, who or what are they to obey? It must be said that soldier-writers have a complex relationship to obedience. "It's not that you set out to oppose authority," Paley and Gallagher remind us. "In the act of writing you simply do." Likewise, Snowden and Nussbaum speak out against the authority of twentieth-century binary logic and the authority of Cold War common sense. Cosmopolitanism, so easy to dismiss for so long, is now experiencing an intellectual renaissance in light of planetary crises and the digital age. "Cosmopolitanism," far from providing a retreat into "[t]he New Cold War," "offers no such refuge," according to Nussbaum. "[I]t offers only reason and the love of humanity, which may seem at times less colorful than other sources of belonging."¹⁰⁰ So how does one draw out this missing color?

If the key recruitment tool for this new kind of patriotism or "belonging" is a "colorful" rhetoric, how does the writer develop a chromatic voice that makes sense? The martial cosmopolitanism on display in the post-9/11 soldier-writer community offers an ostensibly simple answer: deploy personal narratives that create space for the erased voices in the official narratives. But, to be clear, what Snowden's memoir demonstrates is far from a patchwork of manifesto and story. When, narratively situated in Hawaii, Snowden finally elects to blow the whistle on the NSA, the writer himself is situated in Russia with an entire field of discourse about his life on display over the "world wide web" or the "electronic frontier." The Russian-Hawaiian-American zone between the writer and his audience, like the forest of Arden in Shakespeare, is a space of scrambled identities that only the most deft readers of humanity can negotiate and even they, at times, will find confusion. This "frontier," where Snowden and reader meet (perhaps on a page, perhaps on a screen), is full of color and costume, the tastes and smells of Hawaii. But when it comes time to place his reasoning for his transgressive act, Snowden drops the dissensual mask, that narrative space where senses clash.

The preface to Snowden's key moment of parrhesia is constantly laced with "narrative," but the prose act itself is almost entirely "rhetoric," if I might be permitted, via quotes, to highlight the absurd binary of these categories and the way so many critics wish to divide the intellectual world (and English departments as well) between one way of writing and another. Of course, these divisions and academic specialties often serve individuals and institutions well, but Snowden, like Walton's child at play, exploits the exception. His narrative capitalizes on the exigence of binary assumptions about narrative and rhetoric, sense and sensibility, story and manifesto. Just as he scrambles the scrambling notion of dissensus with his own terminology ("human encryption"), Snowden, in the chapter titled "Whistleblowing," offers his own definition of a "whistleblower." Just before clarifying the truth-telling rationale he has been encrypting with narrative for the entire book, Snowden conceals his motives even further by reconfiguring the terms of the debate. A "whistleblower," according to Snowden, "is a person who through hard experience has concluded that their life inside an institution has become incompatible with the principles developed in—and the loyalty owed to—the greater society outside it, to which that institution should be accountable."[101] When this whistleblower finally decides to disidentify with the state in the name of the nation, he not only redefines the nation-state on his own terms, but he also redefines the whistleblower. One is tempted to sentimentally suggest that this is a story all Snowden's own, but that would be missing the point, the dissensual pattern, the contrarian spirit that travels like D.H. Lawrence's archetypal American snake and Wallace Stevens' serpent, shedding and sloughing its way out of Eden, through Arden, across the frontiers of the old West, and clear into the fog of the dark web.

As if to clarify such fog—the very scrambled narrative space he himself has cultivated—Snowden sets setting aside in the chapter titled "Whistleblowing." After defining "whistleblower" with his own terms, he does not beach the reader in scene, a token moment at a window in an apartment overlooking the ocean or the shopping malls of Hawaii. Instead, in his moment of decision he breaks utterly and decisively with his own narrative pattern. He abandons scene, that creative writing workshop mandate of "show, don't tell." And because he does, and because he has been rather disciplined in applying a narrative enamel to his "manifesto," one can, paradoxically, feel his anger, the unmooring of a self spent by the sense-stripping environments of what Snowden himself labels "the machine."[102] After leaving mainland America by choice but before being forced into asylum in Russia, Snowden spends a year in Hawaii, but he abandons this "paradise." Like a pioneer, he leaves behind the comforts of home. At the moment of uprooting, far from nostalgically looking back at palm trees, hula skirts, and sunset breakers, Snowden's story, instead, stares "the machine" (itself a metaphor) in the face and speaks to it in the mechanical language of logic with yet another metaphor shipped in: "This motive of restoration I take to be essential to whistleblowing: it marks the disclosure not as a radical act of dissent or resistance, but a conventional act of return—signaling the ship to return back to port, where it'll be stripped, refitted, and patched of its leaks before being given the chance to start over." Dissenting with Lagasnerie's construction of Snowden's dissent as a novel act of revolt, Snowden here "sets the record straight" about his "motive." If dissensus is an aesthetic of dissent, then, ultimately, it even takes issue with dominant constructions of dissent and dissensus. Years after dropping a trove of classified NSA documents in the hands of journalists, Snowden here explains his "total exposure of the total apparatus of mass surveillance—not by me, but by the media, the de facto fourth branch of the US government, protected by the Bill of Rights."[103] Even here, as he is clarifying, he is scrambling and encrypting, lacing himself in with the very "media" he seeks to separate himself from, tying himself, like a seasick sailor, to the mast of his metaphorical ship, "the Bill of Rights." His "human encryption," like a narrative onion router (the name of his favorite scrambling software), proceeds sentence by sentence, concealing claim with narrative, abstracting narrative from claim, and, further, abstracting self from media before couching that very self back into the nestle of the media. Thus, we, the people—Snowden's readers—might be smart to greet this scramble with the same skepticism as the author. We might be wise to question the simple and singular motive Snowden dangles in front of us like a piece of low-hanging fruit, forbidden only to intellectuals who make a life out of eschewing and forbidding the simple. In the final analysis, which, of course, never exists, Snowden tells readers that he "was resolved to bring to light a single, all-encompassing fact: that my government had developed and deployed a global system of mass surveillance without the knowledge or consent of its citizenry." Whether "a single, all-encompassing fact" exists is, perhaps, up to the reader or a jury in some court of the future. But how such facts or "truths" are handled in the new public sphere is, indeed, Snowden's key concern and, by the same token, the territory of this book; the problem of truth-telling in the novelistic world spaces of our time is, indeed, a major focus of this study.

When post-9/11 veteran-activists disidentify with conventional constructions of race, gender, or nationality, they are not simply reinscribing themselves into the postmodern matrix of deconstruction. The parrhesiac, dissensual, and cosmopolitan pattern I read in this community is not one of treachery, anarchy, cynicism, or recycled postmodern play. Like Snowden with his avatars, digressions, and narrative masks, this "human encryption" is not just "perversity" or fun and games, a casual shattering of a casual construction of a master narrative. The play has a purpose. It returns readers to history with a new spatial imaginary and a new narrative operating system. When Snowden describes himself, in the final paragraph of "Whistleblowing," as surrounded by other men and women like himself in "the Tunnel," he is addressing one of the core problems of contemporary truth-telling: the sense of ahistorical isolation and atomization, the repression of tradition, one truth apparently as good as another. Snowden may or may not be participating in "dissent" or "resistance" when he blows the whistle, but he resists the way readers and writers often alienate truth-tellers by conceptualizing them as "outlaws" or "lone wolves." By placing Snowden's story alongside other truth-tellers and a tradition of courage, this book, also, resists that atomization. "My fellow technologists," Snowden writes, "came in every day and sat at their terminals and furthered the work of the state. They weren't merely oblivious to its abuses, but incurious about them, and that lack of curiosity made them not evil but tragic."[104] And so the reader sees the new Prometheus—the new truth-teller—as both alone and akin. He or she is like the viewers in a movie theater: alone together. He or she is a wave and particle in a narrative cloud. Snowden is encrypted for readers as "one man hunched over a blank blue ocean," and also as one of many "fellow technologists." Presented with such an array of identities or disidentities, the reader is left to him- or herself to decide which mask feels more real if, by real, one means the feeling—the sense—of the truth.

III

The FOB and Beyond: Patriotism at the Limit

Turning to soldier-writers such as Elliot Ackerman and Kristin Beck and to the particular world spaces they canvas, this portion of my book submits that their fictional and nonfictional works embody a new kind of ethos and, accordingly, an "expanded" American patriotism. Specifically, I claim that through the ethos of their lived experience and the aesthetic techniques they deploy in narrative and digital genres, these authors suggest a path forward past limited, territorially defined allegiances and other ideological and emotional components of what Americans ordinarily call "patriotism." This chapter consists of three rather short parts. Through Ackerman's essay, "The Fourth War," the first argues for a new apprehension of American ideals such as democracy and for a more nuanced analysis of the expansive patriotism one witnesses in the post-9/11 soldier-writer community. Part two furthers the study of Ackerman through a close reading of his first novel, *Green on Blue*, which, I propose, is an illustration of the democratic narrative and transterritorial patriotism introduced in part one. Finally, in part three, through Beck's social-media rhetoric and her memoir, I synthesize these claims about patriotic identification and disidentification and ethical remapping and share a close analysis of Beck's collaboration with Dr. Anne Speckhard in the co-authoring of *Warrior Princess*, a politically charged memoir that documents the first Navy SEAL in American history to come out as transgender. To frame my overall argument, I lead off with a short detour through two related texts, *Fobbit*, a novel by David Abrams, and "Names," an essay by Paul Crenshaw. I do so for three reasons: first, because these works survey the spatial category this chapter is focusing on, namely what is known as the forward operating base (FOB). Second, because they describe the system of self-identification, ethical remapping, and potential reimagining of the public sphere of values that is coded into the formal and informal regimens of the American military's basic training, operation, and location; and third, because it is this system that accounts for the identity metamorphoses and resistance potential on display in Ackerman and Beck.

The "fobbit," to begin with, is, readers learn from Abrams's novel, an insider moniker for an American soldier who, like Tolkien's "hobbit" in "the shire," lives in a discrete sheltered environment (the FOB or forward operating base) and therefore does not adequately experience "real" immersion in all of the action "outside the wire." A sort of martial analogue to the suburbanite, the fobbit is a character both inside and outside "the reality" of war. Coined during the early years of the Global War on Terror, the name reveals both a bridge and a divide in the military as well as a tension regarding place in these wars. In his novel, Abrams, a fobbit himself, draws on his experience to show how so many signs of the homeland have been juxtaposed upon the mountain and desert frontiers of this conflict and the identity struggles of the servicemen and servicewomen stationed near the borders. Abrams's novel is populated with fast food restaurants and the linguistic rituals of corporate America. The FOB is a place where soldier, contractor, translator, and adversary alike encounter the red and yellow of Burger King and the blizzards of Dairy Queen, a surreal dynamic space where clipboards, laptops, ping pong tables, golf carts, and Internet porn intersect with the bodies of America's dead. Here at the FOB, the casualties of war are treated, in Abrams's words, like "objects to be loaded onto the back of C-130s somewhere and delivered like pizzas to the United States."[1] Just as Klay, in "The Warrior at the Mall," highlights the contemporary soldier's sense of spatial and moral dissonance with his or her homeland, Abrams's novel reveals that same contempt exported to the spaces of American bases abroad and the men and women who manned them. One is never quite home in a war that is both everywhere and nowhere if, by home, one means a name for a stable place.

And yet there are those soldiers who did indeed inhabit the "real" spaces beyond those offices in the desert. *Fobbit*, with its narrative of clerks, mailmen, programmers, logisticians, and lawyers, may indeed represent the dominant experience of the twenty-first-century American military, but this primary character is defined by its ostensible opposite, a lionized other inside the ranks, a fellow soldier who seems to possess an almost mythic quality: those warriors who dare interface with *the world beyond the wire*. To trouble this binary and preface the work of two such figures, Ackerman and Beck, this part starts at the beginning in the barracks of basic training. For, before traveling to the territorial frontiers of Eastern Afghanistan and the rhetorical frontiers of gender theory, I wish to ground the ethical remapping on display in Ackerman and Beck in the lived experience of Crenshaw, a veteran who never traveled those hinterlands but whose narrative ethos still bears the mark of a moral and political reconstruction of identity—the dynamic of ethical identification and disidentification in worlds and spaces beyond the homeland. As I maintain, Crenshaw's "Names" prepares readers for the fiction and nonfiction of Ackerman, as well as the memoir of Beck's ethically subversive journey to coming out transgender.

Crenshaw's essay describes a process of disidentification and identity reconstruction at a particular moment in American history. Crenshaw enlisted in the Arkansas Army National Guard in 1989. He was at Basic Training when Saddam Hussein invaded Kuwait in August of 1990. Crenshaw, like so many soldier-writers, writes with a voice steeped in a particular American tradition. But as I have emphasized throughout, the outspoken, worldly, and dissensual "turn" is not a simple binary response of "yes" or "no," a static position against a single war or a singular institution like the Guard, the CIA, or even the United States. What I come across in Crenshaw's "Names" is perhaps the fundamental distillate of the dissensual pattern I encounter in post-9/11 narratives of soldier-writers. Through the tally of onomastic transformations his fellow soldiers endure during basic training, Crenshaw lays the foundation for the evolutions readers will be witnessing in Ackerman and Beck. Crenshaw uses a rich vulgate of perverted nicknames to register a hieratic argument that the military, on its most basic level, really operates as a *system of identity disidentification and reconstruction*, an ethical remapping in the name of a world beyond the individual. In other words, the dissensual turn, far from imputing treachery to the soldier-writers of the "Forever War," is in many ways the mark of their training continuing its evolutionary course.

"Names" takes readers back to the beginning of the soldier's story and maps the territory of change, the remapping to come. Crenshaw describes how the American soldier is *compelled* by training to morph, to alter his or her name, often by nothing more than a letter. Crenshaw, like Klay in "Psychological Operations," notes nuance in the military experience, a multiplicity where many see little more than a monolith. Like Klay, Crenshaw recognizes a diversity in the terrain of vulgar nicknames that populate basic training. "Keller was Killer and Weaver was Weiner and Penn was Penis or just a dick," he writes in the first sentence of "Names," laying the groundwork for a Whitmanian tally of names and narratives, the grand enterprise of a platoon or a crew requiring that individual details be packed into their narrative space just as tightly as if they were in the hull of a ship or the barracks of a base.[2] But neither vulgarity nor narrative inventory necessarily implies an absence of nuance, sophistication, or purpose. The deliberate process Crenshaw describes could be called one of indoctrination.

Erik Edstrom, in *Un-American*, a memoir of serving during the Global War on Terror, writes, "I was not born for the military; I was heavily configured for it."[3] Like Crenshaw, Edstrom describes a process of self-identification-cum-identity reconstruction:

> Through repetition, servicemen have their values, behaviors, and identity recalibrated with the ultimate aim of making them willing to kill or be killed in political violence without thinking about it too much. It is the construction of blind faith in the state and the deconstruction of any critical thinking that could stand in opposition to the state's aims.[4]

The method of "deconstruction" Edstrom and Crenshaw detail in their work proceeds both logically and dynamically. This is a pedagogical, psychological, and linguistic operation, the subject's resistance to message softened by the disarming poetry of the vulgar. "Clapp was too easy," Crenshaw writes, "and so no one even bothered changing his name, only put 'the' in front of Clapp, and Syphers couldn't escape syphilis any more than any of us could escape Fort Sill where we found ourselves in the summer of 1990."[5] In this "real world" of Fort Sill, before even the base became trivialized as not real enough in the face of an actual war, Crenshaw describes a cast of characters who are complicit in the development of their own indoctrination, an identity reformation that is both individual and institutional, granular and grand. However, just as basic training breaks the men down to serve the state, it also, more broadly, builds them up to serve an entity other than the state:

> We were all dysfunctional, we thought, for we were told so by the drill sergeants all the time, from the first long days when we arrived at Fort Sill and cried sometimes in this harsh new place, through the hot afternoons of drill and ceremony, marching in big round wheels under the summer sun, all the called commands a way to discipline us, make us move as one unit instead of fifty different men, like the naming was to break us down so we could pull closer together.[6]

The double-spirit Crenshaw portrays here of an institutional program that serves two collectives simultaneously (state and platoon) illuminates the contemporary quandary. Which is to say, what readers witness in the space of Crenshaw's first-person plural essay is a variation on the same drama of dissent they will find throughout the troubled wartime and remote geographies of Ackerman and Beck. As the divide Snowden describes between state and nation widens in the context of the Internet's expansion and the continued pursuit of the Global

War on Terror, so does the dissensual pressure on the soldier-writer. In many significant ways, this pressure began in the summer of 1990 as the country shifted its mythological binary focus from the evil of Communism to the evil the state names terror or terrorism—the new "other."

The voice that marks Crenshaw and the other soldier-writers of post 9/11 America is an evolution of the empathically unsettling voice one discovers in the writers of earlier epochs, as well as voices from beyond America's "vaporous" borders. This is a voice that is dissonant but not "isolate." Like the Chris/Kristin readers will meet in *Warrior Princess* and the Aziz Ackerman constructs in *Green on Blue*, this voice is not just that of a man or an American, and it is not purely contemporary either. Novel as it may seem, the contemporary soldier-writer's voice is rooted to a long-standing "republic of letters" that disrupts the reader's common-sense assumptions about geography, literature, nation, and place. This voice encourages us to ask at this point: what are the material and ethical limits of American patriotism, and how does the real and imaginary spatiality of American soldier-writers retrace them? If the fiction, nonfiction, and digital rhetoric of this community of veteran-activists does indeed challenge pivotal assumptions about location, territory, national identity, and ethical values, how can readers and writers evolve their understanding of these categories and thereby map the way they play out in narratives located beyond the borders of the nation and the FOB?

To answer, let me reiterate first that Rancière and Nussbaum, in particular, steer readers toward a new concept of democracy. Rancière challenges readers to return to Athens and questions the original Greek rhetoric of democracy and dissent. Quoting Pericles as "paraphrased in Plato's *Menexenus*," he writes that "the government of the Athenians is a democracy by the name, *but* it is actually an aristocracy, a government of the best with the approval of the many."[7] Leaning on the dissent of a soldier-orator, he questions a basic principle of Athenian governance and, likewise, a principle that informs so much American patriotism: the ideal of democracy, the rule of the "people." Most of us think, of course, that "democracy" applies to and describes America, but does the name truly apply to our republic and the worlds so many Americans are creating with globalized partners? Are Americans like the Athenians, democratic only in name? How should scholars address this disconnect between name and ideal? "The problem, then," Rancière argues, "is how to conceive of this 'but' that inserts a disjunction between the name and the thing."[8] Like these soldier-writers, Rancière is not simply cynical or nihilistic. He seems interested in solving problems, exploring this "but" that reveals the gap between name and thing and the possibility that "democracy" is "something other than a kind of government."[9] Like Snowden, Rancière pushes his reader to reconceive spatiality, or the place ordinarily understood as democratic, and decouple statal territoriality and the state generally from his or her conception of democracy. But then he pushes us farther. The philosopher suggests that democracy is not just "a form of government or form of social life," but instead "the institution of politics itself," and that "politics itself" presents a paradox given that

> politics seems to provide an answer to the key question as to what it is that grounds the power of rule in a community. And democracy provides an answer, but it is an astonishing one: namely, that the very ground for the power of ruling is that there is no ground at all.[10]

In a study seeking to ground the ideas of a community of veteran-activists in rhetorical concepts that originated in ancient Greece, this assertion of groundlessness is unsettling. But Rancière, like Klay, Snowden, and Nussbaum, sees a path forward. Democracy may not be an extant territorial geography, but the ideal remains; *not only that, but it can thrive, re-spatialized beyond that territory.* "The demos," says Rancière, "is not the population, the majority, the political body or the lower classes. It is the surplus community made up of those who have no qualification to rule, which means at once everybody and anyone at all."[11] Stated as a cliché, this is "the power of the people," and because it is not grounded in a particular state office or particular public square or any particular national-geographical territory, it is a spatial variable, affording reinventions of democracy outside its traditional, domestic spaces and predictable routines, and in that disruptive and protean sense, it embodies the dissensual.

1. Democracy in No Man's Land: Elliot Ackerman's "The Fourth War"

When Grace Paley argues that "[i]t's not that you set out to oppose authority. In the act of writing you simply do," she suggests that there is something fundamentally dissensual about a *certain* kind of writing.[12] Through radical acts of unnaming and renaming—by opposing the assumptions that root readers' understanding of democracy and by binding a new concept to "a practice of dissensus" and the "act of writing"—readers can begin to establish a framework for mapping the new patriotism Nussbaum imagines and the one on display in the works of Ackerman. What both Nussbaum and Rancière urge their reader to reconceptualize in the name of a truer democracy is the idea of a private and public, national and transnational space where patriotic values emerge and remerge transformed. It is the dissensual spectacle of this transformation that draws me to Ackerman. The discussion of his essay "The Fourth War" sets the stage for an engagement with his novel.

A soldier-writer, Marine, and spy pretending to be a journalist, the protagonist of "The Fourth War" travels from his apartment in Istanbul to the edge of Syria for a conversation with a former member of Al-Qaeda. Far from the American homeland and removed from the fortifications of American bases, Ackerman and a man named Abu Hussar sit down for tea. The shared, public space this conversation generates is unusual in the history of narratives emerging from the Global War on Terror. Both men fought in Iraq. Both men have traveled all over the world. And both betray a profound curiosity about the other. Rather than erase, torture, or hire this foreign voice, Ackerman listens and creates a space for the narrative of the "enemy." By doing so with a voice attuned to cartography and the liminal zones of the war, Ackerman changes the reader's relationship to these borderlands beyond America and the FOB. With a deft attention to name and place, Ackerman supports and complicates Crenshaw's "Names" and makes a bold case for Nussbaum's core rationale for a cosmopolitan education.

When Ackerman locates his narrative diplomacy in Turkey, he offers the reader a spatial parallel to the numerous geographies where America has not declared war but is actively at war. Just as drone attacks and secret renditions take place all across North Africa and in countries like Yemen and Pakistan, Ackerman's Turkey both is and is not a coordinate on the cultural map of America's Global War on Terror. Thus, the extent to which his prose embodies a repurposing of this boundless dynamic is also the extent to which one might suggest, as I do here, that his work is in the service of the new, arguably cosmopolitan mode of *placing*, contextualizing, and recontextualizing patriotic values and their role in how we redefine ourselves and others. In the public space of "The Fourth War," Ackerman constructs a dialogue between equals where the place of their discourse is a neutral village. Ackerman places the reader in the village of "Akcakale, a crowded Turkish town with a single main road."[13] Ackerman and the man known as Abu Hussar find a cafe in Akcakale, but public as the cafe may be, the two men want privacy and are, therefore, "taken up a narrow stairway" and to a "picnic table," and because Ackerman finds himself unsure as to "who should go where," he ends up "sitting next to Abu Hussar, the two of us on the same bench."¹⁴ The shared space is the point.

To get a handle on this intimate environment that is simultaneously public and private, American and not, it is worth recalling that, in making her case for cosmopolitanism, Nussbaum offers four reasons for a "cosmopolitan education." She argues that "[t]hrough cosmopolitan education we learn more about ourselves." She adds, secondly, that teachers and students "make headway solving problems that require international cooperation" and, thirdly, "recognize moral obligations to the rest of the world that are real, and that otherwise would go unrecognized." Finally, and fourthly, Nussbaum writes that a cosmopolitan education makes "a consistent and coherent argument based on distinctions we are really prepared to defend."¹⁵ Let these four parameters serve as a legend for the map of "The Fourth War," a term that derives from Ackerman's paraphrase of Albert Einstein, who famously said that "the Third War would be a nuclear war, but that the Fourth War would be fought with sticks and stones."¹⁶ Thus, while the territory for my reading of Ackerman's text is a cultural map triangulated around the three concepts whose interplay informs the overall inquiry of my project—parrhesia, dissensus, and cosmopolitanism—the dominant emphasis here will be on the cosmopolitan, the United States, and an exceptional geographical territory just beyond the Turkish border and the sightline of Ackerman and Abu Hussar.

This territory is Syria. Here and elsewhere, this particular geolocation is instrumental in configuring one's ethical standing, what values are already in play and in place, and how they are displaced or replaced in that very place; how they change. The Civil War in Syria and the worldview Abu Hussar urgently communicates to Ackerman has an unsettling American quality to it. The first tenet of Nussbaum's new patriotism highlights an echo of capitalism's core value: self-interest. "Through cosmopolitan education," Nussbaum argues, "we learn more about ourselves." Therefore, this worlding and worldview with its attention to the other are not simply an apology to the tortured, the purged, and the colonized of the past. This first justification is not framed as an act of white guilt but instead as an appeal to self-improvement and self-interest, an evolution of that distinctly protean American identity whose granular originality has long been the terrain of the country's most daring literature: the individual. But note the first-person plural of "we" in Nussbaum's tenet and that implicit suggestion of a plurality nested in the code of individuality. How does one learn without the other, otherwise, and elsewhere? In what kinds of spaces can a cosmopolitan education take place? Westphal writes that "[t]he travel writer takes part in the only meaningful image of the world, reflecting the abstract spaces through which he or she moves and forming representations of human spaces."[17] Ackerman is certainly a travel writer, among other things, and his journey to this particular abstracted space invites the reader into an exchange that is both "sensual" à la Rancière, descriptive of material culture's distribution to a specific area, and cosmopolitan, values-oriented.

Interestingly, just before the conversation begins, the waiter at the cafe, having heard Ackerman's voice, asks a single one-word question: "Français?" In this one word is an expression of sensory scramble and an impression of individualism's paradoxical nature when viewed through the lens of nation. The American traveler, famously known for sticking out when abroad, stands out to such a degree here in the environment of this cafe at the crossroads to both Europe and Asia, East and West, that he is perceived by a stranger to be French, which brings to mind the second tenet of Nussbaum's cosmopolitanism: "We make headway solving problems that require international cooperation." In view of this tenet, Syria is certainly a problem. Ackerman, pretending to be a journalist and perceived to be French, embodies the pattern of disidentification that so recurrently marks this soldier-writer community. By virtue of these veils, what the American comes to learn about himself and the problem of Syria is that the sacred concept of democracy is not so simple when played out in the "real world" of geopolitical conflict. Ackerman and Abu Hussar sit in the cafe, two veterans of the Global War on Terror on the same bench, in the same sensory space: "A pink tulip sits in a glass of water on the table."[18] A translator named Abed sits with them and "fills his mouth with a piece of baklava."[19] Ackerman then begins the conversation with a story "from the First World War. The first Christmas on the Western Front."[20] The soldier-writer's gambit is to travel back in time and into a narrative, an account of men from other countries in another war:

> The day of the holiday, it snowed. In the cold, the German and British soldiers climbed out of their trenches at a place called Mons. They met in no-man's-land and spent the day swapping small gifts and playing soccer. This Christmas truce became very famous in the West.

The story creates an opening between the men—an ethical interstice inside the physical Turkish interval. "What did they do the next day?" Abu Hussar asks, clearly engaged by the tale, the parallel context. Ackerman acknowledges that the soldiers "[w]ent back in their trenches and killed each other for another four years."[21] Both men laugh, but Abu Hussar claims he does not yet understand the point of the story. It is then that Ackerman invites rhetoric and narrative into the same room. "The story," he says, "is our conversation." In other words, these two veterans of Iraq—a country that did not belong to either of them—derive their sense of belonging in this moment from the transterritorial identity of storytelling. The third tenet of Nussbaum's cosmopolitanism, the reader will recall, defies time, space, and codes of membership based on geography, race, and religion. Like the Germans and British soldiers who, in a national-geographical limbo, told stories during the First World War, this American and Syrian soldier drink tea in a liminal zone with their primary ethical identity being simultaneously literary and rhetorical. The story and the cosmopolitan space it opens up are the point here. A special sense of duty to a distant other is foundational to cosmopolitanism, and as Ackerman and Abu Hussar's shared narrative progresses, it becomes apparent that both men learn a great deal about the thorny issues facing the web of nations deployed to Syria, the country just beyond the cafe. The problem of the Syrian war, much like the Global War on Terror at large, is complex for a number of reasons. Why, I ask, is it that some American soldier-writers express a passionate identification with the warriors in this war, especially when so many of their adversaries have demonstrable ties to Al Qaeda? Conversely, why do so many Syrians construct their concept of "revolution" in American terms? How can one account for such improbable associations and identifications?

To answer this question about the importation of American ideals, it is noteworthy that, at one point in the conversation, the translator "excuses himself and goes to the restroom," leaving Ackerman and Abu Hussar alone at the picnic table.[22] Here, without the yoke of language, "the space between us becomes awkward," and so, like a cartographer, Ackerman begins to draw:

> I sketch out a long, oscillating ribbon running from the top left to the bottom right of the page: the Euphrates. Abu Hussar quickly recognizes this. He takes the pencil from my hand and draws the straight borderline between Iraq and Syria, one that cuts through a tabletop of hardpan desert.

Without an interpreter to facilitate rapport, the soldiers are left with images of spaces, drawings of water and land. Ackerman and Abu Hussar return to that most primitive of linguistic enterprises: topography, symbols of places, lines representing land and water. Tracing the line Abu Hussar draws, Ackerman writes "a single name: al-Qaim."[23] And next to this name Abu Hussar writes a date. Using the coordinates of name, place, and date—time and space—these men begin to cobble together a new history, a shared history, and a novel map. If literature is to afford a new space where divisions can be challenged and bonds forged, it must be a spacetime or Bakhtinian chronotopy, if you will, an "interval of time," or "tempuscule," as the scholar Maria Luisa Dalla Chiara Scabia calls it.[24] The "tempuscule" challenges readers to disidentify with the idea of time as a series of discrete points, places, or homes in return for a dimension of exchange, threshold, and shared locations and histories. This is precisely what the dissensus concept stages, namely, a dilation of time's space. Through a litany of dates and toponyms like "Haditha," Ackerman and Abu Hussar build a "log," a logic, a "common language."[25] Both men have been to many of the same places, and as they sit on the same bench in the contact-zone of the cafe, they recognize this commonality, but through the articulation of time—dates—they also notice their difference: the fact that they were never at the same place at the same time. And so a problem presents itself, perhaps the quintessential cosmopolitan paradox. Cosmopolitanism is, as Bruce Robbins argues, "perpetually torn between an empirical dimension and a normative dimension," which is to say, between a concrete cultural space and its norms.[26] If cosmopolitanism asks readers to "recognize moral obligations to the rest of the world that are real, and that otherwise would go unrecognized," then what kind of geopolitical "community of fate" can give shape to such obligation? Strangely enough, it may be the very geopolitical enterprise that sought to erase and subjugate these bonds. Through the boundless Forever War, a bridge has been built in a spatial and moral sense.

I read Ackerman's conversation with Abu Hussar as a literary moment that is cartographic in this twofold sense. Writing out *against* the erasure of his adversary, Ackerman shares a physical and narrative space with Abu Hussar, and through the common coordinates of their travels, he establishes a code of ethics beyond the code's territorial—domestic and partisan—encoding. He evolves the "no man's land" of the First World War into a new narrative space that includes the ethnic others who fought in the Global War on Terror, a storied space where new individuals can shed their weapons and allegiances and break bread—or baklava—with their fellow man. But this powwow between the American and Al Qaeda is not all roses and candy. As Nussbaum's fourth tenet suggests, conversations such as these may indeed inculcate in the writer and reader a sense of special responsibility, but Nussbaum's cosmopolitan proposal also prepares the American to construct "a consistent and coherent argument based on distinctions we are really prepared to defend." Abu Hussar and Ackerman have both fought for their people. They are both capable, even without a translator, of establishing rapport, a shared discourse based on the primitive but always evolving coordinates of time and place. But their relation reaches an impasse—a crossroads—as the two soldiers confront the destabilizing possibility that the idea of democracy might "invade" the people of Syria. For, beyond the forward operating bases of the United States' Global War on Terror lies the American notion that is, itself, repurposed from Hellenic provenance: democracy. But what does "the demos" or "the will of the people" mean as Ackerman's readers approach the twenty-first century and an increasingly globalized context? In Athens, "the people" did not include women and slaves, just as in the United States, where for a long time, these categories of people were excluded from the rights of suffrage, pay equity, and equal protection under the law. More to the point, what are the limits of American patriotism when "the people" begin to include new categories of human beings such as the transgender veteran, Kristin Beck, or the large swaths of Islamists who may well represent a majority in countries like Syria? When America announces that it wishes to support freedom and democracy around the world, what happens when the Kristin Becks, the Palestinians, and the Abu Hussars of the world say, "We want that, too!"

The questions Ackerman raises in this Turkish cafe reveal real problems for scholars of politics, geography, history, rhetoric, and literature. When American soldiers travel beyond the borders of their country and their FOB, and the discourse of spreading democracy all over the globe does, indeed, spread all over the globe, are these soldiers prepared to defend the new manifestations of democracy? When America's aspirational documents and history lights the fires of revolutionaries in places like Cairo and Damascus, are Americans truly prepared to support the will of the people in these places? For the purposes of this study, these questions refine into the problem and possibilities of a politics and an aesthetic where American authors seek to *enlarge the public space* of their narratives—to set up a fictional public sphere so as to include the previously uncounted citizens of the world. Specifically, Abu Hussar, as a former member of Al Qaeda, one-time political prisoner of Assad's in Syria, and supporter of the Islamist revolution in its search for a transnational caliphate, embodies precisely the kind of voice traditional politics and the rhetoric of patriotism seek to silence. Artists, unlike police, seek to give vent to these voices, and sometimes merely in the name of disruption, but what characterizes so many post-9/11 soldier-writers is a *spatially fostered ethical code* for including these voices. Like the code drilled into the enlistees in Crenshaw's story, the code on display in "The Fourth War" is one that extends brotherhood to a tribe of men beyond territorial nation-state and its kinship affiliations. Strikingly, the tribal expansion in Ackerman's essay locates this brotherhood in a fellow soldier outside the national unit. However, Ackerman seems to reach the limits of this expanded sodality when Abu Hussar challenges him on the notion of America's support for "the people" of Syria. "Just imagine if we had weapons like yours now," Abu Hussar says. "Assad would be dead within a few weeks. If Obama armed the Islamists, he wouldn't have to worry about Putin and Khamenei's games."[27] Just as Ackerman challenges the American reader to consider the humanity of the other, so does Abu Hussar challenge Ackerman to more deeply consider that same humanity. What if the revolutionaries from Syria indeed possessed the same weapons as the soldiers from the United States? "Right in his face," Ackerman writes, "I laugh."

A laugh can blur the borders of thought and emotion. Laughter is a rare commodity in the literature of recent wars, and in this case, I suspect few readers will share in Ackerman's outburst. However, in the context of the horrors he has experienced in war, I imagine his laughter as an authentic excess, a sensory demonstration of surprise that reveals what could be read as the current limits of American patriotism. "You think it's funny," Abu Hussar says, "but it's the truth."[28] Indeed, this disconnect between a rhetoric of democracy and a willingness to honor the will of people both at home and abroad may well be "the truth" if by truth one means an exigence, a hole in the discourse, a profound problem demanding address. This aspect—what Chomsky calls "the crisis of democracy"—may indeed be the elephant in the room. When unnamed others abroad count on support from the American revolutionary tradition, who does America include in its roll call of international enlistees? Ackerman's narrative diplomacy hits a wall here, a textured moment of literary space that is both democratic and skeptical of America's democratic marketing or outward projection into other spaces and cultures. "It has often been said," Ackerman writes,

> that the test of a first-rate intelligence is the ability to hold two opposing ideas in thought at the same time while still retaining the ability to function. Based on that criteria, the way most Syrian jihadists and activists think about the United States makes them some of the most intelligent people I've ever met.

In an essay whose cultural map establishes coordinates in the "no man's land" of the First World War, Ackerman here bookends his narrative with a paraphrase of F. Scott Fitzgerald, a post-First World War era writer. Repurposed in "The Fourth War," Fitzgerald's observation from his essay, "The Crack-Up," serves to relocate the fissure of one man and one generation into a globally schismatic condition with repercussions for both Americans and those abroad whom readers might wish to call Syrian or Iraqi but who themselves challenge the Western nomenclature of nation. Instead, Abu Hussar, like many of his fellow soldiers, wishes to map his tribal identity in terms of a transnational geopolity—the caliphate. "Like most in the Arab world," Ackerman writes, people like Abu Hussar "are deeply suspicious of American interventions in the region—the invasion of Iraq was criminal to them. But held in opposition to this outrage, those same voices now clamor for a similar intervention in Syria."[29] The ultimate political fate of these "voices" lies beyond the purview of this book. But the narrative problem of truth-telling—a process that identifies and disidentifies, associates and disassociates—is in this context my study's domain.

Ackerman's essay, like Crenshaw's, maps a process of disidentification and identity reconstruction—an ethical remapping. Defiant in the face of twentieth-century colonial notions of national identity, "The Fourth War," at the same time, relies on twentieth-century history to present a vision of alliance for the twenty-first century. Ackerman's essay is an exercise in democratized narrative, a dilation of the public narrative space afforded to the precarious others who exist beyond the borders of America's Forever War. But the limits of the patriotism he allows his own narrative avatar to exhibit are just as troubling as they are liberating. When the waiter "wanders over" at the end of the conversation between Ackerman and Abu Hussar, he seeks to obtain from Ackerman the identity of everyone but the translator. Ackerman, at this point, is the only one left at the table to receive the waiter's questions. The waiter tries to determine whether Ackerman's companions are Syrian ("Syrie?") and whether or not Abu Hussar belongs to the rebel tribe, "Jabhat-al-Nusra."[30] Ackerman does not confirm or deny Abu Hussar's membership in Jabhat-al-Nusra. He shrugs. When the waiter, "seemingly confused," asks Ackerman if he himself is American ("Amerikee?"), Ackerman replies with, "New York," a place name that is at once a confirmation and refutation. He describes the waiter, in response to the utterance of this city's name, as one of casual bafflement. New York, the city whose attack triggered the start of the Global War on Terror, registers to the Turkish waiter who "shakes his head knowingly, as if to intone the words *New York* is to intone a universal spirit of anything goes." Thus, as the conversation and the story conclude, the reader is confronted with a host of problems about geography and ethics. Like an ancient traveler poised to cross a moat between one kingdom and another, Ackerman and his contemporary American readers stand on the shore of one nation and look across a thin dividing line into the world of another. From a Turkish cafe on the edge of Syria, Ackerman is asked if he is American and responds by identifying with that most cosmopolitan of American cities: New York. What does it mean to choose a specific city name over a nation name, and how does such a moment of identification push back against the cosmopolitan assumption that a "universal spirit" is little more than a code of "anything goes"?

In the following chapter, as Ackerman crosses the moat and takes readers deeper into the life of one who lives beyond the borders of America and its forward operating bases, I continue to explore the intertwined stakes of identification and disidentification and the paradoxical democratizing power of narrative transgression. Prior to venturing into Ackerman's first novel, *Green on Blue*, and Kristin Beck's memoir, *Warrior Princess*, it is worth pointing out, though, that the geographical complexity of Ackerman's situation in "The Fourth War" does not alter the fact that, politically speaking in this moment, he remains a citizen of the United States. Choose as he does to identify with New York over "Amerikee" and allow, as he does, for the humanization of Abu Hussar, an Islamist with ties to Al Qaeda and rebel networks who have worked with ISIS, Ackerman himself still remains a citizen and soldier, a double identity in which the former category, according to Klay, trumps the latter. Ackerman, like Klay and Snowden, speaks out in public. Just as Beck will "come out" as the first transgender SEAL in *Warrior Princess*, Ackerman, in the public space of an essay collection, places dissensual public discourse above the codes of classification that have "renditioned" men like Abu Hussar, stripping them of the rights of citizens. When Ackerman names Abu Hussar and sits next to him on a bench at a cafe in a country on the border of Syria, he does not, by virtue of such naming and proximity, condone the flying of airplanes into corporate office buildings nor does he condemn the use of torture at Guantánamo Bay. What he does endorse in the narrative space of "The Fourth War" is a *new public sphere* of sorts, one that is not constrained by the FOB or the national boundaries that were once drawn by the West for the countries of the Middle East shortly after the First World War. This new public sphere does not place the stories of men like Abu Hussar in tiny national boxes. Instead, Ackerman models a discourse in which conversation is story and a man who desires a caliphate is not deprived of his voice simply because he does not accept the demarcations of nations like Iraq, Iran, Turkey, Syria, Pakistan, and Afghanistan. The names of these nations, like the civilian names of the newly enlisted soldiers in Crenshaw's "Names," are skins to be shed in the name of an expansive future and geopolitical realm organized by a code of brotherhood and, as readers shall see in Beck, sisterhood, too.

2. Empathic Unsettlement: Ackerman's *Green on Blue*

Who has the right to tell the story of American history? What are the risks, for the storyteller, of mixing identity categories as if they were nothing more than paints from a palette? These questions are not simply "academic." In the American military, such questions have urgent legal traction as the country struggles to decide how to handle a new generation of transgender enlistees. Furthermore, in the realms of intelligence operatives, choosing a believable second self, or alias, is often part of the trade. As Snowden writes in *Permanent Record*, "The Intelligence Community tries to inculcate in its workers a baseline anonymity, a sort of blank-page personality upon which to inscribe secrecy and the art of imposture."[31] Like Snowden, Ackerman knows this world of "imposture." He has "been there and done that." But like all the other writers here in this space, Ackerman's work is only eligible for study due to his specifically national pedigree. Even more relevant to this segment of part two is the repurposing of that pedigree—the ethical remapping at play in his fiction. According to the first edition of *Green on Blue* (2015), Ackerman

> served five tours of duty in Iraq and Afghanistan and is the recipient of the Silver Star, the Bronze Star for Valor, and the Purple Heart. He is a former White House Fellow whose essays have appeared in The New Yorker, The Atlantic, The New Republic, and Ecotone, among other publications. He currently lives in Istanbul, where he writes on the Syrian Civil War.

There is nothing radical about noting the way this particular bio highlights the military service of its author and highlights his national identity. One need not be steeped in the theories of cosmopolitanism, history of the book, or global literature to see how a paratextual element, like a bio, might be used to brand a national soldier as a global writer. But Ackerman is not just a solitary figure that happens to have traveled all over the planet as both a soldier, intelligence officer and a writer. He is also part of an evolving global network of veteran-activists.

Ackerman's lived experience as an American soldier, coupled with the pattern of disidentification one finds in his narratives, both fiction and nonfiction, suggests an author who is cultivating a transterritorial ethos. Ackerman is no fobbit. The authority of his work derives from the frontier substance of his institutional service, the quality of his prose, and his willingness to speak against the very state institutions he has served in his time overseas. This contrarian ethos synthesizes the poles of discourse on ethos from ancient Greece and the evidence for this synthesis can be found all over the map of Ackerman's works. When one flips over to the back of *Green on Blue*'s jacket, one sees more paratextual elements at work: the blurbs: the "Advance Praise for *Green on Blue*." Among the writers and soldiers praising Ackerman's first novel (such as Azar Nafisi, bestselling author of *Reading Lolita in Tehran*), one finds Klay—the subject of Chapter 1, part one and two—who writes: "In all too many accounts of the Afghan War, the Afghan people caught in the cross-fire are rendered invisible. Elliot Ackerman's eye-opening *Green on Blue* places them front and center."[32] Klay and Ackerman are "friends" on Facebook. They follow each other on Twitter/X. They often retweet each other. Klay interviewed Ackerman for *The Rumpus*. Ackerman sat with Klay to discuss "Love and War" on YouTube. Together, I see in them a series of patterns unique to their generation of veterans. They are members of a community akin to the Beats and the Lost Generation. The soldier-writers of "The Forever War" represent a genuine literary movement, and I read Ackerman and Klay as two of the leaders, much in the way Kerouac and Ginsberg were viewed as the standard-bearers for the Beats. But unlike their obviously countercultural predecessors, there is a strangely restrictive biographical requirement for this literary movement: to belong, one must have served. To counter the unworldly culture, some say, the military has been poised to impose on the world, it seems that one has to be a member of that very minority and its flagship institutions. To disidentify with a narrow nation-state commons and speak out for precarious others and redistribute the sensible realms of public space, one must be a citizen with a certain degree of access to the worlds and characters behind the curtain. And so questions about the paradox of authority emerge. The ethos of this community of authors is certainly about more than Aristotle's definition of ethos: "character as it emerges in language."[33] So how does one determine and practice authority and character in this novel and paradoxical tribe? How does an evolving literary marketplace decide which authors have the authority—the public trust—to roam freely from character to character, place to place? Ethos, in this soldier-writer community, much like that literary marketplace and like the Cynic school of philosophers from ancient Greece, is increasingly haunted by not just the paratextual but the transtextual: ethos is logos.

In the ethical mapping readers witness in the soldier-writer community, one sees an evolution of the Cynical ethos, a new liminal mode that is just as much akin to Aristotle as it is to the model of ethos described by Diogenes and the Cynics and by rhetoricians like the Attic orator, Isocrates, who claimed that "the argument which is made by a man's life is of more weight than that which is furnished by words."[34] Isocrates and Diogenes, with their emphasis on the speaker's "way of life," serve as useful foreshadowers of the identitarian age and its emphasis on lived experience. In a book whose cognitive map is influenced by Hellenic discourse, this Greek notion of authority and credibility—ethos—seems worth considering for a moment before diving down into Ackerman's appropriation of the identity of an Afghan soldier. As one thinks about the new rhetorical patterns one witnesses in this community of writers, the question surfaces: How does one construct the concept of authority that enables the outspoken imaginative leaps afforded by these authors? The moat—the conceptual space—between Aristotle and Isocrates is instructive. Aristotle, who does not emphasize biography and geography in the same way as Isocrates, was perhaps conscious of his citizenship—of his territorialized status. As with Foucault and Ion, the story returns to the crucible of place and citizenship. Isocrates was an Athenian. Aristotle was not. This territorial, political, and biographical coordinate within the discursive map of "ethos" reveals a discrepancy that did not just suddenly emerge in the twenty-first century with this generation of American veteran-activists. What is unique about these artists is the way in which they both inhabit and wander away from the haunt of their authority. Writers like Klay, Snowden, and Ackerman seem to be at home in "the art of imposture." This community of authors both embodies and troubles the patriotic ethos and the space of the national soldier by embedding dissensual narrative elements within their texts. What is particularly noteworthy about Ackerman's novel and its distorted mirror is the way in which he deploys this spatial aesthetic in a landscape and a character—an other—far beyond the pale of American borders.

Ackerman, like Klay, seeks a new kind of camouflage. Like Klay, he begins his story in the voice of the other. Far from the mall, the FOB, and the fobbit, Ackerman's gambit orients the reader to both a different time and a different place. Just before the reader enters the first chapter of *Green on Blue*, they encounter the words of Imam Al-Bukhari: "Allah's Apostle said, 'War is deceit.'" Al-Bukhari was Muslim and an eminent Persian scholar of the ninth century who wrote a number of revered Sunni texts. His father, who died when Al-Bukhari was young, was a Zoroastrian. Thus, in Al-Bukhari, the reader sees the seed of the novel's narrator, Aziz, whose father also dies when he is young, and a window into the timeless world of identity projection, affiliation, and reaffiliation: the son who disavows the old faith and joins a new movement, Islam. But Ackerman does not include these biographical details about Al-Bukhari in his epigraph. These are the only words that are present: "Allah's Apostle said, 'War is deceit.'" Note the Chinese box of this epigraph, the box within the box. This is Ackerman quoting Al-Bukhari who is himself quoting "Allah's Apostle," Muhammad, without uttering the prophet's name. Thus, prior to the introduction to Aziz, readers are introduced to the liminal virtue of deceit, the fundamentally ethical subversion that is literary fiction. This is what one means when one argues that a certain kind of literature is inherently dissensual. Literature is often the pastiche of the particular conceits and deceits of a man attempting to survive in his individual war with the world. But what if literature and war are both fundamentally dissensual enterprises, their convergence an increasingly dislocating and reorienting, identity-making and remaking double helix? Where else does one find oneself so violently and inextricably awash in otherness and estrangement but in the literature of war? In *On War and Writing*, Samuel Hynes argues that modern wars introduce soldiers to "anti-landscapes" and "antirhetoric"—*other* spaces, and value discourses—but is careful to add that "[o]ne war generation will be separated from another by the character of its wars."[35] Hynes, whose book was reviewed by Klay and Ackerman's mutual friend, Gallagher, seems to suggest here that there is an arc of evolving separation, a progress of dislocation and detachment in Western war narratives that travel from the First World War to the present wars. The sincerity with which young men entered the trenches and machine gun fire of the First World War (think Rupert Brooke) yields the ironic tones of the Second World War (think Joseph Heller and Norman Mailer, *Catch-22* and *The Naked and the Dead*). By the time readers arrive at Ackerman and the war in Afghanistan, one can see a kind of "full circle" or perhaps a broad dialectical map for the student of the American soldier-writer: sincerity splintering into irony, irony splintering further into a sincere appropriation of the other, Ackerman's placement of the Afghan and tribal soldier "front and center" as a way of decentering the traditional white male narrative and also keeping with the tradition of pushing war literature's ethical thrust toward the dissonance of the "anti-landscape" and "antirhetoric." As Hynes writes of the Second World War generation,

War had detoxified them, and they had returned to write down their hangovers. The young men of the next generation would not go to their war quite so innocently, or use the Big Words so easily, or return so bitterly, but would manage to combine in their remembrances the Rightness of their war and its Reality, its rhetoric and antirhetoric.

This synthesis of "rhetoric and antirhetoric," of landscape and "anti-landscape," achieves a new dissensual pattern in the current wars, a spatial mark one finds all over the cognitive map of *Green on Blue*.

I borrow the cartographic notion of cognitive mapping from Frederic Jameson, who uses it in his attempt to define the way a subject situates himself or herself in a "totality" that is unrepresentable. For Jameson, the cognitive map was a heuristic dependent on what he referred to as the "cultural dominant." "If we do not achieve some sense of a cultural dominant," Jameson argues, "then we fall back into a view of present history as sheer heterogeneity, random difference, a coexistence of a host of distinct forces whose effectivity is undecidable."[36] In other words, critics who sense the stir of a new aesthetic recognize, like the writers whose art they chart, a sensibility that is at once pointed and disoriented. But forging an orientation is the challenge of the cognitive map. It is this sense of direction, or of redirection, rather, and of the attendant new spatializations of culture, values, and identity that I see in Aziz and Ackerman. If there is a cultural dominant in the contemporary moment that gives readers purchase in the histories of the present, I argue one more time here that it can be found in the fluctuating sum, the wobbling dot—the tempuscule, the compass bead—of a voice that is dissensual (not monolithic), parrhesiac (not obedient), and cosmopolitan (not nationalist). This is a quantum voice that pushes beyond the geography of the fobbit and pushes back against what Jameson calls the "canonized rhetoric of temporality."[37] Where time once was, arguably, the modernist dominant, these writers join others in making a case for an expanded space not for spaces's sake, to be sure, but for the American values that can be revaluated and "expanded" in this space.

A case in point, Ackerman's Aziz possesses a number of liminal markers that locate him as a character beyond the bounds of nationalist narrative and discursive maps. He is not merely a "green," as the Americans called themselves, or a "blue" as the Americans marked the Afghans. In other words, Aziz is not, first and foremost, an Afghan. Just as the Global War on Terror erodes respect for national sovereignty, so does Ackerman's novel—notably, with an ethically transgressive turn. Like the stereotypical American soldier who derides all talk of geopolitics by swearing that his oath is to his "band of brothers," Aziz also identifies not with the national goals of Afghanistan, but with his actual brother, Ali, who sustains, early in the story, an injury that leaves him bereft of genitals. It is this wound that compels Aziz to seek money to keep his brother alive in a hospital, and it is in this convalescent setting that Aziz runs into a man named Taqbir, who has money to spare. Taqbir is himself a liminal character. He serves as an intermediary between an American named Mister Jack and a "Special Lashkar" force of Afghans who, primarily, fight against a Taliban warlord, Gazan. When Taqbir offers Aziz a position in the "special" joint force, the reader witnesses Aziz attempt to find geopolitical foothold in the offer, a sense of exactly for whom he is being asked to fight. Taqbir tells Aziz that his men "fight against the Taliban to uphold Pashtunwali" and that this "special" force "protects the border."[38] "So you fight for the government," Aziz asks. "We fight for the nang of our homes, but for no government," Taqbir responds as he "stuck his chest out in his clean American uniform," green and blue one in this mercenary head-hunter, as if America and its government simultaneously symbolize nang (individual honor) and "no government," a substatal ethic.[39] The significance of this exchange is to be found in the tension between the national and the local, the disavowal of the former in the name of the latter while the whole national/local dilemma takes place in the context of a war made up of a coalition that is not just multinational but sometimes a pairing of a nation and a tribe triangulated through a security corporation.

But that is just the tip of the iceberg when it comes to Ackerman's play with geography, identity, and ethics. The tribal-minded (Pashtunwali) men that the American, "Mister Jack," cobbles together through his intermediary, Taqbir, are themselves divided into two camps: the Comanches and the Tomahawks. Just as the Saudi Arabian Al Qaeda leader, Osama Bin Laden, was dubbed "Geronimo" by American special forces, dislocating the name of the Chiricahua Apache Chief, so do readers see here a former American special forces officer appropriating the identity of an Afghan soldier whose narrative identity, on its more granular level, is not just tribal but a graft of the tribes American military forces once conquered on the "frontier" that was once national but is now global. Of course, even that generalization begs troubling, for the original American "frontier" was not simply a binary of one nation versus many "tribes" but a multitudinous contention between many nations (America, Mexico, France, England, Comanche, Shawnee, Apache, etc.). In other words, the spatial complexity of the American identity has always been there, and so it is only befitting that Ackerman's novel charts a course between linear national history and a complex present of tribal relationships as they evolve on the challenged turf of Eastern Afghanistan. This territorial reorientation, marked by attention to a porous and complex spatiality and permeable and playful tribal identities, embodies the kind of cultural map Jameson imagines. Ackerman, like Jameson, attempts to ground the reader in the dynamic spatiality of the present. If the Global War on Terror is both a totality and a constantly shifting narrative and rhetorical frame, a cultural map of its domains must capture the dynamism of its names and places, its evolutionary legend. Ackerman's Eastern Afghanistan accomplishes this difficult task and provides such a guide.

The cognitive map of *Green on Blue* riddles the reader, leaving character after character unsettled as he or she tries to find traction in the shifting sands of a landscape at war. Thus, what we see in *Green on Blue* is a constant negative, as in a photographic proof revealing an apposite and yet aptly opposite orientation—a precise disidentification. If Hemingway is America's most canonical soldier-writer, and the tragically maimed Jake Barnes from *The Sun Also Rises* his most memorable protagonist, then the similarly maimed brother of Aziz serves a subversive function as a peripheral figure in this American novel where the only American character, Mister Jack, is little more than a bag of national cash used to pit one tribe against another. In other words, the American and the archetypal wartime wound of the American protagonist have both been decentered in *Green on Blue*. Ackerman, like Hemingway, witnessed the complexity of the frontline. He bore witness to the ironies one finds when a national enterprise yields to a platoon's code and the intimate details of an individual's mind, but he did so in his own war, and this new war demands its own forms. What Hemingway and Ackerman do have in common, aside from castrated characters and a spare lyrical prose, is the ethos of a personal history that intersects with a political history. Hemingway's biography matters, and so does the fact that Ackerman himself served in the position of "Mister Jack." Ackerman was that bag of cash, although maybe not that particular bag. Ackerman did, in fact, serve as "the primary combat adviser to a 700-man Afghan commando battalion," and, in spite of this ethos, the *New York Times* critic, Michiko Kakutani,[40] takes him to task in her only complaint about his work, which seems to be that his rendering of the American presence was flat, a "reductive cartoon of the oblivious American." But what if one of the sure signs of a proper humanization is showing the other's ability to dehumanize? What if this particular species of leveling and dehumanization is part of what Rancière means when he talks about narrative democracy and its dissensus component?

Dissensus, I have observed in the introduction, begins when artists "make the invisible visible, and make what was deemed to be the mere noise of suffering bodies heard as a discourse concerning the 'common' of the community."[41] But more than just a concept that plays out in content, dissensus is also a structuring mechanism. Describing the Greek teaching of parrhesiac techniques, Foucault seems to recognize what Rancière and other contemporary philosophers of narrative also acknowledge: these techniques constitute narrative operating systems designed to address "suffering."[42] To heal the traumatic divisions, the wounds, the rifts between places and people and other intervals created by the rhetoric of terrorism and its attendant trope of nationalism, the writer must alter his or her approach to character, plot, and sensory language. To break down the partitions between the people of the planet, the writer must cultivate a new technique of subjectivity, that is, of an intersubjectivity that makes "the invisible visible." To accomplish this task and master this technique, one might assume that all an artist has to do is bring all voices into a perfect egalitarian polyphony. But such a simplistic solution is not what Rancière has in mind. The dissensus Rancière recommends to counter the culture of pseudo-consensus is not just a symmetrical evening up of voices that some algorithm could accomplish. What Rancière argues for is something deeply human and new. The first modernist aesthetic, which was profoundly responsive to the technology, politics, and particularities of its time, must evolve. The twenty-first-century fobbit must travel beyond the FOB. The gestures of fragmentation and dissonance must now go further in the post-9/11 era and not toward some perfectly even ratio or some explosion or erasure of the privileged white other but, instead, in the direction of what Dominick LaCapra calls "empathic unsettlement."[43] Daniel O'Gorman utilizes LaCapra's discourse of "empathic unsettlement" to emphasize the importance of unsettled territory (wilderness and frontier) in the American identity and the consequent need for a new identity structure that honors that heritage. Evolving Jameson's cognitive mapping and borrowing from Derek Gregory's concept of "imaginative geography," O'Gorman suggests that the emergent identity we are beginning to see in innovative war fictions does not simply reproduce an "us versus them" binary. Instead, what O'Gorman documents are a series of authors creating "connective dissonance" between Americans and their putative enemies. Utilizing the language of music, Gorman's rhetoric of dissonance and connectivity seems appropriate to this critic for framing the bridge-building of writers like Ackerman. The narrative and rhetorical pattern here is at once centripetal and centrifugal, a speaking out and a taking in much like a "dissonant musical chord occupies an ambiguous space between notes."[44]

What the dissensual soldier-writer attempts to do, then, is travel further and further away from the canonical center and venture out beyond the frontiers of whiteness, masculinity, and nationalism. Ackerman, through Aziz, has undertaken such an act of spatial expansion, ethical remapping, and "empathic unsettlement." He has crafted a convincing and subversive portrait of the other and his monolithically constructed hideout: Afghanistan. But monoliths, complete with their assumptions, emerge in every sentence, dissensually entangled with their challengers. Aziz is not the other whom readers already know or at least know of. This is not Martin Amis's studied but stable portrait of Muhammad Atta from "The Last Days of Muhammad Atta" or Don DeLillo's Hammad, Atta's accomplice in *Falling Man*. Well beyond the circle of the 9/11 hijackers and their substatal conspirators in Al Qaeda, Ackerman locates and creates space for the largely illiterate young men who had nothing to do with Al Qaeda or the Twin Towers but suffered the vast bulk of America's singular urge for revenge. To do so, he takes the reader into the specific "topological" or spatial dimensions of the other one finds in the mountains of Eastern Afghanistan. His story creates a "connective dissonance," a subversive I/thou pairing, the American soldier now in the skin of the Afghan, the language of Aziz folded "dissensually" into the English text.

Perhaps the most recurrent Pashto word in Ackerman's novel is "badal," which roughly translates to "revenge." He introduces other Pashto terms like "nang" (honor) that help the reader understand that the American mission to exact revenge in Afghanistan is anything but exact. *Badal*, Ackerman demonstrates, is a phenomenon much like the golden spiral, a thing that circles out, a local villager's vendetta caught up in a tribe (the Special Lashkar) organized around vendettas and funded by a global superpower (America) that is itself seeking both vendetta and a third Pashto term Ackerman describes at length: "ghabban." Over the course of this story in which he seeks revenge/badal for the maiming of his brother, Aziz comes to realize that his commander is not what he at first appears to be. "In Pashto," Aziz explains, "Commander Sabir's type of war is called ghabban: this is when someone demands money for protection against a threat they create. For this type of war, the Americans don't have a word. The only one that comes near is racket. Our war was a racket."[45] The reader here experiences, I would suggest, the "connective dissonance" of dissensus: prose where I and Thou meet in sensory juxtaposition. The American reader now possesses a new coordinate, a novel word for the war they have co-produced: ghabban. Ghabban and racket sit side by side in Ackerman's novel, his disidentification with the macro of the Global War on Terror and the micro of the tribal wars it fuels serving as a planetary plea for a higher logic, a planet of nations and tribes and cities and villages organized around something larger and more ethical than badal and ghabban, revenge and racket. Notably, Aziz goes to work for Commander Sabir in the name of badal—for the purpose of avenging his brother. But in the end, when Gazan, the very tribal leader who ordered the attack that led to the maiming of Ali, is in a Toyota Hilux with Aziz, Mister Jack, and a wealthy Afghan villager named Atal, Aziz kills them all. This is not the mass shooting of a man who simply believes in violence, the old ways of badal and ghabban, racket and revenge. The literary activism on display in this study is not a repackaged advocacy for tribalism and revenge. The killing at the end of *Green on Blue* is not simply a dislocated rehash of 9/11. Prior to the slaughter of the Afghans and the American (while in a Japanese truck), Aziz openly turns away from badal when he hears that his brother's attacker (Gazan) is himself prepared to turn away from the old code and abandon war entirely. Before Aziz and Gazan pick up Mister Jack and Atal, Gazan tells Aziz that he will work for peace through Mister Jack: "If he can bring the peace, I'm for him," Gazan says. To which Aziz responds, "Then I could be for you."[46]

It is interesting to note here the narrative power Ackerman achieves by defamiliarizing the advocates for peace. By placing the reader in the shoes of Afghans who are tired of war, his spatial aesthetic achieves a different effect than if his characters remained fobbits or American soldiers located *on American soil*. For, as history shows, American territory has not been continually attacked during these past two decades of the twenty-first century. To speak for peace through an American character during the Global War on Terror is to risk the cliché of the stateside "Jody," the Quaker or the hippie, the figures ostensibly without skin in the game. The American soldier who argues for peace is often constructed as a hypocrite, subversive, or a traitor, while the American civilian is regularly constructed as "at the mall" or out of touch. But the Afghan who has been compelled into badal by an American vendetta that orchestrates tribal wars for the sake of war itself—ghabban—marks a different kind of ethos. This is the political and aesthetic power of dissensus. More to the point, this is parrhesia: an American speaking out through lived experience. And, in turn, this parrhesiac moment is cosmopolitanism: the voice of one who has been all over the world and has brought the world back home.

Dissensus is not mere dissent, a "no" in the face of war, neoliberalism, or global injustice. It is not a crypto-Marxist struggle of emancipating the international proletariat. Dissensus, with the veteran-activists of this "Forever War" generation, is a "philosophico-politico-aesthetic scene" where the modernist pattern of "defamiliarization" works to redistribute the voices of the public space and reorient the legends of narrative maps and, thereby, construct an ethical vision of a common humanity. When Mister Jack and Atal enter the crowded space of the HiLux and the geopolitical negotiation begins, Aziz is prepared to be less "patriotic" or "tribal," and thus disidentify with Pashtunwali, his desire for revenge and the kinds of traditional death-centered narratives such codes enable. But reflective of the real historicity of the war and its real intersections of East and West, this negotiation "went South," as Americans say. Ackerman's dissensual narrative defamiliarizes the death-centered narrative. The classic pleasure of "the bad guys" dying is here infested with a bug— the exception Aziz takes with the fact that all of the parties in the HiLux are engaging in deceit, a fiction within a fiction. All of the talk about a transcendent future without war is nothing but bait for Aziz and the reader. One can feel Aziz drifting from naive hope to complicated rage in the claustrophobic environment of the "foreign" truck. Mister Jack claims he admires "a man who wants peace for his village," but "now is not the time."[47] The American plan to create a peaceful global village cannot be sustained without war, and even though Atal seems to know the American desire to do right is a classic deceit, both he and Gazan feel powerless in the face of the money the Americans are willing to spend to keep the war going.

Right and wise as Atal may be, cash is king in this imaginative moment, and so Atal and Gazan cave to the American. But it is only then, after a pronounced narrative pause fraught with hesitancy and ethical deliberation, that Aziz intervenes with a violence beyond badal and shoots Gazan, Atal, and Mister Jack:

> The restraint I'd felt toward Gazan left me. If the war was for him, he was for the war. If peace was for him, he was for the peace. There could be nothing larger in him, and I felt the fool for hoping there could be, in him, in any of us. What moments before had seemed unclear was now obvious. There was no cause in this war, at least none larger than oneself. And what I did next was natural, and yes, easy.

For the reader, the digestion of this violent scene is not "easy." When an Afghan shoots an American on American soil, the first word many Americans probably think is "terrorism." But when Aziz shoots Mister Jack, Atal, and Gazan in a Japanese truck in the liminal mountainous space between an Afghan village and an American base, the audience response—the aesthetic quality—might be more than a bit dissonant. For here, in the defamiliarized zone—far from the Twin Towers, the Pentagon, and the Green Zone of Baghdad—American readers and readers from all over the world receive both the classic satisfaction of the death-centered narrative and the dissonance that comes from locating the act staged in such a liminal space. Remarkably, in trying to understand his own actions, Aziz cannot help but see them in terms of a confused map: "And as I thought of all the ways one could be killed in this war, and of all those who could do it, I couldn't think of a single way to die which wasn't a green on blue. The Americans had a hand in creating all of it."[48] This spatial reorientation, both away from and toward America, complicates and thereby renews the reader's perception of the world. This aesthetic remaps America's war, the "ghabban" that continues to challenge those who wish to tear down the old codes and old walls in the names of a more ethical planetary future. This harrowing ending could have conceivably been delivered by a fobbit or someone other than a veteran, but the fact that it comes to the reader from a soldier with Ackerman's particular stripes makes the narrative space all the more ethically claustrophobic and charged. There's no way out but further in. The cognitive map here does not direct the reader to a fantasyland beyond earth and history, but it does not countenance a simple linear or nationalist history either. Ackerman's ethos, coupled with his granular construction of space, instead, causes *Green on Blue* to be precisely the mess it claims to be. This is not Green versus Blue. This is *Green on Blue*, a story that throbs with the unique power of dissensus, a mode of parrhesiac disidentification that both engages and troubles the current "consensus of fear."

3. The Sheepdog: Transgender and Trans-space in Beck's *Warrior Princess*

Ackerman and Beck are both a part of and apart from the new American military with its increasingly "special" character. They have both spent time overseas among the most classified "special forces" of the Global War on Terror. I pair them together not just because they both navigated the geographical frontier of these wars but also because of the contrast between these secretive operations in Afghanistan and the brazen quality of their public rhetoric on an Internet that has fundamentally altered both the maps and the territories of state and literary expression. Additionally, much like Ackerman, Beck cultivates a transgressive voice that draws from the authority of her military experience, challenges that very terrain and, thereby, remaps the reader's concept of patriotism. Shortly after the 1990 US invasion of Iraq, Beck enlisted in the Navy and signed up for basic underwater demolition (BUD/S) training. Beck graduated at the top of class 179 and thereby became a SEAL. Beck participated in "Operation Iraqi Freedom" in 2003 and was chosen, in 2005, to be part of the elite Naval Special Warfare Development Group (DEVGRU). Beck "was the primary Subject Matter Expert in the Pathfinder UAV technology demonstration and was instrumental in development of the Small and Medium class UAV in use by Special Operations Forces to this day."[49] Beck's background is relevant for this discussion, for this soldier did not just "serve." Beck led, both on the battlefield and in the laboratories, cultivating the innovative technologies and strategies that map the architecture of the Global War on Terror. In 2008, Beck "received a special assignment" as a "source handler" on the border between Afghanistan and Pakistan, received a Bronze Star and Purple Heart for service in the Afghan theater, and, in 2009 became the Senior Enlisted Advisor to USSOCOM's Science and Technology Directorate. Beck's work was "critical to providing cutting edge technologies to SOF personnel in support of Special Operations Forces worldwide."[50] If the American military is the most empirically observable power structure on the planet, then the arc of Beck's career serves, I contend, as a unique trace coordinate, a marker that has traversed various spaces and war theaters in unprecedented fashion. Beck's biography is indeed "a profile in courage," as Colonel Carl Castro has written, and that "courage" is partially a function of Beck's location on and across the frontiers of geography, battle, technology, and identity. In the public space of *Warrior Princess*, Beck's memoir, the author repurposes and respatializes these frontier territories in the name of a transgressive alterity—a new territory of identity and storytelling.

The disidentification and expanded patriotism readers find in Nussbaum and Ackerman is taken further in Beck's collaborative memoir. On February 9, 2013, Beck issued a press release in which the soldier announced "his long-standing gender identity as a female."[51] According to the release, "Chris respectfully remained silent regarding her gender identity—following the U.S. military's 'Don't Ask/Don't Tell' policy current during her service—but since retirement has decided to announce her decision to live openly and as authentically as possible."[52] Like Ackerman, Crenshaw, Klay, and Snowden, Beck can now be found in what is arguably the new public sphere: Twitter/X. However, Chris Beck is no longer Chris Beck. Just as the whistleblower Bradley Manning is now Chelsea Manning (author of the 2022 memoir, *README.txt*), the SEAL Chris Beck is now the civilian, Kristin Beck, and in *Warrior Princess: A U.S. Navy SEAL's Journey to Coming Out Transgender*, Beck tells her story with the help of Dr. Anne Speckhard. As a narrative that is fundamentally collaborative and transgressive, *Warrior Princess* represents a frontier case study for the patterns of dis- and re-identification and ethical mapping and remapping readers witness in the public rhetoric of America's post-9/11 soldier-writers. In "Names," Crenshaw describes, as we know, a cast of young soldiers who collaborate in an identity reformation based in nickname. This informal training in identity gamesmanship, inscribed within the formal "basic training" of the military, is initially framed by Crenshaw as a move toward correction and development, conditioning individuals to serve the collective over the self. However, just as basic training breaks the young men down to serve their state, one might also argue that it builds them up to serve a conceptual space *beyond the state*. As Snowden and Brand repurposed their collaborative military training in cybernetics and systems from a territorial spatial orientation to a transterritorial orientation, so do readers see the classified operations of Chris Beck transform into the public rhetoric of Kristin Beck in her cooperation with Speckhard in the spaces of the memoir.

Critics took note of the bold rhetorical project that is *Warrior Princess*. In 2013, *OutServe Magazine* described Beck and Speckhard's story as "one of the smartest and most important books of the year" and added that "where Kristin's experiences differ from the readers, Speckhard subtly exercises her understanding of psychology and sociology to bridge the gap."[53] This artful bridging of "the gap" that exists between the rarefied experiences of America's all-volunteer military and an increasingly alienated citizenry is why I read Speckhard and Beck's co-authorship as such a significant narrative tactic. In their collaborative challenge to the conventions of genre, identity, and the codes of secrecy one finds in the Special Forces community, Beck and Speckhard offer a rhetorical model for the path forward in the unique narrative aesthetic I pursue in this book—one defined, to reiterate, civically and politically by the dissensual and parrhesiac and culturally and ethically by the cosmopolitan. Like Ackerman's, Beck's experience and story challenge readerly expectations about geography, identity, and ethics.

Her biography and public rhetoric take us farther into the uncharted territories of a new subjectivity and its intersection with digitality. I argue, however, that Beck pushes the boundaries of the contemporary rhetorical moment even harder than perhaps any other soldier-writer when she leverages her "coming out" narrative into a digital presence on Twitter that simultaneously defends and challenges the American state. By switching genders and going public in the generic space of a co-authored memoir, Beck defies her commander-in-chief, his "transgender ban," and constructs for herself a liminal "sheepdog" identity poised to defend the new patriots of America's future, a move Beck further complicates by detransitioning in 2022.[54] In other words, through the public spaces of her collaborative narrative and her new media presence, Beck expands, I contend, the limits of American patriotism.

Warrior Princess, according to Dina Titus, "challenges the American principles of liberty and equality on the battlefield of gender expectations."[55] Titus's blurb suggests the pages of a book to be a new kind of space or "battlefield." I might add that her review, rather than splashed on the cover, can be found on the memoir's first pages, even before the title page and copyright information. A gathering of blurbs at the beginning of a book is not a novel paratextual characteristic, but Beck's and Speckhard's blurbs make for a unique feature in this particular text. Before anything else, the reader is asked to consider the reviews of *OutServe Magazine* and a number of other similar endorsements. Of course, there is nothing inherently dissensual or avant-garde about gathering a dozen reviews at the beginning of a text. But just as this book offers brief biographies of soldier-writers for a unique rhetorical purpose, so do the blurbs in *Warrior Princess* serve a unique spatial and symbolic function. Readers go back and forth between transgender publications (*OutServe*) and Army Colonels (Castro), this coordinated split of sensibilities offering a spatial gambit that culminates with Titus. The cumulative weight of these blurbs begin the bridge a former man attempts to build by telling her soldier's story alongside a woman who happens to be the author of *Talking to Terrorists: Understanding the Psycho-Social Motivations of Militant Jihadi Terrorists, Mass Hostage Takers, Suicide Bombers and "Martyrs."* In other words, readers cannot fully appreciate Beck's project unless they understand her as a former soldier who has elected to tell her story with the help of a woman whose scholarly focus has been the humanizing of America's enemies. What is more, after the advance praise, dedication, table of contents, foreword, press release, and preface, Beck and Speckhard give readers a prologue. But before one can even engage this seventh tier of pretextual text, "one" is given a black-and-white photo of "Chris in gear in Afghanistan."[56] And gear does matter. Beards matter too. Quite often, to be an American soldier is to dress up like "Chris in gear" and to perform masculinity. When one studies the black-and-white photo, one cannot help but note the "rough and ready" image of an updated Natty Bumpo. This is not the profile of a fobbit. Chris Beck, before she became Kristin Beck, knew how to play the part of the one beyond the wall and the pale, that ostensibly simple role that harkens back to America's history on the frontier, her battles with the French, the Indians, and the imperial Brits.

But the "wild and wooly" look of the SEAL on the frontlines of the Global War on Terror can be deceptive. After the veils of paratext unfold, Beck and Speckhard take readers into the real theater of war, that troubled geography where America's ethical commitments blur. The co-authors describe the "half-sleep" of American men who inhabit their costumes as if they are skins, "the sleep the guys forced on themselves when the unknown overcame their mind's ability to grasp anything else but fear."[57] But, like Klay and Ackerman, Beck has a map of this unknown. That is to say, *Warrior Princess* unveils a deliberately *cartographic rhetoric*. Beck and Speckhard frame their narrative as a kind of guide, a legend for the map of negotiating identity. In this particular scene, Chris is indeed "looking at a map" as his unit is getting ready to "go from sitting down in the helo [helicopter] to a full-out sprint off the back into a hot landing zone."[58] In a study of veteran-activists, many of whom were low on the chain of command, this flagship case study spotlights a soldier who was near the top of the chain, a Navy SEAL giving orders in a primary theater of the war. Beck's location, in terms of geography, identity, and rank, offers her narrative a lens that is spatially and rhetorically novel. She was with others beyond the confines of the American FOB and her worldly observations engender a sense of moral obligation that both affirms and expands what it means to be American.

Building this kind of ethos early on is essential to Beck and Speckhard's spatio-rhetorical project. Using the third-person POV, they describe a soldier whose very training has given "him" the detachment to fight not only the terror of war but also the terror of being trapped in the wrong body:

> Chris had moved into combat mode—totally detached from emotions and from his physical body. In this mode, he and the guys beside him seemed less like bodies and more like souls, fighting side by side—fighting other souls. Moving like a machine, Chris felt time slowing down as he entered a calm peace amidst the combat.

Note the description of a hive mind spatiality and a profound sense of disembodiment. Much like Lagasnerie's and Snowden's descriptions of the Internet and the way it denationalizes "minds and imaginaries," military training itself does something quite similar, emphasizing the collective over the individual. At the conclusion of this particular operation in Afghanistan, Chris survives, but one of his men, John, does not. Chris, "inside his head," screams, "It should have been me!" and not just because he cared for John. Like Chelsea Manning who writes, "if there was a uniform, I wouldn't have to think about gender presentation at all,"[59] Beck and Speckhard describe a soldier who "thought if he had died there would be no more battles with trying to live a man's life while inside a transgender female."[60] Thus, in this tempuscule, two identities alchemize in a crucible of anguish, demonstrating for the reader the ethically transgressive power of wishing you were someone else.

Warrior Princess is a study in the way a body maps the gaps between geography and ethics. The memoir travels through the tragic stories of Beck's military family, the tales of other hypermasculine men who grew up in different theaters of war. Chris's grandfather, Sam, was a veteran of the Second World War who returned home and became an alcoholic and "kept his pain bottled up and didn't let anyone in."[61] Chris's conservative Christian father, Luther, witnessed Sam's pain but was confused about the "demons."[62] Chris's own struggle, as viewed by many who do not take the time to read his story, could simply be chalked up to trauma, nothing more than a replay of Sam's "demons." But, to pair a doctor with a soldier challenges conventional categories and, by the same token, conventional perception. The discourse of biology, coupled with the discourse of combat, builds a unique collaborative narrative ethos that triangulates, much later in the story, with the work of George Brown, M.D. But before readers arrive at Brown's research on transgender service-members, let them look more closely at the very particular story of Chris Beck becoming aware that she is Kristin Beck and the ways in which both Speckhard and Beck serve as guides for different communities of readers and the way their collaboration shepherds readers through the frontier of a new subjectivity.

Instrumental to this innovative sensibility is an awareness of the relationship between identity, ethics, and geographical location. Prior to deploying to Iraq and Afghanistan, Beck knew she was different. Unlike her grandfather, her "demons" cannot be constructed as a simple "snap" or a before/after binary in response to war. Beck and Speckhard are careful to challenge the territory of the conventional "war story" and the domination of trauma narratives by spending significant time away from Iraq and Afghanistan. After the paratextual pileup of blurbs, foreword, press release, editor's note, preface, and prologue, the authors tell the domestic homeland story of a son and a brother growing up in the space of a Christian home in the American South. Young Chris Beck, surrounded by quiet, conservative Christian elders, had a slightly older sister named Hanna. Well before his tours of duty, while still a child, Beck recalls a "habit of taking Hanna's clothes and then late at night when no one could catch him doing it, he put them on. Dressed in her clothes he got back under the covers to sleep as a girl" and remembers praying, "Please let me wake up in Hanna's body!"[63] This intersection of space (the American South), time (childhood), religion (Christianity), and gender (dysmorphia) challenges conventional discourse that locates stories like Beck's in the "consensus of fear," the binary play between trauma and a culture putatively plagued by liberalism and moral relativism. Beck does not chart her journey toward womanhood on a binary map of feminism versus capitalism, conservatism versus moral relativism, and so forth. Beck's parents "didn't want their children to be exposed to the liberal and sinful ways that seemed to be sweeping the country in the late sixties and early seventies," so they sent their son to Lynchburg Christian School where Luther, Chris's father, taught.[64] But even in this sealed pedagogical space, Beck could not escape a sense of being different.

What Beck achieves through a dissensual aesthetic that regularly juxtaposes the discourse of gender with the landscapes of Afghanistan and a private Christian school in southern Virginia is a cumulative image of a geocultural space at odds with itself, a representative sensibility Chris's mother describes as her son's "weird sense of justice."[65] Young Chris Beck wears his sister's tights and stands up for bullied children at school not just because of a war wound or a repressed and traumatized grandfather or a desire to be as free and as loved as an older sister but because of all of these things and more. If dissensus is about anything specific, it is about a privileging of the sensibility that was once in the background; it is a blending of seemingly disparate sensory details that complicate class, race, and region divisions, linear plotlines, binary constructions, and monolithic characterizations. Far from a mode of erasure, dissensus, instead, pushes back against "the myth of the given" and seeks to make visible the fractures in the "given" conceptual categories that mediate sensory impressions. In one of Rancière's most famous examples, Flaubert's *Un Coeur Simple*, dissensus manifests in the character of "a poor illiterate servant" named Felicity and the needle of a barometer this maid encounters every day of her life.⁶⁶ Felicity is not a soldier, a CEO, or a famous diplomat, and yet Flaubert slows narrative time for her. The author's attention to the illiterate servant and the "needle of the useless barometer" that marks her days confer upon Felicity "the grand intensities of the world" and gives symphonic space to the routines of her life.⁶⁷ Likewise, *Warrior Princess*'s attention to domesticity and gender studies, broadly, and to the tights of a sister, specifically, redistributes the sensible territory of the soldier story, yoking together the tights of a girl in Virginia with the warpaint of a SEAL in Afghanistan. In short, Beck and Speckhard tear down the walls between men and women, home and abroad, and author and editor. As a political aesthetic, dissensus welcomes these connections as diplomatic openings. It invites previously ghettoized voices and compartmentalized impressions into a new public sphere where the line between location and dislocation is often unclear. Through dilation, complication, and a rejection of any single cause as sufficient for explaining the struggles of the individual, dissensus invites the reader to imagine a more diverse and embodied life dynamic. Dissensus is not a divorce from nation, race, philosophy, English, ethics, rhetoric, narrative, gender, Marxism, socialism, capitalism, or any other conceptual category. It is not the divorce of time from space, truth from beauty, or man from woman. Like parrhesia and its potentially cosmopolitan upshots, dissensus solicits the reader into an outspokenness, a sensory environment unpoliced by the standard divisions. Beck and Speckhard do not play the dominant culture game of blaming Chris's problem on a "lone wolf" of one "ism" or another because, as they see it, *Chris does not have a problem*. Beck has a story and an evolving character. And the dissensual name Beck and Speckhard elect to describe this character is "sheepdog."

Like all of the authors in this project, Beck seeks to unname and name—to disidentify and reidentify—so as to locate a discourse for a new sensibility. In so doing, she both affirms and complicates the parrhesiac tradition. Beck lived the vast bulk of her adult life on a kind of frontier, a pastoral zone between the sheep and the wolves. This American author played all the parts. Beck and Speckhard make expert use of the photographs they include in *Warrior Princess*, particularly the sequence titled, "Second Life—Navy SEALS 1991-2011." Here readers see a beardless Beck "as a young SEAL team guy in Panama," and then readers see "Chris and Karl Borjes—'At the laboratory, building a new automated mortar system,'" and after a number of other costumes, readers see Chris with a dyed black beard and indigenous regalia, the caption reading "Chris in his uniform of the day in Afghanistan."⁶⁸ Cumulatively, these photographs build on the archetypal Natty Bumpo image to suggest a lonely but timeless warrior who understands that the fundamental element of warriorhood is the hood—the mask—the ever-changing uniform and the correspondingly evolutionary character. Such a subjectivity presents a paradox in the discourse on parrhesia.

In his lectures, Foucault discusses Plutarch's construction of the parrhesiac individual as one who possesses a stable identity and a steady character. The *parrhesiastes* are those characterized by harmony, not dissonance. "First," Foucault writes, "there is a conformity between what the real truth-teller says with how he behaves." Second, he states, there is a "permanence," "continuity," and "steadiness," to this truth-teller, "regarding his choices, his opinions, and his thoughts."[69] But if Plutarch is right and this is true, then what are readers to make of the many masks of Beck, specifically, and this protean pattern they see in the soldier-writer community? I argue that the paradox is resolved by the recognition that flexibility, self-effacement, and "the art of imposture" are stable, fundamental components of basic training, particularly for soldiers in special forces, *those who must live in other spaces and among the spaces of the other* and, thereby, perhaps come to the conclusion that there is no other. This pastoral "sheepdog" pattern translates well from space to space, from battlefield to book. Beck and Speckhard simultaneously complicate and clarify their argument through the hybrid "sheepdog," a descriptor for Beck's character that captures his liminal identity and his "weird sense of justice" while also grounding that weirdness in sensible space: a dog that stands against other dogs in order to protect the sheep.

For Beck, the sheep may be other suicidal soldiers, other trapped men performing hypermasculinity, or perhaps her own children. After the stories from Beck's time in "The Forever War," one gets the feeling that the author has found a mission beyond state missions. As the narrative approaches its close, the intimate third person turns increasingly polyphonous and discursive. Speckhard comes out from behind the curtain just as Beck is coming out as transgender. Together, they help the reader understand the utility of the "sheepdog" in a world of wolves Beck sometimes labels as "rednecks and bigots."[70] Speckhard's voice, in these moments, seems distinct, but the authors elect to couch her in the third person:

> Anne thought that Kris sounded suicidal her whole adult life: the way he as a SEAL kept going back into war, trying to leave his life insurance for his boys. But Kris's sentiment of wanting to embrace life was right on. It isn't her fault how her mind and identity were shaped—whether it be from DNA, chemicals in our

environment, or early childhood. Her responses to trauma, family dynamics and all the things that shape an identity were not choices, but were shaped by things done to her, Anne reflected. And she had struggled so hard, for so many years to overcome it—marrying and divorcing twice and all the ruin that went with that.

The story of one man has suddenly become a space for two women. In *Places and Names*, Ackerman describes a location on the edge of Syria where two men discuss the "no man's land" of the First World War. But here in *Warrior Princess*, the story of one man has suddenly itself become "no man's land," a narrative space inhabited by two women. These separate but conjoined voices stage dissensus in *Warrior Princess*. They overthrow patriarchy with a powerful literality. If "all the things that shape an identity were not choices," these "things" can still be made part of that shape through transgressive narrative moves. If there is a monolithic nationalized identity at war with a more multitudinous transnational sensibility, such a struggle for identity reconstruction has a strong case study in the warrior princess and the sheepdog, two double-identities here united in the persona of Chris/Kris Beck. Speaking directly to Speckhard, the narrative now overtly dialogic, Beck continues to rail against the "rednecks, Christians, and bigots" who wrap themselves patriotically in the American flag while subverting American ideals. "'Life, liberty and the pursuit of happiness. I fought for the first two—can I have the third?' Kris asked, referring to the inalienable rights that all human beings are endowed with—for the protection of which they institute governments."[71] Thus, like Snowden and his carefully elided co-author, fiction writer Joshua Cohen, Beck and Speckhard mark a disconnect between America's founding principles and its current institutions and citizenry. They inhabit both a text and a growing community of signifying practice where public speech and writing itself serve as the bridge between America's divided tribes, as well as those tribes beyond: "I am going to start a blog," Beck says. "Maybe I will be able to help a few of the younger kids out there with gender issues. I want to go to high schools and give talks; I am a sheepdog after all. I can keep the wolves at bay."[72] Beck, in this narrative instance, calls for the staging of a conciliatory bridge between man and woman, as well as between two kinds of mythic animals: the sheep and the dog.

Like a sheepdog, a soldier-writer and veteran-activist are two things at once, maybe more. Beck and Speckhard disrupt conventional binaries as well as the more sophisticated binaries of biological determinism. However, their disruption is not mere nihilism or a pivot toward epistemic anarchy. Instead, they point readers toward a sense of collective cohesion—toward a more expansive patriotism. As Beck and Speckhard note, discourse on gender and identity is evolving quickly in the twenty-first century:

> [U]ntil very recently, the American Psychiatric Association (APA) classified transgender and gender-nonconforming identities as mental disorders. But then in 2013 the APA removed their previous categorization of "Gender Identity Disorder," revising the diagnostic category to "Gender Dysphoria" to reflect the emotional distress that can result from a marked incongruence between one's experienced/expressed gender and assigned gender. This is in recognition that a person's identity is not disordered, but that some transgender people have severe symptoms of gender dysphoria that can be treated successfully.

The work of George Brown shines a light on how these evolving conversations apply to Beck's story and also functions as yet another instance of a service-member breaking with code to evolve that code and uphold the ethos of a transgressive narrative. For this study itself to bridge the gap between a remote geography and a reinvented ethics, the case must be made for an intersection between the cultural maps showcased in narratives and that cartography's presence in the public spaces of the new media. Beck situates herself at this intersection. This is where she makes her own case, where she presents the ideal frontier study. Her story and her public rhetoric on Twitter directly challenged her commander-in-chief's prohibition on transgender soldiers. On April 10, 2019, the US military instituted a ban on transgender service members. On that same day, Beck began her rhetorical insurgency through the creation of an uncanny contrarian pair. Beck, the SEAL/woman who worked with Speckhard, the scholar who humanizes Islamic terrorists, tied herself to the tweet of Robert O'Neill, the SEAL who took out Osama Bin Laden. On the day of the ban, before directly addressing the policy, Beck engaged the assassin by tweeting with comment atop O'Neill's post. Now a public intellectual with a regular spot on Fox News, O'Neill tweeted out to the world on April 10: "Stop getting distracted by things that don't affect you at all."[73] Such rhetoric, with its implicit faith in discrete categories, embodies binary thought. This is not the rhetoric of outspokenness. This is the language that advises the individual to stick to his or her caste. Incidentally, Beck and O'Neill both served on SEAL Team Six, the unit responsible for killing Bin Laden. Therefore, it is hard to gauge and unpack, with complete certainty, the words Beck types atop O'Neill's tweet: "YES YES YES/THIS, Do this!!!" Is Beck speaking sincerely to O'Neill? Is she collaborating in the construction of rhetoric that demands people stay out of certain conversations that don't affect them at all?

A study of the evolving relationship between place and code must penetrate those new policed public spaces where amplification, silencing, and censorship go hand in hand. Twitter/X is certainly one such space, and, like with her memoir, Beck's speech there maps a pattern that is instructive for the students of both narrative and rhetoric. Beck's challenge on the transgender ban supplements her story and extends its rhetoric. In her April 2019 threads, she moves from a cryptic engagement with a Fox correspondent and a former SEAL teammate to an explicit conversation with Representative Joe Kennedy of Massachusetts about the ban. The pattern of the next twenty-four hours essentially becomes a dialogue with supporters and opponents, many of whom see Beck as the standard-bearer for this issue of transgender service. Kennedy opposes the ban. Beck quotes him saying "I cannot promise you that we will win this fight by Friday night, but I can promise you that we will win. #FightTheBan #LGBTQ #TransRightsAreHumanRights." Beck delivers the closing line on the tweet: "Navy SEAL 20 years … tell me #transgender people aren't 'capable' of military Service!!!!"[74] and then provides two photographs beneath, one of deployed Chris in beard and fatigues, the other of Kris with long hair in a blue dress. Thus, readers see this veteran-activist's narrative as the beginning of a public conversation in a collective dialogic sphere where the story continues to evolve with history if, by history, one means a public record of speech acts.

Through both her memoir and her digital presence, Beck, like Snowden, challenges her reader's apprehension of American patriotism. With Trump's transgender ban still hanging over her head, Beck goes further with her challenge to the supreme commander of her country's military, but her tweets are not simply discrete acts of dissent against Trump or the current government. Like in her memoir, Beck's speech betrays a useful ambiguity when it comes to the military's relationship to American ideals and the nation's relationship to the state. On April 11, she tweets, "I'm not sure who fights for us. Our nation is adrift in a political war of Right vs Left and the military is a PAWN."[75] Ignoring the code of silence, just as O'Neill did by selling a book about killing Bin Laden, Beck challenges this silent "PAWN" identity in her own way. Then, leveraging her ethos to amplify the dissent of other communities like the military podcast, *Zero Blog Thirty*, Beck retweets an interview with herself from *Zero's* podcast. Five days earlier, in anticipation of the ban, the podcast tweeted: "Navy Seal Kristin Beck fought for freedom and liberty; she won't tolerate people trying to strip hers. To hear the full interview with @valor4us listen to today's pod."⁷⁶ At the conclusion of this tweet is a link to an interview with Beck where she slams the "super religious" and the "GOP" for violating the constitutional separation of church and state by using religious principles to strip individuals such as herself of "liberty." This word, "liberty," is a dominant hashtag in Beck's Twitter history, often coupled with "justice." In this new public sphere of social media, Beck speaks with and through countless others, constantly repurposing their posts. As the transgender ban sends ripples of horror and enthusiasm throughout the various silos of social media, Beck studies the discourse and intervenes strategically. She builds on popular and scholarly discourse. Like her memoir, her new media presence is a dissensual collage of voices that bridge together the warrior and the healer, the sheep and the wolf, the military and medical community. On April 11, she tweets: "Fact: The AMA has said repeatedly that there is no medically valid reason to exclude transgender individuals from military service."⁷⁷ Again, on that same day, she retweets a story from November 24, 2018, from "NowThis," a site with over two million followers that highlighted Beck's opposition to Trump with the following tweet: "President Trump says trans people don't belong in the military. @valor4us knows firsthand how wrong he is."⁷⁸ The tweet then links to an interview with Beck, but before moving on to one final tweet, note the mass media bricolage of voices. Bricolage is an artistic tool used to bring a diverse array of materials together in unifying fashion. Beck's tweets do precisely this both individually and collectively. Her campaign culminates, briefly, on April 12, with Beck's retweet of a civilian who possesses no military pedigree: "#KristinBeck is a fearless Navy SEAL!" writes Maggie Allaga-Kelly, before punctuating her tweet with a meme of Beck in a dress with her medals pinned to her left breast and the following words floating over her shoulder:

Kristin Beck—Navy Seal
Transgender Woman
To Trump ...
Tell me to my face
I'm not worthy of
serving!

IV

Extraordinary Renditions

Mohamedou Ould Slahi, author of the 2015 *Guantánamo Diary*, is not an American veteran-activist. He is not an American citizen either, so he does not fit the author criteria of this project. And yet, he does. My book's fourth chapter opens with a reading of *Guantánamo Diary* for two reasons. The first should be obvious since this section of my study focuses, as announced at the outset, on narratives of dissent and cosmopolitan aspiration situated in particular spaces, namely at specific sites of detention. The second has to do with how Slahi handles dissensus in his text. Like the other writers I examine, he uses literary genres to speak back to the US government and deploy, accordingly, a parrhesiac ethos bolstered by unique lived experience. Specifically, he takes an established literary genre, in this case the memoir, and destabilizes its traditional use through various oppositional techniques. Homing in on them, part one of this chapter attends to *Guantánamo Diary* as an ideal case study for the staging of dissensus. Building on this introductory analysis, part two of this chapter offers a close reading of Kevin Powers, author of *The Yellow Birds*. Like the *Diary*, Powers's innovative story travels all over the world, speaks truth to power from inside the carceral space of a prison, and binds the reader to the sensibility of the invisible men of the Global War on Terror. Lastly, part three returns to Guantánamo Bay through an analysis of Joseph Hickman's *Murder at Camp Delta*, an ethically subversive narrative that shines light on a secret interrogation site at Guantánamo Bay called "Camp No." Repurposing this classified place name, this part of the book concludes by discussing the ways in which Hickman's story challenges the norms of narrative space, speaks up for inmates like Slahi, and thereby expands the patriotic code of care its author learned from his training in the American military.

1. Staging Dissensus

Before I offer a reading of Hickman and Powers, let us briefly turn away from this cast(e) of white soldier-writers. By binding Slahi's *Diary* to *The Yellow Birds* and *Murder at Camp Delta*, I would like, first, to highlight once more the governing cultural logic of my project and the escalating structure of this book. Rather than approaching Hickman and Powers as sites of binary clarity—they versus the "system"—I see in their narrative rhetoric a spatial reorientation, a staging of dissensus and a recognition that the detention places of recent military conflicts mark a gap or what Giorgio Agamben calls a "state of exception," which is to say, a "threshold at which logic and praxis blur with each other and a pure violence without logos claims to realize an enunciation without any real reference."[1] Designed to punish in the name of a "norm" or a law, the site of extraordinary rendition, instead, is a paradoxical space where *law is suspended in the name of applying the law*. These are world places where human rights, such as right to a fair trial, are denied in the name of an American nation-state ostensibly dedicated to such rights *urbi et orbi*. With an imaginative pattern of cosmopolitan dissent, Powers and Hickman challenge their country's faltering commitment to these rights and push readers to see, in these very correctional spaces outside the homeland, a need for domestic correction. Far from reinforcing the suspension of law that seems the fundamental premise of the ongoing war, Powers and Hickman, instead, suspend narrative time and democratize diegetic space to dignify the lives of the dead as well as the lives of invisible men like Slahi.

A Mauritanian accused of being a soldier for "the other side," Slahi was detained for nearly fifteen years without charges before being released from the "Echo Special" unit of Guantánamo Bay in 2016. Again, Slahi is not an American, and therefore, via binary thinking, one might argue that this Mauritanian should be banned from literary works focused on American soldier-writers. But the *Diary* casts a nuanced light on the pattern of disidentification and ethical remapping described throughout this book. More to the point, I contend that Slahi's book is useful in terms of helping us come to grips with US soldier-writers' use of negation—or with what Hugo Friedrich calls "the negative categories"—for, indeed, the soldier-writers of this study participate in the modernist stylistic tradition of disidentification with dominant cultural codes through a political art of negation. I show how this art informs one of the most insightful "extraordinary rendition" accounts. Of course, this quoted phrase is itself relevant. "Extraordinary Rendition" repurposes a name from the policies, strategies, and practices of the Global War on Terror. "Extraordinary Rendition" refers to the abduction of human "targets" from countries in the theater of conflict and the transfer of those "targets" to "sites," like Guantánamo Bay, where the United States could circumvent its own laws on detention, interrogation, and torture. By including Slahi's narrative in the conversation, my book sets out to disrupt and evolve its own structural logic and reveal a more complete map of the most secretive truth-telling geographies in the recent wars. Furthermore, I read Slahi's *Diary* as a narrative of exception, evidence of how the old national identity markers no longer serve as reliable coordinates.

I view Slahi's text as illustrating narrative, non-fictional dissensus as a site of interdisciplinarity, an intentional breaking down of discursive walls. This memoir is a place where conversations about geography, geopolitics, technology, style, ethics, film, history, literacy, narrative, and human rights intersect. In this segment of my argument, I demonstrate how *Diary* offers readers a number of valuable lessons on the staging of dissensus. I focus here on a close reading of two particular sections of the book to explore the dissensual properties of the text and the cosmopolitan ethos Slahi cultivates. Like Snowden's *Permanent Record*, the *Diary* follows a computer specialist along a seemingly simple timeline. Structured around events from 2000 to 2005, *Guantánamo Diary* travels from Mauritania to Jordan, and then from Afghanistan to a place that is neither quite Cuban nor American: Guantánamo Bay. However, just as Hawaii represents a troubling and dissensual geographical territory in *Permanent Record*, Slahi dilates his experiences in Jordan by returning to that country in the middle of his tale and the torture he experienced there. Slahi's prose, like Snowden's and the other soldier-writers, is impossible to separate from his whereabouts and his biography and, thereby, dramatizes the impossibility of this separation. This is important in that it establishes the narrator's ethical status, beginning with his reliability, an attribute that, I would emphasize, is a function of place, of world spaces with which the author and narrating protagonist proves solid ties. In addition to these geographical and cultural territories, Larry Siems, the book's editor and a human rights activist, offers the reader chronological traction as he or she moves blindfolded through the darkness from site of rendition to site of rendition. But Siems's footnotes are not the only crucial paratextual elements. Like Beck and Speckhard, Slahi and Siems bring the multitude of the book's background into the foreground and stage a deft collective of voices that enhance the credibility of the hero and the book. As Slahi lands in Jordan, the reader begins with Siems's footnotes and his references to documents obtained from Human Rights Watch who discovered that "from 2001 until at least 2004, Jordan's General Intelligence Department (GID) served as a proxy jailer for the US Central Intelligence Agency (CIA), holding prisoners that the CIA apparently wanted kept out of circulation."[2] Slahi's editorial team circulates the story of the prisoner the CIA "wanted kept out of circulation." Through this collective, with Slahi as the spearhead, the reader is able to locate the writer in time and space, even as Slahi himself tells readers that "I still hadn't adjusted to Jordanian time."[3]

To be adrift in time and space—to trouble the reader's relationship to spatialization—is fundamental to the staging of dissensus, and nothing, stylistically, captures this dissensual drift like "the negative category," or language, on the sentence level, resistant to common sense notions of nation, time, space, and narrative. As a Mauritanian speaks out about torture in Jordan from an American prison leased from Cuba, the attentive reader shares in Slahi's disorientation. Slahi's own family, at this time, did not know the location of their kin, and as Siems's footnotes relay, the family only found out through an article, a year after the fact, that was published in *Der Spiegel* titled "From Germany to Guantanamo: The Career of Prisoner No. 760."[4] Thus, as the hood is removed from both prisoner and reader, two sensible experiences are staged simultaneously: the narrative of useful confusion and the scholarship of troubled locations. On pages that are intermittently broken up by black bars of redaction, deepening the simulation and revelation of secrecy and censorship, readers witness the dissensual voice of a man who is being held against his will by people he thinks of as American, Jordanian, and his own. This latter category of kinship on account of religion and popular culture (Slahi's identification with Muslim captors and American movies) is fundamental to the subversively inclusive logic of dissensus.

Slahi's Jordanian interrogators, contracted by the CIA, present the problem of identity and nationalism head on. "I scanned both back and forth and wondered about these guys," Slahi writes, following a black bar of redaction. "The whole problem of terrorism was caused by the aggression of Israel against Palestinian civilians, and the fact that the US is backing the Israeli government in its mischiefs."[5] Whether one agrees with Slahi's geopolitical claims or not, the point he makes about the pedigree of his Jordanian interrogators is causally linked to his musings on history:

> When the Israelis took over Palestine under the fire of the British Artillery, the invasion resulted in a mass migration of the locals. Many of them ended up in neighboring countries, and Jordan received the lion's share: more than fifty percent of Jordanians are of Palestinian origin.

Slahi's interrogators, therefore, appear in his narrative in the same way Slahi himself does: characters whose national identity categories disrupt the cultural map of the story. In an overarching geopolitical narrative in which thousands of Muslims were rounded up by bounty hunters contracted by the United States, this is not merely a rhetorical point about the complexity of the human condition. The problem of monolithic identification led to war crimes. This is a human rights issue that includes torture, unlawful detention, and cruel and unusual punishment. Slahi's dissensual narrative strategy dramatizes these narrative and legal problems at nearly every turn, constantly holding a dark mirror up to peripheral characters and to the reader himself or herself. Along with the inclusion of foreign languages and the deployment of negative phraseology, this dilation of sensible narrative space on behalf of the others one encounters marks the staging of dissensus on the level of style. Dissensual style also tends to compel uncomfortable encounters through dialogic moves. Slahi, who regularly deploys the second person and consistently calls out his "Dear Reader," "shifts the discursive context from the violence of interrogation to the conversation of the book."[6] As the reader discovers Slahi in his cell in Jordan, Slahi does not permit his audience a detached spectatorial gaze. The redactions themselves, originally designed to conceal data from the reader, now work together with Slahi's invitational rhetoric to inspire questions about gaps in the historical record.

This book—right here, right now—is also concerned with gaps. How does the Global War on Terror, with its "state of exception," complicate the writer's relationship to space, place, and ethics? How—right here, right now, during a frantic geopolitical moment where the United States seems to be shifting its attention away from Iraq and Afghanistan and toward Ukraine, Gaza, Russia, and China—does a writer account for the ways in which narrative warfare constantly splinters the reader's attention, inviting the reader to forget the fact that America's torture gulag, Guantánamo Bay, still remains open? Prior to arriving at Gitmo, Slahi waits in the limbo of another dark liminal site where his Jordanian/Palestinian/American interrogators remain nameless, the black stripping of identifying markers now repurposed by "Prisoner No. 760" and his editorial team. As the interrogators get down to the business of extracting intelligence from Slahi, it becomes clear that a portion of their interest in their captive derives from his digital footprint and that the writer, in turn, has an interest in understanding the footprints of his captors. What seems to baffle Slahi is the US Intelligence Community's strange allegiance to figures from a foreign country. It is the digital link—his work in computing—that he reads as illuminating why "the FBI trusts the Jordanians more than the other American intelligence agencies."[7] In this section of the book, Slahi recapitulates his capture or how he was working in computer programming when he voluntarily turned himself in to authorities shortly after 9/11. At that point, he narrates, "[T]he FBI confiscated my hard disk."[8] Slahi, taking a break from torture at Guantánamo Bay, tries to recall his torture in Jordan and the foreign intelligence officers who provided him with "enhanced interrogation" in that liminal territory of the Global War on Terror. He writes that he cannot quite understand why "the FBI would cooperate more with foreign organizations than the domestic ones, but I do believe that the Intel industry is like any other industry: you buy the best product for the best price, regardless of the country of origin."[9] Slahi frames his captivity as a traumatic experience, and like with so many traumas, exact recall is sometimes impossible, but Slahi's struggle to situate his story is not merely a function of trauma. The complexities of identity in the twenty-first-century globalized economy are made visible in this story. Even as the United States seeks to erect barriers at home, it needs to break them down abroad to prosecute war and commerce, and a fundamental aspect of that prosecution is stylistic nuance and interpretation, language, and translation.

The problematic relationship between geography and ethics cannot be tackled without attention to the way languages both morph and migrate as they pass over borders. Slahi, who himself speaks four languages, reads translation as the key to understanding the US intelligence's dependence on Jordanian torture workers. After he is captured and his computing materials are seized, the writer confronts the most basic form of encryption: a foreign language. So were the Jordanians up to the cosmopolitan task of deciphering a Mauritanian's code for their American employers? Slahi admits to reservations:

> [M]y original emails were in German, and the Americans translated them into English and sent them to the Jordanians, who in their turn translated the English versions into Arabic. Under these circumstances, the original text suffered and the space for evil interpretations widened with every translation.

This widening of space is stylistically mirrored and repurposed in the spatial dilations enumerated in Slahi's text. Just as the globalized economy generates porous borders for foreign workers, so does the cosmopolitan writer generate porous borders to capture traces of truncation and a ghostly semblance of all that is lost in translation. At the same time, like the Iraqi al-Tawhid in Klay's

"Psychological Operations," Slahi encounters strange cultural crosscurrents and endures a cavalcade of insults with, again, specific attention to the genitals of women: "You are not a man!" they tell him after slapping him and shoving him against a wall. "I am going to make you lick the dirty floor and tell me your story, beginning from the point when you got out of your mother's vagina."[10] Although he can recall portions of the interrogation vividly, much of the ordeal seems to have escaped Slahi's memory. After a certain point, all he can recall is the answer he gave, over and over: "Ana Bari'a," or *I am innocent*.[11] In spite of detailed descriptions of torture and a story full of reasonable doubt concerning the narrator's guilt, what is decisive in establishing Slahi's credibility is the transformative parrhesiac variable in Euripedes: citizenship. What Euripedes makes clear in *Ion* and what Foucault emphasizes in his study of this play is that Ion's story lacks the ethos of the narrowly defined Athenian citizen, and it is this absence that compels the excess in Ion's acts and speech. Like Ion to Athens, Slahi to America stages the excess in order to prove he belongs.

Nowhere is this performance of excess and exceptionality more powerful than in Guantánamo Bay. So it bears asking: what is the relationship between this place and truth-telling? Prisons, like the barracks of basic training, compel fundamental identity shifts as individuals assume numbers and nicknames and the new codes of the institutions to which they are indentured. But what unique cosmopolitan identity transformations are set in motion by the particular post-colonial space of Guantánamo Bay, broadly, and "Camp No," specifically, later in this part of my argument? As readers move from "the homeland" to "beyond the FOB" and now, in this second section of *Guantánamo Diary*, to the Cuban-American real estate that continues to serve as an incarceration center for America's Forever Prisoners, the dissensual politics of place comes into sharp relief, foregrounding my attention to this place in Hickman's *Murder at Camp Delta*. In Chapter 7 of *Guantánamo Diary*, titled "Gitmo," Slahi confronts American soldiers on the grounds of the prison the United States leases from Cuba against Cuba's will, the American occupation of this geography viewed, from the Cuban side, as a violation of international law. Slahi writes from this contested territory through the extraterritorial confines of a book that now travels around the world. In this final chapter of the *Diary*, the classified captors and named captive (Slahi) hold forth on America itself while sharing a geography that is American, according to the Americans and Cuban, according to the Cubans. Slahi and his interrogators discuss this strange place that positions both turnkey and terrorist in Cuba. The guard and the guarded debate the Global

War on Terror, racism, body image issues, sex outside of marriage, freedom of religion, and cinema. At one point, Slahi writes that "if Americans can be proud of something, they can be proud of their motion picture industry."[12] This is not a casual concession by the prisoner-writer. The aesthetic techniques Slahi deploys in this final chapter reveal a student of American culture repurposing the humor, outspokenness, and metacognitive techniques one discovers in American movies like *Groundhog Day*, a comedy Slahi references that tells the story of a man who is forced to live the same day, over and over, until he gets it right.[13] Prior to the *Diary* being adapted into a major motion picture in 2021, *The Mauritanian*, Slahi himself demonstrates a cosmopolitan understanding of American film on the pages of his memoir. By turning the mirror on nameless (redacted) American soldiers from within a secret American prison that forces Slahi to produce the same fiction, over and over, through torture techniques that include waterboarding, rectal force-feeding, and sleep deprivation, Slahi flips the Hollywood narrative. He repurposes the comedy of insane repetitions one finds in *Groundhog Day* into a tragedy published against the country that produced both the story and the invisible prison Slahi inhabits. With a voice that is both worldly and uncannily American in its web of references, *Guantánamo Diary* offers readers a Mauritanian voice from Cuba that spars deftly with American interrogators about American culture and America's ongoing military exploits abroad. What is perhaps most startling about Slahi's memoir is the degree to which the author exhibits an understanding of the American military and American culture that far exceeds the wherewithal of his soldier-captors.

As the book approaches its close, Slahi's fearless speech tackles the very institution that confines him at Guantánamo Bay. "Many young men and women join the U. S. forces under the misleading propaganda of the U. S. government," he writes, "which makes people believe that the Armed forces are nothing but a big Battle of Honor."[14] However, instead of raging against these "young men and women" who have tortured him, Slahi offers empathy, as if to highlight the innocence of their youth and the true target of his parrhesia: the state institution. Slahi begs the reader to "look at it from the interrogator's perspective. They were literally taught to hate us detainees."[15] Slahi possesses compassion for the victims of American propaganda. Thus, his words have that much more power when they attack the source: "[T]he U. S. government bets its last penny on violence as the magic solution for every problem," he writes, "and so the country is losing friends every day and doesn't seem to give a damn about it."[16] The nameless American soldier fires back at Slahi's critiques, the absence of the American's identification part of the repurposed power these entwined narrative spaces create. "Fuck them Terrorists," the interrogator says. "Ok," Slahi replies. "But you should find the terrorists first. You can't just go wild and hurt everybody in the name of terrorism."[17] The American soldier does not appreciate Slahi challenging him. In a moment of devastating irony, the soldier argues back that "Al Qaeda is using our liberal justice system," as if Slahi had chosen to be part of America's "Extraordinary Rendition" program. As if the prisoner-writer were deliberately embedding himself in a secret torture facility for the purpose of publishing a subversive narrative. But here, rather than challenge his captor directly, Slahi addresses the reader: "I really don't know what liberal justice system he was talking about: the U. S. broke the world record for the number of people it has in prison."[18] As one of those prisoners, as a victim of torture and censorship, and as a member of a prison community where no one is ever brought to trial, Slahi's accurate and worldly critique of America's incarceration system has a unique power that is a function of the geographical and narrative space that it inhabits. In *Guantánamo Diary* geography and place are as bound together as captor and captive.

Therefore, in Slahi's story readers witness the ideal case study for a germane sensibility that must be nonetheless marginalized by the conceptual parameters of this project. Here, in this prison and on the pages of this memoir, readers find a writer "whose very constitution is bound up with that of his readers" but also one whose authority is anchored in the citizens of the very military that sanctions his precarious legal status.[19] *Slahi lives in the state of exception geographically and legally at once, that is, in a territory designed to hide spatially the very juridical gap dissensus seeks to publicize.* Guantánamo Bay, like the oracle at Delphi, is a setting beyond the walls of the state. Just as Ion goes to Delphi for the truth (about his lineage), so do the Americans take Slahi to Guantánamo Bay to extract the truth (about his ties to Al Qaeda). But Apollo lies to Ion and Slahi lies to his captors both in Guantánamo and Jordan. As Foucault points out repeatedly in his study of parrhesia, there is a decisive relationship between parrhesia, place, and citizenship. The "political destiny" of an individual depends not just on a discovery of the truth, but the articulation of that truth in a public space by credible sources. If Ion cannot determine his parents, he cannot determine his citizenship status, and without the status of citizen, he cannot speak freely and forcefully in public: "I pray my mother is Athenian," Ion says, "so that through her I may have rights of speech. For when a stranger comes into the city of pure blood, though in name a citizen, his mouth remains a slave: he has no right of speech."[20] Likewise, Slahi's free speech is both censored and unleashed by a particular class of American citizens, and it is only through the dissensual pairing of Slahi with his ostensible American adversaries that readers begin to apprehend the full weight of his disclosures. While the military seeks to torture truth out of prisoners in a no-place between Cuba and the United States and between law and illegality, the tortured reach out from that *same* liminal place and through that *same* military to reverse the rhetorical dynamic.

Yet Slahi remains a Mauritanian. Even with the paratextual assistance of multiple American citizens, including one Lieutenant Colonel Couch, Slahi's citizen status still keeps him off the roll call of the veteran-activists in this study. He is offering his experience in war; he is speaking back to the US government and military; like Snowden and Beck, he is using the literary aesthetic techniques of memoir to make his rhetorical argument. But, unlike Snowden and Beck, Slahi is not a US citizen. This disqualification emphasizes the paradoxical significance of a clear identifying national marker. In juxtaposing Slahi with other soldier-writers like Powers and Hickman, questions arise: Is there only one way to be American? What does it mean to be an American in a globalized world? In the original binary phrasing of the Global War on Terror, George W. Bush did not set forth a membership criteria based on citizenship so much as on performance and allegiance: "You're either with us or against us," Bush said in a joint press conference with Jacques Chirac on November 6, 2001. "A coalition partner must do more than just express sympathy, a coalition partner must perform," Bush said. With the rhetoric of that decree, Bush invited American corporations, Jordanians, Eritreans, Iraqis, Afghans, Chileans, Australians, Brits, Pakistanis, Ukrainians, the French, and numerous others to join in the American effort, just as Slahi and other Mauritanians once joined in the American effort to defeat the Soviet Union in Afghanistan.

What seems essential to mention about a place like Guantánamo Bay is the way it houses so many men who once partnered with America. And now that partnership echoes back with the story of this prisoner-writer from the "Echo Special" unit of this notorious prison. Because Slahi chose to speak out, others spoke out with him and amplified his voice. Because Slahi wrote, others wrote with him, echoing his claims and building a Greek-like chorus. In spite of the fact that Slahi did not serve in the military, members of the American military, like Couch, saw it as part of their service to step away from their commitment to secrecy and to write publicly about a prison beyond America's borders. Couch's collaboration, according to Alexandra Schultheis Moore, was essential toward convincing her American college students of the reliability of Slahi's narrator.[21] The dissensual narrative that is *Guantánamo Diary* is, therefore, a testament to free speech, censorship, and an expanded collaborative concern for American ideals. As a primary document that interweaves secondary sources and stories and languages from around the world, Slahi's narrative is a place to study style, human rights, contested speech, and global literature. Furthermore, Slahi's memoir is a place to reimagine literacy itself and what books belong on what shelves. Here is the timeless question of the scholar, as well as the student and the librarian of the future: where to place this story? Where does the scholar house the rhetoric that leaks from the hidden spaces in the state of exception? How do teachers respond to students who "describe the book as a thriller, memoir, autobiography, imagined diary (addressed to Dear Reader, rather than Dear Diary), individual and institutional memoir (that tells Slahi's story and/as that of systemic transnational racism), and as literary testimony"?[22] If the *Diary* resists the standard disciplinary mechanisms of critical identification, how might a new transdisciplinary criticism build a home for such a story? In the next two parts of this chapter, through a close reading of *The Yellow Birds* and *Murder at Camp Delta*, I deepen the reader's immersion in the transgressive narratives of the soldier-writer community and, in closing, suggest a path forward.

2. Stay Deviant: Powers's *The Yellow Birds*

The Yellow Birds is a frame narrative or an intercalated story. Such narratives serve a number of purposes by embedding one or many strands within a larger structure. Embedding multiple narrative lines within a stable frame can set the stage for destabilizing a traditional chronological plot. In Powers's novel, that larger frame is the story of a soldier telling a particularly "situated" story—a story narrated, that is, from a "detention facility" in Kentucky. Rhetorically outspoken, politically resistant, and cosmopolitan in its ethics, *The Yellow Birds* exhibits an American soldier writing publicly about an American soldier-prisoner confined to a prison set at a strategic narrative location. The location of this prison and this narrative frame, like location in this book, is more than instructive. For these American soldier-writers, space is indeed the final frontier but not that Star Trek space beyond the "vaporous borders" of the planet. These veteran-activists chart an interior and textual space that they intentionally expand to create more room for the other. Thus, at the center of this project is a study of forbidden narrative territories and a "neogeography" that acknowledges people and places the official narratives of the Global War on Terror have rendered invisible. *The Yellow Birds*, situated as it is within an American prison and a global war, provides a powerful case study for exploring this spatial turn.

The relationship between geography and the kind of truth-telling Powers and his narrator, John Bartle, undertake is complicated by the fact that Powers's own story, or biography, operates as a kind of frame all its own. In the first line of his review of *The Yellow Birds* in the *New York Times*, Benjamin Percy writes that "[a]t the age of 17, Kevin Powers enlisted in the Army and eventually served as a machine gunner in Iraq, where the sky is 'vast and catacombed with clouds,' where soldiers stay awake on fear and amphetamines and Tabasco sauce dipped into their eyes, where rifles bristle from rooftops and bullets sound like 'small rips in the air.'"[23] In fact, nearly every review of *The Yellow Birds* begins with or draws heavily from a snatch of Powers's biography, his service in this social group. The brief biographies in such reviews call attention to the complicated ways in which identity serves as a critical anchor for soldier-writers. Increasingly, identity matters and twenty-first-century texts and criticism highlight this value by creating more space for the lived experiences of authors, marginalized characters, and even the reader himself or herself.

But if the soldier is a sacred identity category, what are readers to make of the soldier-writer whose soldier-character comes to the reader from prison? How does Powers's frame narrative, grounded in an identity category heralded for service and obedience, become troubled by its outlaw location? A pattern of spatial and geographical awareness, play, and reconstruction, and ethical remapping operates within this community of writers. Their ethical subversion of identity and practice of disidentity politics constitute an aesthetic of disidentification. Dissent is a binary; a discrete yes or a discrete no. Dissensus, on the other hand, is a pattern, an aesthetic, a complex style of distortion and resistance. In that sense, Powers confirms and complicates Rancière's claim that humans are in the midst of a spatial and ethical turn and that ethics is "the kind of thinking in which an identity is established between an environment, a way of being and a principle of action." "The contemporary ethical turn," Rancière argues, "is the specific conjunction of these two phenomena."[24] However, unlike Rancière, who seems dispirited by the role of identity, I argue that the politics of identity continue to evolve in unexpected ways and that the evolution of the disidentity politics readers witness in the soldier-writer community offers rational grounds for arguing that readers are in the midst of a consequential challenge to the norms of nationalist narratives, of identitarian discourse, and of the fundamental ways authors spatialize prose.

Powers's novel, and the haunt of his lived experience, magnifies this political-aesthetic from the beginning of *The Yellow Birds*. His frame narrative invites the reader into an affiliation with the dissensual, a permeable first-person plural POV that runs counter to the "The War" the author locates as agent and adversary in the first sentence of *The Yellow Birds*:

> The War tried to kill us in the spring. As grass greened the plains of Nineveh and the weather warmed, we patrolled the low-slung hills beyond the cities and towns. We moved over them and through the tall grass on faith, kneading paths into the windswept growth like pioneers. While we slept, the war rubbed its thousand ribs against the ground in prayer. When we pressed onward through exhaustion, its eyes were white and open in the dark. While we ate, the war fasted, fed by its own deprivation. It made love and gave birth and spread through fire.

As a dissensual specimen of Powers's prose, *The Yellow Birds* quickly turns away from the first-person plural and into the story of Bartle, a contemporary scrivener, but in its first movement, the book suggests a dynamic of transnational collectives, a single war against a single community of human beings, and those human beings, the soldiers, are against the war.

The Yellow Birds is the fiction of a soldier who has himself crafted a fiction: Bartle tells a well-intentioned lie to a woman, the mother of Murph, a dead soldier from his unit in Iraq. The reader discovers that Bartle has been called to account for his tale, the letter he writes to Murph's mother. Powers's novel takes the reader back and forth between an American detention facility, site of Bartle's punishment, and the Iraqi theater of war. The book describes the tribal condition of Bartle's life abroad and his isolation and alienation at home. As he comes to grips with Murph's death and the trauma of all that he witnessed in Al Tafar, Bartle cannot help but feel that his sense of home has been forever altered by his time in Iraq. At one point, in the first third of the novel and while located in Iraq with Murph, Bartle recalls a conversation about home. In this moment, he remembers "remembering the cicadas fluttering their wings in the scrub pines and the oaks that ringed the pond behind my mother's house in Richmond."[25] As Daniel O'Gorman writes of this "particularly reflexive moment in the narrative," Powers here shows us a soldier "remembering his wartime self remembering home. Although the Richmond to which he has returned is geographically the same Richmond that he previously left,"

O'Gorman argues, "it is no longer 'home' to him in the way that it once was."[26] Powers's prose has a spare paratactic quality and, thus, this "reflexive moment" operates as a "reveal," a removal of the veil from the dominant pattern of lean lyrical prose. The minimalist music of Bartle's voice fugues and evolves in these dilated moments. "The space between home," Powers writes, "whatever that might mean for any of us, and the stretched-out fighting positions we occupied, collapsed."[27] O'Gorman observes in this revealing scene the "connective dissonance" he maps throughout his study of the "transnational 9/11 novel," which is part of the pattern I witness in the narratives of the American soldier-writer community.

The dissensual aesthetic both shows and, in its revealing, occasionally tells of the collapse, the disintegration of the old categories. Just as the Global War on Terror mapped a borderless war in search of an emotion, so does the dissensual aesthetic of the soldier-writer chart a mission that defies the binaries of politics and aesthetics as well as nation and state. This defiant political aesthetic is a narrative pattern that operates throughout the frames of *The Yellow Birds*. Bartle is constantly writing, constantly leaving the "real" frame of his prison. Bartle and Murph are perpetually walking away. Whether it is Murph from a base in Iraq or Bartle from a base in Germany or his own home in the Richmond frames, this is a story of exile and defection, but even that description is defective. Echoing Crenshaw, what gives Powers's novel such destabilizing force is the institutional instruction—the training—Bartle and Murph receive from their higher-ups, particularly the character of Sergeant Sterling. "There's only one way home for real, Private," Sterling tells Bartle. "You've got to stay deviant in this motherfucker."[28] Like Crenshaw's privates in "Names," the young soldiers of *The Yellow Birds* develop their "deviant" sensibilities as an organic result of their training in the US military. The way "home" is not simply "away." When Sergeant Sterling tells Bartle "you've got to stay deviant in this motherfucker," he is not giving simple geographical orders to redeploy or stay on one side of a fence or another. Like the public soldiers labeled privates that Crenshaw describes disavowing their own names, the soldiers Powers describes are being told by their superiors to obey the order to disobey a certain species of order. They are being trained in the art of unlearning. The military ethos on display in both Crenshaw's story and Powers's novel describes a sensibility adept at deconstruction, reconstruction, and a "deviant" path of negotiating the no man's land, those pastoral zones between statal identities that can get a soldier saved or killed in the theaters of war.

This in-between space takes the reader to an uncomfortable place. About halfway through *The Yellow Birds*, Bartle returns to Richmond, Virginia. Or, rather, Powers takes readers recursively back to Richmond, the former capital of the Confederacy. *The Yellow Birds* is a haunted novel, a story built with the rhythms of older stories. In this particular section, Bartle returns to the river, the James River, and using the paratactic language pattern of the King James Bible, he connects to a river abroad, dilates narrative spacetime, and shows a man alienated from old American friends upstream with whom he is both present and absent. The spatial and ethical subversion is on display in the narrative landscape, and the paratactic sentence here and the way clauses flow together like the liminal cartographic feature—the river—demonstrate a contrarian style at work:

> [R]eally it doesn't matter because by the end you failed at the one good thing you could have done, the one person you promised would live is dead, and you have seen all things die in more manners than you'd like to recall and for a while the whole thing fucking ravaged your spirit like some deep-down shit, man, that you didn't even realize you had until only the animals made you sad, the husks of dogs filled with explosives and old arty shells and the fucking guts and everything stinking like metal and burning garbage and you walk around and the smell is deep down into you now and you say, How can metal be so on fire? And where is all this fucking trash coming from?

Here and elsewhere in Powers, the paratactic can be a democratic tool, a leveling device that works in contrast to the hypotactic style one finds elsewhere. In the paratactic moments, the reader must be the one to create space and make distinctions—to pause for meaning and relief. In a sentence such as this, if the reader does not provide the space for themselves, he or she may find themselves swept away by musicality. Perhaps that musical quality of union or indistinction that emerges from a rhythmic chant is the desire of some readers. Powers redeploys the mystical sentence structure of the Bible in his secular prose. When the paratactic clashes with the hypotactic and is removed from its religious context, it maintains a haunt—an echo of its prior dwelling—in its new contrarian domain. The historicity of *The Yellow Birds*—its time in space—is part of the cartography that continually evolves the seemingly simple Biblical style and pushes the parameters of literature.

Critic Brian McHale writes of the "interpenetration between reality and its representation" and refers to this "flickering effect" as the "heterocosm" of literature.²⁹ Why does Powers employ the paratactic in his contemporary chronicle? How does this stylistic choice enhance the "flickering effect" and return the reader not just to history or Iraq but to the traumatized body-mind of one who has "been there"? In *The Yellow Birds*, the reader finds Bartle at a particularly complicated juncture of time and space. In August of 2005, during the heart of America's war with Iraq, Bartle returns to Richmond, Virginia, and he is quite literally sinking. He is floating in the James, water rushing all around him. Bartle is sinking in the river at home and his thoughts in this sinking come to us in the prose—the "old arty shells"—of the Bible. Only in *The Yellow Birds*, readers hear the story of one man from a war waged in the old holy lands but reflected not just in America but the capital city of the rebel state—the Confederacy—that once challenged the legitimacy of the United States in the Civil War. *The Yellow Birds*, therefore, is a novel haunted by disidentification and "the flickering effect." Yes, it is the story of Murph, Bartle's friend, who abandons his American base in Iraq and is killed outside the wire. But it is also the story of Bartle making sense of Murph's story in a Kentucky detention facility and remembering how he nearly drowned in a river in Richmond, Virginia, the former capital city of a country that signifies the only organized military revolt against the United States in its history. Bartle is literally in the state of revolt, the dwelling of a rebellion that still haunts America as a monument to the dark side of identity politics: white supremacy.

Like the Confederates, Powers rebels, but in the other direction. He embraces the other. Like Ackerman, Beck, Klay, and Snowden, Powers disidentifies with a narrow racist nation-state commons to expand his ethos and the territory of American patriotism. Powers fights against one side in a global conflict while speaking out against his own. Powers's cosmopolitan parrhesia is dissensual: he does not abandon his side but instead foregrounds a contrarian tension; he evolves this pattern of worldly spatialization and disidentification—this international and internal Civil War—by eventually bringing it home to Germany, the most famous twentieth-century locus of fascism, and Richmond, Virginia, the old haunted capital of the Confederacy and, therefore, the haunted house of white supremacy. But beyond (or within) these clear geographical fractured sites sits an imagination on the page. Bartle writes to the reader as a kind of "figurative refugee," in O'Gorman's words. After his friend, Murph, dies beyond the wire in Iraq, Bartle returns to Germany and Richmond with an imagination shaped by memories from beyond the wire. Murph's abandonment of his post, resonant of Bo Bergdahl's famous abandonment of his post on the Afghanistan front of the Global War on Terror, known in military nomenclature as DUSTWUN (Duty Status Unknown), leads the reader into the believable consciousness of a soldier imagining precisely what Murph (and Bergdahl) might have imagined: the life of the other. The tug of empathy certainly qualifies as getting "deviant in this motherfucker," for nothing is more diametrically opposed to the training of the soldiers of the Global War on Terror than allowance for the humanity of the enemy. As Hickman describes in the next text of this section, military training often cautions soldiers about identifying with the other: "Our instructors spent much more time explaining Stockholm syndrome," Hickman writes, "than helping us understand our captives. Stockholm syndrome is when captives start to sympathize and identify with their captors."[30] In other words, connecting with the enemy is the clear and present danger. But in a war at such cross-purposes, empathy—deviance—is also a solution, a strategy that is, in Powers's case, simultaneously aesthetic and political. His show of resistance to his own side in a public space is a narrative act that is brave, worldly, and innovative.

Powers reveals a literary identity standing at a crossroads. He inhabits this zone as an author, character, and historical textual artifact that intersects with the lived experiences of his ever-evolving communities of readers and writers. His work is a testament to the worlds of their time and the struggles for change in the times to come. The war, broadly and specifically Powers's war in Iraq, promised a change of "hearts and minds" and prescribed such psychological operations overtly through a specific textual artifact, the Army's famous field manual known as *Counterinsurgency: FM 3-24*. Given by JSOF forces to this author while embedded in Al Anbar Province, Iraq, *FM 3-24* runs counter to the traditional training manuals of pre-Vietnam military operations and seeks to assert, instead, a new set of fundamental principles in counterinsurgency (COIN) context.[31] This was the one book given to me by the lieutenant in charge of the Joint Special Operations Force I documented as a journalist and later in my memoir, *The Mysteries of Haditha*, and it is a text that exhibits the nuanced ethos of an entire generation engaged in a new kind of war. When Powers portrays Sergeant Sterling instructing Bartle to "stay deviant in this motherfucker," he is not describing a traitor or an outlier from the higher ranks, but instead a figure like Beck, a reflection of the complex contrarian identity of the modern American military in the Global War on Terror. Torn between traditional and evolved training doctrine (which privileges political or diplomatic action over offensive military action), the American military, not surprisingly, has produced a generation of soldier-writers whose narratives are political, "deviant" and contrarian, constantly engaged in an internal counterinsurgency in which they find themselves at war with themselves and the value of empathy. Bartle, by the conclusion of *The Yellow Birds*, is just as "disassembled" as the gun Murph left "scattered in the dust" on the night he abandoned Bartle's unit. Murph "was gone but we didn't know it yet," Powers writes at the end of the novel, revealing a tension between surface and depth that has transferred, like a ghost, from Murph to Bartle. Like a legacy passed down from Melville's Wall Street scrivener, this "gone" quality ("I prefer not to") manifests in the end as a portrait of a soldier becoming a writer in Fort Knox, Kentucky. Kentucky here seems to serve two purposes: one figurative and one literal. Kentucky is the site of Bartle's punishment for the lie he tells Murph's mother (assuming Murph's identity in a letter home), but this state is also the location of the old American frontier and thus locates the reader in yet another haunted liminal territory. Kentucky, like Germany and Virginia, is a spectral landscape of flickering effects. The concentration camps of the Nazi regime operate in tension, as noted above, with the capital of the Confederacy in *The Yellow Birds*, and this tension is both heightened and resolved in the novel's final movement. The ghost of the modernist sensibility is indeed encoded in the counterinsurgency manuals of the Global War on Terror and the way this text questions and problematizes traditional training doctrine. To truly get "deviant in this motherfucker," Powers not only describes this dialectical tension but synthesizes it and evolves it by resolving his story in the geography that used to exist "beyond the wire" of the original United States. But where once there was a frontier, readers now find a prison.

Again and again, this book returns to the fundamental principle of geography and real estate, to location and its bearings on discourse. After the American Revolution, when the United States was once again at war with itself (its prior British self) in the War of 1812, its soldiers fought an eastern front and a western front, and the west was marked by the Kentucky territory. In Chapter 2 of this book, I describe the "frontier" as Barlow's metaphor for the early (and ideal) Internet and the ways in which Snowden troubled this conceptual territory that has often been discursively constructed as distinctly American. The national-geographical frontier was always a shifting thing, moving westward and north, from Kentucky to California to Alaska to space. But now, in Powers, it moves inward. What the soldier-writer community represents, with Powers as one of its most subtle prose stylists, is an insurgency at home. At the conclusion of *The Yellow Birds*, the reader finds Bartle in the space one would expect to find a militant, an enemy combatant, or an insurgent.

Powers's prose spatializes Bartle's imprisonment in careful ways. Fort Knox, Kentucky, operates as a "heterocosm," a cosmopolitan history agitating in the grain of this seemingly singular space. Space dilates at the end of the book and solidifies into place. Time slows down. As Westphal writes, "space turns into place when it gains definition and becomes meaningful … [p]lace is a landmark upon which the eye pauses when it surveys a general scene, 'a point of rest.'"[32] Powers, in the end, settles the reader down on the old frontier. Where once there was the plot of a homestead, there is now a prison. Bartle, in the end, is located in the middle of the contemporary United States at a site that was once its border. Powers locates his soldier-writer at a "Regional Confinement Facility" where he has "been pleasantly forgotten about by almost everyone."[33] Powers's prose in this place embodies the tension between the paratactic and the hypotactic. The reader witnesses here the absence and presence of coordinating conjunctions and the elision and imposition of connection between concepts. Here, in this space, Powers's voice seems torn between the descriptive and the abstract, the personal and the political, the emotional and the logical, the dissensual ethos as the embodiment of the war between the languages of narrative and rhetoric. Halfway to the end of this final chapter, Bartle tells the reader, in hypotactic fashion, that he "spent a lot of time trying to piece the war into a pattern" and that he came to wonder if "all choices are illusions, or that if they are not illusions, their strength is illusory, for one choice must contend with the choices of all the other men and women deciding anything in that moment," and though this piecing together continues, what is noteworthy for this argument's purpose is the word "for."[34] Powers is not a purely paratactic prose stylist. The paratactic is merely the dominant in his novel. Powers's protagonist is struggling to find meaning in the war and, thus, his prose is at war with the "for," the language of telos: ideology. At the end of this hypotactic paragraph, Bartle confides in the reader that "I eventually accepted the fact that the only equality that lasts is the fact that everything falls away from everything else."[35] This principle applies to America's national identity and has been borne out as an accurate description of the nation's protean national ethos from the very beginning. Like the young men shedding their names in Crenshaw, so do readers here, in Powers, find the confined voice of an American, once again, abandoning old America. But the pattern of disidentification in the character of Bartle is both unique and representative. The ethical and stylistic code of the soldier-writer community is not nihilistic or simply postmodern. There is a compass here. There is a "for" here, not just a bleak tide of "against" or a desert of elisions. "I don't want desert," Bartle writes, harkening to the appeal of the arid lands of the old frontier and, perhaps, the deserts the Global War on Terror:

> I don't want prairie and I don't want plains. I don't want anything unbroken. I'd rather look out at mountains. Or to have my view obstructed by a group of trees. Any kind would do: pine, oak, poplar, whatever. Something manageable and finite that could break up and fix the earth into parcels small enough that they could be contended with.

Powers's hunger for mountain and clear border is inscribed as an aesthetic antidote to the "unbroken" space of the desert, the past of both Iraq and the old American deserts of the West. But this fixation on mountains can also be read as a belief in an ideal, the mountain as the archetypal sublime site of achievement, vantage, and imagination. It is appropriate too that Bartle, haunted by the old frontier, describes a new imaginative frontier that is again marked by mountains. The US prison within the old US frontier, far from being a geographical binary organized between the poles of America past and America present, is triangulated in the novel's final movement as a space that includes Iraq. Rhetorically parrhesiac, *The Yellow Birds* concludes with an American soldier-writer writing publicly about an American soldier in an American prison writing about a map of Iraq given to him by the mother of his dead friend. Alternating back and forth between describing the site of his confinement as a "cell" and "my new cabin," one thing that is certainly noteworthy about this final place is that visitors are allowed. This is not Guantánamo Bay, and this is not Camp No, either. That is why I place Powers after Slahi and before Hickman. The Kentucky facility is a contested space but not the most contested. There is a very permeable border between the public and the private. Murph's mother is permitted to visit and gives Bartle the map of Iraq where he sees "a section magnifying Al Tafar and its surrounding landscapes."[36] Like we see in Klay, Snowden, Ackerman, and Beck, the soldier-writer narrative here is shaped by a cartographic imagination.

The ethical remapping these soldiers execute with their narratives is covalent with the attention paid to geography within the space of their stories. Murph's map of Iraq "seemed so foreign and imprecise. Just a place scaled out of existence on a map."[37] This map, as an objective correlative, is not a zone of certitudes or a comforting return to the mountainous American territory Bartle longs for just outside his window in Kentucky. Murph's map of Iraq, like the text of the novel, is a tangible space unto itself with "creases that ran straight along a very small section of the Tigris."[38] If Murphy's law is that everything that can go wrong will go wrong, Murph's map charts that law on a very particular landscape: Iraq. But Murph's map does not just grid the country or the city of Baghdad the American media uses as a stand-in the same way Hollywood uses New York or Los Angeles as a stand-in for the United States. This specific portion of this dead soldier's map points Bartle and the reader toward two things: Firstly, a detailed riparian portion of a country that is occupied by Americans but not American in terms of sovereignty and, secondly, a self-consciousness about geography, the ever-evolving constructs of time and space.

The reader, in other words, observes the map of Iraq along with Bartle but also thinks about this map, specifically, and maps, more generally. Powers's prose, in the end, embodies the relationship between history and geography, time and place. His careful spatialization of his story splits the senses of the reader between multiple sensibilities, multiple ideologies, and multiple geographical coordinates. "That map," Powers writes, "like every other, would soon be out of date, if it was not already. What it had been indexed to was only an idea of a place, an abstraction formed from memories too brief and passing to account for the small effects of time."[39] At this narrative coordinate, the reader studies a domain of coordinates and, perhaps, thereby, absorbs a meta-awareness of the plotted course of his or her journey. Like Bartle, the reader has traveled all over the world in the very real social space of words on a page (or screen) transformed by a reader into the unique territories of the imagination. *The Yellow Birds* itself, like Bartle's map, may "soon be out of date" and Powers's novel, like every novel, only offers readers "an idea of a place, an abstraction formed from memories." Thus, as Bartle struggles with the map of Iraq as a territory unto itself—as a precious sensory artifact within the deprived spartan quarters of a "cell" that is also a "new cabin"—the reader enters into a precarious literary space. Murph's map is the final dissensual territory of Powers's story, representing a magnified and dilated zone of time and space that shepherds a river in Iraq into a room in Kentucky, as well as the ever-changing geography of the reader.

In this triangulation of places, the faces of the dead resurface: "I saw Murph as I'd seen him last, but beautiful," Powers writes. "Somehow his wounds were softened, his disfigurement transformed into a statement on permanence."[40] The "flickering effect" and the "ethical dissonance" of this final moment confront the reader with a reterritorialized vision that is both past and present, here and there, phantasmatic and, at the same time, grounded in the historical spaces of the Iraq War. The map gives rise to Murph. Murph is suddenly an American body swimming through non-American names and places while his friend resides in a prison that is both a "cabin" and a "cell." Bartle, in the end, is telling the truth about a lie. Bartle, Powers, and the reader, in this metafiction, watch the disfigured Murph as he "passed out of Al Tafar on the slow current of the Tigris, his body livid, then made clean by the wide-eyed creatures that swam indifferently below the river's placid surface."[41] Like those "wide-eyed creatures," the reader is invited into an encounter with a body that is "livid," Murph's frame both animated and dead. Powers's contemporary readers, like those who may study or enjoy his novel a hundred years hence, do not conclude their reading experience in America. Instead, like Bartle the soldier-writer, they abandon their immediate confines in Kentucky and dream a map to life. They see "the Shatt al Arab in summer" and "the broad waters where the Tigris and Euphrates marry unknowingly," just as a corpse wanders "unknowingly."[42] They witness an American abroad, an insensate Western figure disfigured in the Middle East, his body lifeless but still traveling, "passing through the cradle of the world as it greened, then turned to dust."[43] In many linear death-centered narratives, the hero dies in the end and the bell tolls for both protagonist and reader. But in Powers the soldier lives and is left to mark the paths of the dead, as well as his role in the dying. This is a profound difference in terms of the reader's relationship to time and space. Far from simulating death in the repurposed cadence of the Bible, Powers's prose takes the soldier-character's death one step further. Prompted by a cosmopolitan sensibility, Powers does not let the reader escape to "the other side." Powers's protagonist does not abandon his senses. He does not drift out of consciousness. Bartle remains alive and awake and dissensually stages the death of a friend in the sensible space of a diegetic Iraq. He speaks out in his American prison and imagines his dead friend with his "injuries erased to the pure white of bone."[44] Murph's wounds have been "erased" and his body will "finally break apart near the mouth of the gulf," but, in the end, the bell does not toll for Powers's reader or the reader's vicarious self that splits and silts in this visionary current on the other side of the world. The consequences of war remain vivid and estranged for both Bartle and the reader, even as the character of Murph—the AWOL American—floats far beyond the walls of a prison that was constructed atop the forts that once marked the border of the Western frontier.

3. Camp No: Hickman's *Murder at Camp Delta*

No site embodies Rancière's "consensus of fear" or Agamben's "state of exception" more than Guantánamo Bay. America's most notorious secret prison grounds a number of pertinent questions about the relationship between law and location, race and space, and naming and place. Guantánamo Bay is the site on the global map that most powerfully demonstrates (grounds in the demos) the consequences of the US Patriot Act and the ways in which this law, according to Agamben, "radically erases any legal status of the individual, thus producing a legally unnamable and unclassifiable being."[45] These precarious phantoms, "enemy combatants" or "insurgents," stripped of national status and the protections such status entails, are now like the landscape they inhabit: liminal. Guantánamo Bay is not quite Cuba and not quite the United States. It is a place in between, a "no man's land" where democracy itself is excepted in the name of preserving democracy.

In *Murder at Camp Delta*, Joseph Hickman shines a light on the deaths of three young men who allegedly committed suicide at Guantánamo Bay. Reviewing for *Newsweek*, Tim Dirven calls attention to *Murder at Camp Delta* and its unusual concern for people most Americans would like to forget. "In the official literature," Dirven writes, the men Hickman speaks out for are "often referred to by their Internment Serial Numbers, the prevailing nomenclature of the Guantánamo Bay detention center: 588, 093, and 693."[46] But Hickman gives these men more than just names. He gives them a story and includes his own and that of scholars in the telling. *Murder at Camp Delta* begins with a map of Guantánamo Bay. Hickman's book begins in cartography. This paratextual preface is a multimedia stylistic move and visually locates three primary coordinates for the reader: Camp America, Camp Delta, and Camp No. Camp America is the military name for the prison portion of the base that both is and is not American. Leased from Cuba on February 23, 1903, and formally recognized by both the United States and Cuba as sovereign Cuban territory, Guantánamo Bay is legally Cuban but houses Camp America and the extra-legal camps where detainees from the Global War on Terror are concentrated or "renditioned." Camp Delta is the specific southern "area of detail" where Hickman manned the watchtower over a cellblock just off the coast of the Caribbean Sea. Camp No, just beyond the northwest border of Camp America, but still within the leased American territory, is the dark site where Ali Abdullah Ahmed, Mani al-Utaybi, and Yasser al-Zahrani were allegedly murdered by American interrogators on June 9, 2006.

Hickman's geographical foregrounding of these murders immediately raises the question of place.

But before the reader gets to this liminal territory in Hickman's narrative, the author begins his story by classifying his identity as explicitly nationalist: "I am a patriotic American," Hickman writes in the first sentence which reads as both literature and investigative journalism. To travel from the fiction of Powers's rendition to the nonfiction of Hickman and his supervision of rendition is to journey through both geography and genre. Like all of the soldier-writers in this study, Hickman repurposes his military credentials, his biography serving as a legend for a map that guides the reader beyond the borders of the United States to look back on that land and its most challenging ethical precepts. Hickman's story in the context of its own unique geography is juxtaposed with his narrative as a subverted genre, like Slahi's *Guantánamo Diary*. As such, *Murder at Camp Delta* is a text that provides a unique window into narrative as rhetoric, identity as dynamic, dissensus as style, and global literacy as a new kind of ethics. When Hickman says, "I am a patriotic American," in the first line of his book, he begs the reader to wonder when he or she will arrive at the *but*; the territory Agamben defines as "the state of exception."

Just as the border between the United States and Cuba is contested and permeable, so does Hickman's narrative form, like Powers's and Slahi's, embody this porousness with its self-conscious narrative rhetoric. In the words of rhetorician Lloyd Bitzer, a work of rhetoric "comes into existence for the sake of something beyond itself ... Rhetorical works belong to the class of things which obtain their character from the circumstances of the historic context in which they occur."[47] Fundamental to Bitzer's concept of rhetoric is the notion of "exigence," which he describes as "an imperfection marked by urgency; it is a defect, an obstacle, something waiting to be done, a thing which is other than it should be."[48] The exigence is the very "state of exception" that marks Guantánamo Bay. When Hickman establishes his national and military credentials by saying "I am a patriotic American" (and thereafter spending several pages detailing his decades of national service), he is foregrounding his service in this exigent territory where individuals belonging to substatal organizations are tortured by multinational corporations subcontracted by the US government.

Hickman's book is the final case study of the imaginary pattern I read as operative and dominant in the innovative literature of post-9/11 soldier-writers. This pattern is simultaneously literary and rhetorical, a new subjectivity and a novel exigent discourse that is both protean and historical, personal and political, parrhesiac and collective, dissensual and cosmopolitan. Hickman's patriotic and transnational voice is the negative of "the Global War on Terror," a reversal of the "declaration of war on terror" that "is the exemplary speech act of sovereignty for our era."[49] Hickman, like Ackerman, Beck, Klay, Powers, and Snowden, establishes his national ethos in order to speak up for an idea of the American "nation" that both embodies and transcends nationalism. To articulate this new expansive national ethos, Hickman takes the reader through the life of the soldier, "the training days," the simulations—the fictions—that are a constant part of the soldier's life. These war games or revolutions serve a purpose for the soldier and the soldier-writer who deploys them for the reader. To witness Hickman's training regimen is to witness an identity formation that plays out over and over again in the US military and, likely, most militaries across the globe. But something has changed in this particular regimen in this particular war. Hickman, as part of a Marine unit (the 629th Battalion) that was about to deploy to Guantánamo, begins his simulations but is surprised to find an exception in his company's training, a break with historical pattern. His company commander, Captain William Drake,

> organized the company along racial and socioeconomic lines. Instead of mixing up the country boys and city boys, he kept nearly all the Western Maryland guys from the original 629th in Third Platoon. First Platoon and Second Platoon contained all the guys from the Baltimore units, mostly urban white guys like me from blue-collar backgrounds, along with Latinos, and blacks.[50]

The significance of this break in identitarian pattern cannot be overemphasized. As Hickman writes, "even as far back as 1983, when I joined the Marine Corps, I had never seen any unit deliberately segregated by race."[51] The division and concentration of identities embodied by this training regimen are a mirror of the racist regime embodied at the Guantánamo Bay prison. There are no white men in the cells of Camp Delta. Hickman, perhaps by accident, was that rare figure whose class status trumped his racial status, enabling this white man unusual proximity to a group of dark prisoners with whom he was trained not to identify. What Hickman's instructors seemed most terrified of was "a sort of reverse Stockholm syndrome" in which the captors began to identify with captives.[52]

Those commanders' fears bespeak the tenuous nature of the enemy-construction in the war. To keep a largely white population at war with a largely dark population, isolation and division—segregation—are essential. What makes the identity of the twenty-first-century American soldier-writer so fundamentally novel is their territorial and transterritorial exposure to the other, the double-helix of the Internet, and the segregated lands of invasion and occupation. Cuba is one such territory and one such cyber domain. The digital element of Hickman's narrative will become apparent shortly, but it is first important to trace Hickman's path from servile silence to whistleblower, from soldier to veteran-activist, and to understand how that path in no way undermines his cosmopolitan construction of what it means to be "a patriotic American." Hickman was the first soldier to blow the whistle on the deaths of Ali Abdullah Ahmed, Mani al-Utaybi, and Yasser al-Zahrani. But prior to witnessing the events of June 9, 2006, and before speaking out against his government, Hickman prepares the reader for his expanded vision of patriotism by mapping his lived experience as a dutiful soldier. After his patriotic gambit and establishing America's racist training protocols with an evocative, character-driven voice, Hickman begins to unwind the patriotic ideal from the very real acts and very real setting of Guantánamo Bay. He describes atrocities from his unique vantage in the Guantánamo watchtower:

> I didn't see my first beating until my second week ... I was about sixty feet away in the tower and could see everything happen clearly as they entered the cell block. As soon as they reached the detainee's cell, the guard slammed the luckless inmate into the outer wall. An instant later the guard punched him in the face. The detainee went down, and two other guards who were on duty in the cell block rushed in and started kicking him. After a good minute there was blood all over the floor.[53]

Hickman's witness, in this incident, is inextricably tied to place. His evocative outspokenness is a function of his station. No one but a member of the military could tell this story in a public space. A horde of such abuses are documented in this same bold clear-eyed style. A particularly abusive guard named Monster calls a prisoner a "sand nigger" and kicks him.[54] One detainee, with a prosthetic leg, is kicked over and over again until the prosthetic falls off. What makes Hickman's narrative so authoritative is that one can almost understand, at a certain point, why he would be inclined to not speak up on behalf of the detainees in spite of all the atrocities he witnesses, for he himself is viciously attacked at one point just before the deaths of Ali Abdullah Ahmed, Mani al-Utaybi, and Yasser al-Zahrani.

Prior to Hickman speaking up for these three inmates in the dissensual stylistic way in which he does so, Hickman establishes a rhetorical context for his diegetic argument. Just as he is about to participate in an act of civil disobedience by blowing the whistle on the military, he bears witness to the ethically subversive demonstration of the prisoners prior to the night of suicides. In the winter and spring of 2006, an increasingly large number of prisoners were undertaking acts of civil disobedience insofar as they were protesting their unlawful confinement through hunger strikes. However, the American military circumvented these acts of peaceful protest by force-feeding the detainees through oral and anal tubes. Thus, the prisoners moved from civil disobedience to violent resistance. Prior to the decisive incident of the book, Hickman is called in to put down a "riot" in Camp 4, a location that is described by different personnel as both the most "compliant" and most dangerous place on the base due to the fact that the "compliant" prisoners, by virtue of their compliance, are permitted communal cells. Therefore, in the words of Hickman's commander, Captain Drake, "It's the only place detainees can mass against us."[55] When Hickman and his men arrive at cell block W ("Whiskey Block"), they are told that a prisoner is attempting to hang himself inside, but they do not find this to be the case. What they discover instead is "a volley of piss, feces, and metal objects."[56] The threat of suicide had been used as lure by the prisoners to draw in the guards for a fight. The dilated narration of this conflict situates the reader in a rich and unsettling sensory environment where all barriers between Americans and their precarious prisoners are, temporarily, destroyed. They fight together. They clash in a scatological sensory space that immerses the reader in a prolonged moment of improvisation; action and reaction. "The detainees had smashed apart a security camera in the room, the light fixtures, a fan, and an air conditioner and were using the shattered pieces as projectiles."[57] The harrowing scene that follows details the rarest of things: American soldiers fighting with enemy combatants one on one. This is not the classic Global War on Terror narrative of an IED or a drone assassination picking off distant dots as if they were video game targets or a narrative that stylistically encounters these distant others with a remote POV. The proximity—the intimacy—of this exchange between human beings is virtually unprecedented in the annals of these wars. For a brief moment, the asymmetric dynamic of the war breaks down. The standard and literal lines of attack collapse and so do the divisions of narrative protocol as these sequestered identity categories mesh in a hail of excretions. "The detainees had prepared a small cache of feces and cups of urine to throw at us, and they'd covered the first five feet or so of the floor with soap. As we tried to form our line up," Hickman describes, "we skidded around like Keystone

Kops, clutching at one another to keep from falling over."⁵⁸ A list of the funniest narratives to emerge out of the Global War on Terror might just delight in the comic elements afoot in this scatological melee. Sometimes humor emerges from the darkest of circumstances, that unsettling feeling of the carnivalesque, the high brought low, the witnessing of the powerful Americans rendered temporarily helpless like "Keystone Kops." Hickman, seeing what this reversal of circumstances has enabled, quickly "made the decision to end the fight" and with it the fiction of symmetry.⁵⁹ Seeing that his men were not only in danger but also at risk of "reaching a point where we might beat one of the detainees to death," he commands them to shoot the prisoners with rubber buckshot. What is important to note here is the sudden descent of the meta dimension. After the riot, Hickman is taken into a room where he is told to write his story. However, the officers who read the first draft reject his report. To accept those edits from his superiors is to do his narrowly defined duty. To resist those edits is to expand the territory of American patriotism.

Like all of the books in this book, *Murder at Camp Delta* is a war story, but it also possesses a metafictional quality, a self-conscious style. This is a story about storytelling and how fiction slips into official truth and state documents. "After about ten minutes," Hickman explains, "the senior chief returned with my report. He held it up, crumpled it, and threw it in a wastepaper basket. He shook his head sadly. 'Not good enough. You need to rewrite it.'"⁶⁰ In short, the officers wanted Hickman to lie. They wanted him to commit to paper that his violence was justified because he had "observed a suicide attempt in progress."⁶¹ To tell such a lie would have been utterly in his legal favor, for Hickman, as of that day, was "the first person in the history of Gitmo ever to give orders to fire on detainees."⁶² However, even as Hickman's narrative crosses the desert of empathy and violates the ethical border between soldier and detainee, his character, by the same token, draws a line. He refuses to sponsor the state-sanctioned story. "The navy chief and I went back and forth," Hickman justifies but finally agree to the quintessential political compromise, "the sin of omission."⁶³ Hickman, after eleven hours of drafting his story, allows that he was "told that a suicide attempt was in progress," but "omitted the fact that no suicide appeared to be in progress inside the cell itself."⁶⁴ Thus, the soldier is forced to cave into fiction; drafting and redrafting, combing out the truth. In this moment of Hickman's story, the reader witnesses the American soldier himself as a site of "enhanced interrogation." Prior to becoming a published soldier-writer, Hickman describes himself as the soldier writing and editing a story in the private classified domains of public service. Hickman compares this drafting process to accounts he had "read of people being held in communist Chinese reeducation camps. I had spent eleven hours bending truths into untruths."[65] Such "reeducation" serves as a demonstration of how official fictions become official facts in the Global War on Terror. For students of war, history, human rights, foreign policy, criminal justice, and literature, such moments of narrative transformation are instructive. These narrative acts cannot happen without a worldliness when it comes to history, an awareness of the "reeducation camps" in China. Likewise, such a history is impossible without a willingness to risk the very standing upon which one's story is grounded.

Alongside Slahi's *Guantánamo Diary*, Hickman's book provides a window into history, the process of how history is told, and how geography and genre shape ethics. Student-readers, thus, can study a document and its evolution, a draft of a vocational genre emerging out of a contested conversation and, later, becoming part of a commercial genre one might call journalism, history, or memoir. All of this writing about drafting serves to prefigure the events of June 9, 2006, and the two public narratives that emerge in response to that night: Hickman's and the government. Standing in the watchtower overlooking Camp Delta, what Staff Sergeant Hickman witnessed was, at first, just another day in the life of a guard at Guantánamo Bay. He "went up to Tower 1 a little after 6:30 when the call to prayers was starting."[66] Then something happened. Hickman "saw the white van enter Delta and proceed to Alpha block. Unlike navy guards in the cell blocks, who used plastic flex cuffs to restrain detainees' wrists, the escorts from the white van used metal police-style cuffs."[67] Hickman watches the van leave Camp America. He witnesses the van return and pick up a second detainee and then a third, transporting all of these prisoners in the direction of the facility known as Camp No.

Attention to geography and cartography is essential to Hickman's story. Most notably, his truth-telling takes place in relationship to a site that is not supposed to exist. Camp No was a secret interrogation facility that was not located on any of the official maps of Guantánamo Bay. When Hickman sees it, about "250 yards outside Camp America" while taking a Humvee off-road one day on patrol, he claims that he and Private Jose Vasquez "saw that the facility was surrounded by two parallel fences, typical for detention installations, with brush growing between them."[68] As Hickman and Vasquez get closer to this location that is not located on their maps, Hickman writes that they "could make out six trailer-type structures in two rows of three, with a larger building at the end, about the size of a double-wide trailer. The buildings were covered in aluminum cladding and resembled the newer structures that Halliburton had put inside Camp America."⁶⁹ Staff Sergeant Hickman and Private Vasquez were the soldiers to nickname the site Camp No, a name that has now entered the public lexicon. The CIA's official name for this unofficial interrogation facility, as revealed in 2013, was Penny Lane, but the label "Camp No" reflects the fundamentally dissensual nature of Hickman's narrative and the way that resistance begins on the most granular level—a single phrase—the challenge of a name. Like Crenshaw's soldiers, Hickman's men come up with a deviant name of their own. "One key to surviving military life," Hickman writes, "was to never ask questions or look where we shouldn't. People called it 'staying in your lane.' Neither Private Vasquez nor I was the type to fully adhere to that principle."⁷⁰ Thus, later on the night of June 9, when Hickman sees the white van return to Camp Delta and back up to the medical clinic (instead of dropping the detainees off in their cells), it is no surprise that Hickman begins to ask questions. This basic response to an event is the seed of the rhetorical pattern demonstrated by the veteran-activists of this study. Fundamental to all of the narratives on display is a questioning of American state activities by state actors who have served within the privileged but often contested geographies of the Global War on Terror. Hickman, reporting from the "state of exception" at Gitmo, is no exception.

As stated in the introduction of this book, scholars like Lagasnerie have described a small community of Global War on Terror "truth-tellers" as embodiments of a new subjectivity whose geographical context is the same as their state's war zone: the world. This book seeks to enlarge the aesthetic of dissent Lagasnerie proposes and expand the list of dissidents who belong on that roll. Hickman, like Snowden, exists in a "disposition matrix" and is confronted with a choice that resonates across nearly all vocations: tell the truth of what you see or yield to the gag order imposed by your state, your school, or your corporation. Speak truth to power or let your silence provide consent. For Hickman, this is a decision that is tied to a time, a place, and a series of linguistic choices. What Hickman discovers, along these lines, is that "there was a code red," which is military slang for a harsh extrajudicial punishment.⁷¹ Hickman hears from "Lisa," a member of the clinic staff, that "[t]hree detainees just killed themselves" and that they all "had rags stuffed down their throats."⁷² When Hickman then sees an ambulance arrive at the clinic, he "couldn't understand what it was doing there if the detainees had already died."⁷³ "How could they have died in the custody of navy escorts," Hickman wonders, "with bruises and with rags stuffed down their throats?"⁷⁴ So, after becoming the first soldier to fire on Guantánamo Bay detainees, Hickman now finds himself in the unenviable position of being one of the "watchers on duty when, for the first time, three detainees died at Gitmo."⁷⁵ Given this perilous circumstance, Hickman feels the institutional enticement to lie or accept multiple sins of omission. To tell the truth is to risk one's place. But, at the same time, the soldier-writer possesses a unique parrhesiac duty as a result of his or her place and sworn oath to uphold the principles of the Constitution. Not every American citizen is asked to simultaneously serve their country and sign a gag order. This is a rhetorical quandary unique to the soldier and doubly so to the soldier-writer.

When Hickman is again asked to swallow the official explanation of suicide, he refuses. He is told by Colonel Mike Bumgarner that the official narrative will be that Ali Abdullah Ahmed, Mani al-Utaybi, and Yasser al-Zahrani "committed suicide by cutting up their bedsheets and stuffing them down their throats."⁷⁶ At the conclusion of this briefing, Bumgarner warns the soldiers present that the media will "talk about a different way that these detainees took their lives," but that all military personnel are under strict orders "not to talk about these deaths."⁷⁷ "I need not remind you all," Bumgarner says, "that your communications are being monitored by the NSA."⁷⁸ Which is to say, Hickman tells his story at great risk to his life and career. He leverages his national identity to speak out for the rightless others and against the very national system that forged his identity as a soldier.

In 2008, Hickman delivers his eye-witness account of events to Professor Mark Denbeaux at Seton Hall University. The moment he does, his story evolves into a higher order of dissensual stylistic practice. It crosses a line, both aesthetically and politically. The stranger in one strange land is now the stranger in another, except in this one his medals and credentials demand a certain kind of exile rather than entrance. Denbeaux served as the director of Seton Hall's Center for Policy and Research. When Hickman asks the center to vet his story, Denbeaux demands Hickman subject his account to one of the crucial filters of scholarship: anonymity. Hickman wants to challenge the official verdict of suicide from the Naval Criminal Investigation Service (NCIS). Based on his research into Seton Hall's scholarly *Report on Guantánamo Detainees: A Profile of 517 Detainees Through Analysis of Defense Department Data*, he surmises that Denbeaux is the ideal partner to assess his story. "As the title of the center's paper suggested, Denbeaux's researchers had relied entirely on reports and other data compiled and released by the military."⁷⁹ Like this book in its selection of veteran-activists, Denbeaux's research sets rigorous parameters by taking the military at its word. The Seton Hall project yields to the wartime culture of censorship and seeks to interpret only the redacted documents the military itself provides. As Hickman writes, "They took the government's own data at face value and used it as the basis of their investigation" to report on the seemingly benign question of location: Where did the Guantánamo "terrorists" come from? Of course, this question of geography is far from benign. The public question of place becomes the way into the private places where public servants have outsourced the interrogation of prisoners to private contractors and the corporate space.

Hickman's story of narrative's intersection with scholarship reveals the multitudes of the book's background dissensually foregrounded. *Murder at Camp Delta* expands not just the reader's concept of patriotism but also the scholar's relationship to narrative. Denbeaux meets with Hickman and after hearing his story in person says, "Joe, I don't know what to think. I cannot believe that the authorities at Gitmo would fake a single suicide, let alone three. I don't believe in conspiracies."[80] Hickman is, in fact, one of those authorities, but he refuses to participate in the official fiction. This whistleblower, in this decisive moment of his story, serves as a rhetorical bridge between storytelling and scholarship, fact and fiction, and also between a willfully ignorant nationalism and a patriotism marked by an evolving worldview. The solution Hickman stages on the pages of the second half of his book is the same ethical solution he stages in the first half: he cautiously yields to the other. He trusts his senses at the prison, and he trusts in the work of the scholars at Seton Hall. He is the outside source in a rhetorical realm of propaganda in part one, and he defers to the outside source of scholarly process in part two. In order to navigate the scholarly minefield of their shared interest and responsibly vet a story teeming with shattering implications, Denbeaux begins by introducing Hickman to a veteran and a researcher on his team, Paul Taylor. Just as Hickman yields to Denbeaux, Denbeaux yields to the veteran community and their familiarity with their own discourse. After Taylor claims he finds Hickman's story credible, Denbeaux goes further. He tells Hickman that he will take his case, but that there is a process in place and that it could take months. "I'll turn a document or set of documents over to my students," he says, "and ask them, 'What does this really say?'"[81] Furthermore, according to Hickman, "none of the students would know about my story or even of my existence. This was to ensure that they didn't embark on the project with any bias."[82] Like the other authors in this study, Hickman has, through a process of detachment—through the act of writing—attached himself to the stripped victims of the Global War on Terror and made their classified stories not just his own but a part of a public space.

Furthermore, by building his unique narrative bridge to the lives of Ahmed, al-Utaybi, and al-Zahrani and doing so in a style that is both narrative and scholarly, Hickman expands the aesthetic of dissent. The sensory impressions Hickman shares from Guantánamo Bay reallocate the sensible terrain of the Global War on Terror, revealing shared spaces coinhabited by the figures from "both sides." But by describing his own erasure and inscribing that effacement into the frame of scholarly process, Hickman evolves the reader's concept of dissensus, enlarging it to include not just the marginalized languages of other races and nations but also the linguistic constructions of cloistered discourse. The marriage of narrative and scholarship and the forging of a genre that draws from the ethos of both unifies the narrative and scholarly collaboration the reader witnesses in Beck and Speckhard. Hickman's work with Denbeaux's team, additionally, reveals the institutional identity gaps that exist within the military and stage those spaces as the sites for challenge and change. "The NCIS," Hickman explains, "was an independent agency within the navy, headed and staffed by civilians in order to shield its investigators from influence by navy officers."[83] Thus, Hickman's narrative sensibility penetrates not just the foreign other beyond America's borders but also the embedded civilian other that Klay heralds in "The Citizen-Soldier." The purpose of inserting civilians within the military, in the case of the interrogators at Camp No, is the avoidance of ethical accountability. But the mission of the civilian within the NCIS is precisely the opposite and a mirror of the function of Denbeaux's team as it evaluates the credibility of Hickman's account. If social reality is a spatial system, the ethical remapping Hickman undertakes in *Murder at Camp Delta* can be constructed as an enlargement of narrative's public space. In Hickman, narrative socializes the atomized bodies of Ahmed, al-Utaybi, and al-Zahrani. Hickman makes room for the stories of both the dead victims of the Global War on Terror and the network of diverse institutional scholars who prescribe scientific rigor and self-erasure in the name of obtaining a credible account.

Like Beck with her collaborative memoir, Hickman's narrative creates a public space for challenge from the voices of scholarship. Denbeaux's team, harvested from the Seton Hall law school, evaluated the NCIS documents, setting the stage for students of Hickman's book to do the same.[84] They simulated a crime scene investigation. They recreated the night of June 6, and after failing to see a plausible way for these three men to conduct coordinated suicides while in custody, they came to the same conclusion as Hickman: Ahmed, al-Utaybi, and al-Zahrani did not commit suicide. They were murdered. Hickman's story, censored to avoid an inconvenient truth on one end, leads to the erasure of his story on the other end in the name of revealing the truth and bringing justice to the families of these victims of the Global War on Terror. These three men were designated as low-level enemy combatants. Like hundreds of others at Guantánamo Bay, none of these human beings were ever charged with a crime. After dying in American custody, their bodies were returned to their families with their necks missing. Toward the end of his book, Hickman writes,

> When I arrived at Gitmo with my unit, I believed we were guards protecting America from the worst of the worst. But by the time I'd gathered and sifted through all the relevant documents, I realized that all of us who arrived there, even Admiral Harris, had entered an intelligence operation in which no normal military rules or codes applied.[85]

Hickman here describes a system outside the systems of national and international law. This is Agamben's "state of exception," that zone where "law encompasses living beings by means of its own suspension."[86] Like his fellow soldier-writers, Hickman marches to the frontiers of the Global War on Terror and emerges with a narrative that reverses that state of exception and reveals a war of deceit where the nation's founding principles of freedom, democracy, and justice are narratively deployed to subvert a state run amok.

Like Slahi, the former prisoner of Guantánamo Bay, Hickman, the former guard at this American gulag, speaks up against the state. Like Snowden, Hickman's rhetoric challenges state institutions in public while making it clear to readers that there is a difference between the nation and the state and that a certain species of patriotism privileges the former over the latter. To serve the American people and the nation's original aspirational commitment to human rights is not necessarily synonymous with fealty to American government agencies. All of the soldier-writers of this book share this dissensual commitment to reimagining patriotism and decoupling American ideals, like democracy, from the state yoke. Nowhere is this challenge more rhetorically or legally fraught than in the contested geography of Guantánamo Bay. Whereas the US government, recognizing this geographical exigence or this "state of exception," uses this territory to practice "enhanced interrogation" on a multitude of human beings who, to this day, have never been charged with a crime, Slahi and Hickman repurpose this terrain to stage dissensus, a systemic rhetoric of dissent marked by distinct stylistic moves. Like Powers, Hickman and Slahi reorient the reader's concept of the other or the enemy. When Powers writes that "The War tried to kill us," he deploys the first-person plural POV and rhetorically separates America's wars from America's warriors within the public space of a novel. Likewise, Slahi and Hickman utilize diegesis, the interior rhetoric of narrative, to make a case against "The War." In the sensible realms of "Echo Special" and "Camp No," an American captor and an American captive map the territory of America's secret history in the Global War on Terror, their extraordinary public renditions of events serving as a repurposing of the classified "renditions," or "enhanced interrogations," forced upon the Forever Prisoners of the Forever War. This prisoner and the soldier-writers of this project, through their ethically subversive narratives and decisively cartographic imaginations, offer future scholars and artists a legend for the ever-evolving map of resistance to the war.

V

Conclusion—Ethics, Style, Space: The Soldier-Writer Subculture

I would rather be without a state than without a voice.
                                              @Snowden on January 20, 2021

A new American literary community has emerged in the twenty-first century. The post-9/11 veteran-activists I introduce in this book represent both an evolution and a continuum in terms of the literary and rhetorical devices they deploy across a broad range of genres. However, these soldier-writers are unique in the same way "The Forever War" or the Global War on Terror is unique. Just as these very terms suggest an American enterprise that is boundless in time and space, so have these artists repurposed that boundlessness in narratives that express an American patriotism that transcends national borders. Whether in novels, memoirs, short story collections, social media posts, or works of investigative journalism, these authors write in public about an invisible but omnipresent war whose history has too often been hidden from the eyes of American citizens. With an ethos that is outspoken, worldly, and resistant, Elliot Ackerman, Kristin Beck, Joseph Hickman, Phil Klay, Kevin Powers, and Edward Snowden challenge the reader to travel beyond the borders of the American homeland and bear witness to these conflicts that have displaced tens of millions of people. Their stories, at once dislocating and profoundly attentive to the problems of place and space, beg the reader to value the precarious lives of the Forever War's victims and reconsider what it means to be an American in the twenty-first century. Through storytelling, these authors ethically subvert their basic training and disidentify with an outdated nationalist subjectivity in the name of mapping and serving a larger ideal. Such a project, fundamentally linked to conversations about narrative style, the democratization of literature, and the relationship between geography and ethics, challenges states and individuals alike to construct a new map for the future of storytelling.

This book offers a legend for that map and the communities of conversation about space, style, and ethics that have given rise to this study. Such communities are to the point of this conclusion. Whether their narratives are set on porches, islands, cafes, mountains, a prison in Cuba, or in the prison of the body, all the post-9/11 soldier-writers of this project have one basic thing in common: the techniques on display in their stories were composed among a community of collaborators, editors, and scholars who vetted and refined their work. In some cases, like with Ackerman and Klay and New York University's Veteran Writing Workshop, these collaborations were formal and at least partially designed to address trauma and suffering, the invisible wounds of war. In other cases, like with Snowden and his cooperation with his editor, novelist Joshua Cohen, the process was more informal and private, the code more particular to the exigencies of one particular book. But the result is, in the end, the same: a single digital and material object, a published story both discrete and dynamic in the same twenty-first-century publishing instant—a book. This conclusion to my book brings the conversation about America's post-9/11 soldier-writers into the immediate present of the Trump era, Biden's withdrawal from Afghanistan, and the new wars in Ukraine and Gaza. Furthermore, this conclusion brings together the diverse voices of this study by turning to the processes and practices— the rules—that govern the spaces where the soldier-writers' style develops, and their stories and books take shape. These rules are literary and rhetorical, but as I argue through the work of Dick Hebdige in this final segment, they are also subcultural—they end up producing an entire subculture. The brave, worldly, and contrarian pattern I locate in the cultural maps of these American authors are, in many ways, unique to the historicity of the Forever War and the digital age, but this same evolutionary pattern is in keeping with a tradition Hebdige maps in *Subculture*, a work on which, in closing, I will be leaning briefly as I draw together the diverse diegetic geographies of these post-9/11 soldier-writers and synthesize their efforts to reinscribe the outside, heal divides, and honor dissent. The American authors in this book defy the nationalist geographies of their tradition and, in this systemic dissent, or dissensus, find themselves akin to unlikely others, like their "enemies" and the British punks of Hebdige.

Hebdige's primary concern is the description of an expansive contrarian ethos and the mapping of the processes that mark the sensibility of a particular artistic community. I share in this concern as I document the ways in which this collection of soldier-writers have leveraged their lived experience to expand the discourse of American patriotism and military writing, even as the very terms "patriot" and "patriotism" undergo a dramatic revision in light of the Trump era and the January 6 riot at the US Capitol. Subsequent to this "insurrection," when Jack Dorsey, the CEO of Twitter, deplatformed Donald Trump on January 7, 2021, Dorsey highlighted what Snowden and the authors of this project have emphasized over and over throughout their work: there is an authority beyond the state. In an increasingly digital and cosmopolitan world, the nation-state's hold on speech has continued to weaken or, rather, has continued to change. Before the wars in Gaza and Ukraine and shortly before Elon Musk blew the whistle on Twitter's relationship with American government agencies, an America's commander-in-chief was removed from Twitter's multinational digital platform, possibly as a result of state coercion. Immediately after Trump's removal from Twitter/X, Ackerman wrote an essay about the "politicization" of the veterans and civilians who seemed to be supporting Trump's claims about a rigged election by participating in the Capitol riots and committing what some called acts of domestic terrorism in that hallowed national space. However, Ackerman, who has also recently argued for caution in Gaza and the rapid deployment of diplomacy in Ukraine, does not bite on domesticating the rhetoric of terror. He described the post-election violence as a "collective insanity" "where norms of civilized behavior melt away," a political space reminiscent of the wars he witnessed in Iraq and Afghanistan.[1] Ackerman, unlike Trump, still remains on Twitter/X, one of the unique "rooms" or spaces this study documents; as does Beck, Hickman, Klay, and Snowden. Ackerman, like the former commander-in-chief, defies a certain species of norm or rhetorical order with his words. However, contrary to Trump, what I read in the space of Ackerman's work and the recent public statements of this community is not epistemic chaos or disruption for disruption's sake. Although Trump, as a former commander-in-chief, technically served in the US military, he never participated in that fundamental deconstruction of basic training and was, therefore, never versed in the ethically subversive pattern of disidentification and service that marks Ackerman, Beck, Hickman, Klay, Powers, and Snowden. So alien to Trump, the idea of serving a collective beyond the self is an instrumental ideal of the military and that ideal has been repurposed by this cast(e) of authors. Like the British punks of the 1970s, America's post-9/11 soldier-writers offer a strange but ethical mirror to the contemporary "collective insanity" of their country and the tribal divisions that still plague the nation deep into the first term of Joe Biden.

Punk art is a form of civil disobedience, but not all art qualifies as punk or civil disobedience. Storytelling can be a canvas where the voices of different states, disciplines, and codes clash, deviate, and disrupt the assumptions of contemporary common sense, but not all storytelling is disruptive or activist in this sense. Through the narratives of this book, I argue that readers are in the presence of a new and original subculture of dissent. Instrumental to it is an innovative combat cosmopolitanism. Driving this culture is a novel subjectivity, more specifically, and a collective of digital and narrative voices that do, in fact, challenge the very state they once served and, thereby, expand the reader's notion of service and patriotism. Although it's tempting to unify the core concepts of this public-facing project (parrhesia, cosmopolitanism, and dissensus) and suggest that these veteran-activists synthesize these three techniques to stage truth and reconciliation in the name of peace, such an ostensibly elegant 3-2-1 equation does a disservice to the tension and clash one finds in their art. The challenge to power staged by these veteran-activists is not a simple story. But fundamental to this challenge and tension is the act of writing in public, a process Hebdige calls "signifying practice." In *Subculture*, his study of British punk in the 1970s, Hebdige weaves together a number of tools from across the disciplines to describe how subcultures express "a fundamental tension between those in power and those condemned to subordinate positions and second-class lives."[2] Grounded in Gramsci, Althusser, Levi-Strauss, and others, Hebdige locates his study in England and combines anthropology and Marxism to incisively describe the "deviance" one can read in the aesthetic objects of punks. Like Powers, Hebdige explicitly values deviance which he, Hebdige, defines as a "refusal to cohere around a readily identifiable set of central values."[3] Writing in 1979, I suspect Hebdige would be surprised to see his theory repurposed to map the public rhetoric of American soldiers, but as I have emphasized again and again, there is a difference between a soldier and a soldier-writer.

The soldier is found in the barracks of training, the FOB of the combat zone, and sometimes in militant positions beyond the wire. The soldier-writer, on the other hand, like the punk artist—or maybe even *as* the punk artist—can be found in the workshop, evolving his or her craft. Signifying practice, according to Hebdige, is "a branch of semiotics" that was developed in response to a problem that scholars located in handling the materials of certain artistic communities. When reading the works of postmodern fiction writers or punk lyricists, many reasonable readers may approach the texts looking for a message, a fixed monolithic signifier like "peace." Whether in the workshop or in the privacy of one's encounter with a text in a home, a coffee shop, or a base in Afghanistan, this style of reading may frustrate those who encounter the deliberately diverse, sometimes cacophonous range of voices one finds in, say, the work of Thomas Pynchon or Frank Zappa. Hebdige describes signifying practice as an operating system in which "the simple notion of reading as the revelation of a fixed number of concealed meanings is discarded in favour of the idea of polysemy where each text is seen to generate a potentially infinite range of meanings."[4] Hebdige's theory is not just a tool for a discrete population of scholars, artists, and fans who happen to favor blue hair, sexual sadomasochism, and heroin. Material as these ostensibly subversive elements of style may be, countless scholars have noted how the seemingly stable subcultural markers of punk, hippie, and hip-hop have been appropriated and repositioned by a dominant culture whose regime of the sensible is always in flux. Tie-dye is now found on the Paris runway, and hip-hop has become wildly popular among white privileged teenagers in the suburbs of the American South. Likewise, in punk fashion, the ostensibly square veteran-activists of this study constantly defy the perception of the American military possessing a monolithic identity.

In Chapter 2 of this book, "Disidentity Politics," the reader witnesses a disorienting challenge to conventional assumptions about the American military. As one follows this subculture into the public space of Klay's *Redeployment* and the imagined lives of Zara and Waguih as they play out in a college classroom, one begins to see fractures, trouble with the monolith. Klay, through these characters, turns away from the performative space of the classroom to the more private environment of a porch where his Coptic Christian soldier confides in an African-American Muslim named Zara. Zara reads Waguih wrong. She sees him as a fellow Muslim. Waguih, like Hebdige's punks, rages against the stereotype, the assumed signifier of skin and name. He doesn't like the narrow box. He confesses to Zara but continually protests. Klay's Waguih finally tells Zara his war story and speaks out against the psychological operations he was asked to perform in Iraq, particularly as they pertained to the degrading of women and Muslims. Likewise, Snowden rages in public against the acts he was charged with performing. He turns away from the crimes of the state in his memoir, *Permanent Record*. In this same first segment of the book, with its emphasis on the geographical location of the homeland, readers witness Snowden, while stationed in Hawaii, blowing the whistle on the unconstitutional surveillance practices of his government, but like Klay, Snowden does not leave the reader with easy answers. Instead, through pointed questions and a narrative grounded in the contested post-colonial landscape of Hawaii, Snowden challenges the reader not to abandon the United States but to expand the concept of American patriotism.

His resistance to state crimes compels him to rhetorically decouple the state from the nation or the government from the public. He repurposes the language of the Constitution and the American Revolution to check the oppression of the Global War on Terror. Stationed in Hawaii, between East and West, Snowden juxtaposes the revolutionary ideals of America's founding documents against the acts of the Global War on Terror and is banished from his country for doing so. Like so many citizens of the world, Snowden's story is both expansive and lonely. And yet it is a shared public space, a book where Snowden flies in the face of contemporary common sense. There is, arguably, no act in twenty-first-century history more punk—more disconcerting—than Snowden revealing the crimes of the American Intelligence Community and continuing his "patriotic" critique of America from Russia, his literary activism's resonance becoming more and more dissonant to some as Biden continues Trump's prosecution of Julian Assange, and America's ongoing proxy war with Russia in Ukraine fosters an increasingly censorious social media environment.

Just as Klay and Snowden speak out by evolving the narrative operating systems of the short story and the memoir, Ackerman expands the territory of the novel in Chapter 3 of this study. In *Green on Blue*, Ackerman's Afghan contractor, Aziz, challenges a common-sense assumption about the identity territory of American military writing. Using the capacious environment of the novel, Ackerman does not just speak out for the marginalized and precarious victims of these ongoing wars but speaks out as them, or as one of them, an act that defies trending concerns about identity and cultural appropriation. Leveraging his lived experience beyond the wire in Eastern Afghanistan, Ackerman dares the reader to join him (and Aziz) and, thereby, inhabit that landscape as a native torn between the various tribes in America's war. With a voice and an eye keenly tuned to the cartography of his story and the theater of war in Afghanistan, Ackerman, like Klay and Snowden, blurs borders and challenges the reader to question the relationship between geography and identity. And then Kristin Beck goes even further in her memoir *Warrior Princess*. Fundamental to Hebdige's aesthetic of deviation in punk is, again, the mechanism of "signifying practice." Beck, like Ackerman, Klay, and Snowden, challenges the fixed idea, or the monolith, of what it means to be an American soldier and what such individuals can do and say and what kinds of characters they can inhabit. Pushing the ideal of American patriotism even further, Beck's memoir suggests that soldier-writers can do more than just inhabit the fictional skin of an Afghan. They can also inhabit the flesh of a woman and tell the story of that transgender experience with the public collaboration of a civilian-scholar who happens to be a woman. Beck's alliance with Dr. Anne Speckhard pushes the reader to reimagine discourse on memoir, scholarship, masculinity, patriotism, and identity. The subculture of dissent on display in this book pushes the boundaries of geography, genre, and gender. In Beck's *Warrior Princess*, her dissensual transgender narrative documents an actual marginalized identity emerging from within the bodily confines of the white male monolith, and as Beck does so with help from an editor and co-author who happens to be a woman with a background in scholarship that humanizes "terrorists," a fundamental question surfaces: *What are the limits of American patriotism?*

The penultimate chapter of this book locates the reader and writer in the national and transnational prisons of the Global War on Terror. Through the exclusion of Mohamedou Ould Slahi's *Guantánamo Diary*, the inclusion of Powers's *The Yellow Birds*, and a close reading of Hickman's *Murder at Camp Delta*, this project points to a partition, that place where the rule of law is finally imposed by the state. But even in these narrative spaces that document these confined punitive places, the reader continues to witness the soldier-writer in a state of challenge and pushback. Powers's Bartle, imprisoned in Kentucky for a fiction he told to the mother of Murph, a fellow soldier, is in many ways the everyman of these wars and their aftermath. Powers's novel is a public space where an actual soldier inhabits a fictional soldier who speaks for and against a range of fictions he felt compelled to tell and live. Likewise, Hickman, stationed at Guantánamo Bay, the most notorious prison from the Global War on Terror, refuses to continue with the story he has been charged with telling. His investigative journalism, like all of the books in this book, expands the territory of the genre while simultaneously urging the reader to look at the ways in which specific geographical territories shape the ethics of their storyteller. Hickman resists the culture of secrecy and torture that he witnesses at Guantánamo Bay, a prison that has outlived Bush, Obama, Trump, and now Biden. Hickman pushes back against "the state of exception" that characterizes this unique Cuban-American locale and, by doing so, signifies what Hebdige argued about punks in *Subculture*. Even here, with the prisoners many Americans see as the worst of the worst, there is a problem of perception. Hickman's story begs readers to consider the lives of apparent terrorists as human beings. His outright advocacy for the lives of three detainees at Guantánamo Bay, admirable as it may be, is still not precisely to the point of this subculture of dissent.

To "stay deviant in this motherfucker," as Powers writes, is about more than a single discrete gesture of dissent. There is a difference between isolated acts of dissent and the systemic dissent—or aesthetic of dissent—one finds in dissensus. The community these soldier-writers co-construct, document, and trouble is diverse, and so are the proportions of their separate aesthetics, but two things about this community are stable and invariable: first, the American soldier-writer writes; and second, but equally important, he or she does so *in certain places*. When the reader finds the soldier-writer in Hawaii or Guantánamo Bay, it is not an accident. And when the reader locates the diverse members of this subculture online, one discovers that there is, at times, a familiarity with Hebdige and much of the discourse in this book, but also pushback.

Peter Molin, a veteran who is a Twitter/X follower and Facebook friend of Ackerman and runs the "Time Now" blog and selfsame Twitter/X account, challenges Hebdige. He sees this community as more of a "scene" than a subculture.[5] "The big distinction I would make," Molin said, "is between those veteran-writers who are actively employed in (or hope to gain access to) the literary and publishing industry (and media), and those veterans who identify as members of grassroots, (arguably) more amateurish street-level writing collectives, often for the sake of therapy, exploring experience, and finding their voices and community."[6] Molin sees variability in this "scene," as do I. I see community, scene, and subculture, and I see the stylistic markers of those different realms of discourse throughout the artifactual expressions of the soldier-writers I have encountered as a conference goer, workshop leader, memoirist (whose agent is the soldier-writer, Tracy Crow), and scholar. "There's lots of overlap," Molin said, "and people in the first cohort often start out in the latter, but once a writer senses that he or she has a chance of being recognized on a larger (paying) stage, a lot of things change."[7] An entirely different book could map the hundreds of actual real-time military writing communities and dive deeper into compelling issues of race, gender, and class and the way these meaningful identity categories shape behavior and interactions between soldier-writers. But that is not the purview of this study. Language, broadly, and a particular, "situated"—location-defined—political aesthetic, specifically, is what interests me. I read in Ackerman, Beck, Hickman, Klay, Powers, and Snowden a critical engagement with the narrative and rhetorical patterns on display in this book. Hebdige's framing of signifying practice as a school that treats "language as an active, transitive force" is, in his words, "accompanied by a polemical insistence that art represents the triumph of process over fixity, disruption over unity, 'collision' over 'linkage'—the triumph, that is, of the signifier over the signified."[8] Creative destruction, ethical subversion, and this evolutionary fluidity of identity are the most striking counter-narrative the veteran-activist offers to the discrete veteran and civilian, particularly in an era when ostensibly discrete identities, like transgender individuals, suddenly find themselves forbidden by law from joining the US military. For American citizens in these unique identity positions, or even those veterans now under investigation for terrorism in light of the Capitol riots, the Forever War's "state of exception" continues to invade the conversations and tribunals of the homeland.

Boundless in time and space, these wars have produced veteran-activists similarly unbound by the borders of the nation-state. Whereas the dominant culture once positioned the Global War on Terror in Iraq and Afghanistan, the martial or combat cosmopolitanism of the soldier-writer community, buoyed by lived experience and long study, recognizes the other side of the "global" adjective. This narrative warfare now has tentacles in Ackerman's Istanbul, Beck's Lynchburg, Hickman and Slahi's Guantánamo Bay, Klay's Boston, Powers' Richmond, and Snowden's Moscow. Rancière's conceptualization of the dissensual, variegated as it may be as it moves from medium to medium and genre to genre, is quite clear about its teleology. Dissensual texts represent an "ethical turn," according to the theorist, and the "turn's strength," he writes, "resides in its capacity to recode and invert the forms of thought and attitudes which yesterday aimed at bringing about a radical political and/or aesthetic change."[9] More than just Adorno's "ethical witnessing of unrepresentable catastrophe," dissensus seeks to divorce from "every theology of time" and return "the inventions of politics and art to their difference," and by doing so "rejecting the fantasy of their purity."[10] What I read in the post-9/11 veteran-activists of this study is also what I offer the reader: an expansion and rethinking of ethos *beyond the old borders of territory and meaning*. The patriotism of the American soldier expands further in the signifying practices of the American soldier-writer, and this widening circle, where politics and aesthetics intersect, is mapped in the theory of Hebdige and others. To return to Paley's pithy description of the remapping on display in this study: "It's not that you set out to oppose authority. In the act of writing you simply do." By extension, it's not that the soldier-writer community has set out to collude in the undermining of Western imperialism, American militaristic violence, and the political-aesthetic regimes of oppression. In their collective and most innovative acts of empathy, they simply have and, in so doing, have opened the door to a form of healing.

As Ackerman writes, "The traumas that create post-traumatic stress also create conditions for post-traumatic growth."[11] In *Un-American*, Erik Edstrom confesses to his participation in the "international crime" of the Global War on Terror but also argues that this enterprise has seeded his mind with a new awareness of the planet and that the new mission for America is not another decade of fossil fuel wars but a new planetary enterprise of healing underscored by the message that "investing in climate change is an investment in national security."[12] The scholarly project and a narrative of challenge and healing are one for Edstrom, and the same goes for this book here as we sit on the other side of Biden's withdrawal from Afghanistan after nearly two decades of occupation and are now mired in a new proxy war with Russia, to say nothing of our complicity in the horrors of the ongoing war in Gaza. But this study of contemporary American war literature is not the first place to suggest that the healing of the human divide can be aided and abetted by its mimesis in art and scholarship. In his concluding lectures on parrhesia, Foucault turns his gaze to the environment of the classroom—the very place he stands. The workshop is not just a place to create discrete acts of scholarship or art, Foucault argues. Parrhesia, or truth-telling, is a transcendent technique, according to Foucault. "[S]piritual guidance," he writes, "is the technique of techniques," or the study of these discrete practices in intersection with each other.[13] In other words, in ancient Greece, the classroom was a transdisciplinary place where the arts and sciences—the spirits and techniques—converged. Referring to Philodemus, an Epicurean philosopher, Foucault argues that the classroom was once conceived as a parrhesiac storytelling space, an environment of "mutual confession" or, in Philodemus' words, a space where students might experience "salvation by one another."[14] Foucault is careful to translate here in the presence of such transcendent sentiment. The English word, "salvation," derived from the Greek, "sozesthai—to save oneself—means, in the Epicurean tradition, to gain access to a good, beautiful, and happy life. It does not refer to any kind of afterlife or divine judgement."[15] To be clear, Foucault and Philodemus do not wish to take the student out of the room to some abstract haven away from their senses. Parrhesia, this term that characterizes punk speech and occurs over and over in the New Testament, is about grounding the word in flesh or lived experience and thereby distributing the storyteller's argument in the demotic realms of the sensible. Foucault's attention is not on heaven, hell, death, or a philosophy divorced from the sensible space of the body. Like Rancière, Foucault is focused on what can happen in sensory spaces, those timeless but evolving domains of art. This Greek tradition, like the French scholars and American soldier-writers of this book, seeks to reawaken the reader to the ethos of lived experience all over the new digitally networked globe; to embodied philosophy in the age of computing and surveillance; to a political aesthetic where narrative webs with rhetoric; to a dissensual worldwide space where multiple sensibilities apprehend each other, challenge each other, and heal each other; to a cosmopolitan ethic where the planet itself sits on the table like a bowl of fruit for a workshop of artists.

Notes

Chapter I

1. This tweet posted by @Snowden on January 18, 2018.
2. This tweet posted by @EFF on January 18, 2018.
3. B. Kevin Brown, "To Announce the Good News Boldly: Pope Francis Calls for 'Parrhesia,'" *Catholic Courier*, September 25, 2019.
4. Euripides, "Ion," *Ten Plays* (London: Penguin, 1998), 128.
5. Phil Klay, *The Citizen-Soldier: Moral Risk and the Modern Military* (New York: Brookings Institute Press, 2016).
6. Michel Foucault, *Fearless Speech*, ed. and trans. Joseph Pearson (Los Angeles: Semiotext(e), 2001), 52.
7. Richard Ketchum, *Saratoga: Turning Point of America's Revolutionary War* (New York: MacMillan, 1999), 65.
8. Joseph Hickman, *Murder at Camp Delta* (New York: Simon and Schuster, 2015), 45.
9. Jacques Rancière, *Dissensus: On Politics and Aesthetics*, ed. and trans. Steven Corcoran (New York: Bloomsbury, 2015), 147.
10. Rancière, *Dissensus: On Politics and Aesthetics*, 108.
11. Rancière, *Dissensus: On Politics and Aesthetics*, 108.
12. Rancière, *Dissensus: On Politics and Aesthetics*, 108.
13. Steven Corcoran, "Historicizing Dissensus: Translator's Introduction," *The Lost Thread: The Democracy of Modern Fiction*, by Jacques Rancière (New York: Bloomsbury, 2017), vi.
14. Corcoran, "Historicizing Dissensus: Translator's Introduction," viii.
15. Martha Nussbaum, "Patriotism and Cosmopolitanism," *The Boston Review*, 1994.
16. Nussbaum, *The Boston Review*, 1994.
17. M. Lynx Qualey, "The American Soldier in Arab Novels," *Full Stop*, October 17, 2018.
18. Nussbaum, *The Boston Review*, 1994.
19. Christian Moraru, *Cosmodernism* (Ann Arbor: The University of Michigan Press, 2014), 71.
20. Moraru, *Cosmodernism*, 72.
21. Frederick Jackson Turner, *The Frontier in American History* (New York: Henry Holt and Company, 1958), 2–3.
22. Phil Klay, *Redeployment* (New York: The Penguin Press, 2014), 173.

23 Klay, *Redeployment*, 174.
24 Klay, *Redeployment*, 172.
25 Corcoran, "Historicizing Dissensus: Translator's Introduction," xxxiii.
26 Jacques Rancière, *The Lost Thread: The Democracy of Modern Fiction*, ed. and trans. Steven Corcoran (New York: Bloomsbury, 2017), 17.
27 Rancière, *The Lost Thread: The Democracy of Modern Fiction*, 17.
28 Klay, *Redeployment*, 182.
29 William Carlos Williams, "A Sort of a Song," *The Collected Poems of William Carlos Williams, Vol. 2: 1939–1962* (New York: New Directions, 1991), 55.
30 Klay, *Redeployment*, 170.
31 Klay, *Redeployment*, 201.
32 Klay, *Redeployment*, 201.
33 Rancière, *The Lost Thread: The Democracy of Modern Fiction*, 24–5.
34 Rancière, *The Lost Thread: The Democracy of Modern Fiction*, 36.
35 Emmanuel Levinas, *Time and the Other*, trans. Richard A. Cohen (Pittsburgh: Duquesne University Press), 75.
36 Virginia Woolf, *Three Guineas* (London: Hogarth Press, 1938), 143.
37 Geoffroy de Lagasnerie, *The Art of Revolt* (Palo Alto: Stanford University Press, 2017), 51.
38 Lagasnerie, *The Art of Revolt*, 5.
39 Lagasnerie, *The Art of Revolt*, 47–8.
40 Lagasnerie, *The Art of Revolt*, 110.
41 Matheson Russell, "The Politics of the Third Person: Esposito's *Third Person* and Rancière's," *Disagreement*, vol. 15, no. 3 (2014), 228.
42 Rancière, *Dissensus: On Politics and Aesthetics*, 132.
43 Edward Snowden, *Permanent Record* (New York: Metropolitan Books, 2019), 4.
44 Bertrand Westphal, *Geocriticism*, trans. Robert T. Tally (New York: Palgrave Macmillan), 5.
45 Foucault, *Fearless Speech*, 170.
46 Sebastian Junger, *Tribe: On Homecoming and Belonging* (New York: Twelve Books, 2016), 124.
47 Junger, *Tribe: On Homecoming and Belonging*, 125.

Chapter II

1 Paley's quote found at @MattGallagher0.
2 Paul Giles, *The Global Remapping of American Literature* (Princeton: Princeton University Press, 2011), 16.

3   Giles, *The Global Remapping of American Literature*, 16.
4   Giles, *The Global Remapping of American Literature*, 16.
5   John McClure, "Postmodern Romance: Don DeLillo and the Age of Conspiracy," *Introducing Don DeLillo*, ed. by Frank Lentricchia (Durham: Duke University Press, 1991), 102.
6   Caleb S. Cage, *War Narratives* (College Station: Texas A&M Press, 2019), 108.
7   E. Ann Kaplan, *Trauma Culture: The Politics of Terror and Loss in Media and Literature* (New Brunswick: Rutgers University Press, 2005), 94–5.
8   Wendy McElroy, "Individual Rights vs. Identity Politics," *Ifeminists.com*, October 6, 2004.
9   Jonathan Simon, "Parrhesiastic Accountability: Investigatory Commissions and Executive Power in an Age of Terror," *The Yale Law Journal*, vol. 114, no. 6. (April 2005), 1449.
10 Phil Klay, "The Warrior at the Mall," *The New York Times*, April 14, 2018.
11 Klay, "The Warrior at the Mall."
12 Andrew Brown, "Whole Earth Visionary," *The Guardian*, August 4, 2001.
13 Brown, *The Guardian*, August 4, 2001.
14 Fred Turner, *From Counterculture to Cyberculture: Stewart Brand, the Whole Earth Network, and the Rise of Digital Utopianism* (Chicago: University of Chicago Press, 2008), 73.
15 John Updike, *Rabbit at Rest* (New York: Knopf, 1990), 442.
16 See https://www.eff.org/files/necessaryandproportionatefinal.pdf.
17 John Perry Barlow and Edward Snowden, "A Conversation across Cyberspace," *YouTube*, June 11, 2014, https://www.youtube.com/watch?v=3QrZlHFgxA0.
18 John Perry Barlow, *Mother American Night* (New York: Crown Books, 2018), 255.
19 Barlow and Snowden, "A Conversation across Cyberspace," *YouTube*.
20 John Perry Barlow, "Interview," *The American Spectator*, vol. 34, no. 3 (April 2001), 24.
21 Barlow, *The American Spectator*, 26–8.
22 Brian Doherty, "John Perry Barlow 2.0," *Reason*, vol. 36, no. 4 (August/September 2004), 42–9.
23 Turner, *The Frontier in American History*, 247.
24 Barlow, *The American Spectator*, 28.
25 Dorian Lynskey, *The Ministry of Truth* (New York: Doubleday, 2019), 26.
26 Westphal, *Geocriticism*, 152.
27 Doherty, *Reason*, 42–9.
28 Barlow and Snowden, "A Conversation across Cyberspace."
29 Barlow and Snowden, "A Conversation across Cyberspace."

30 Marshall McLuhan, *Understanding Media: The Extensions of Man* (New York: McGraw-Hill, 1964), 177–8.
31 Walton, *Media Argumentation: Dialectic Persuasion, and Rhetoric*, 144–5.
32 Dexter Filkins, "The Long Road Home," *The New York Times*, March 6, 2014.
33 Klay, *Redeployment*, 241.
34 Klay, *Redeployment*, 85.
35 Leo Marx, *The Machine in the Garden* (Oxford: Oxford University Press, 1964), 119.
36 Klay, *Redeployment*, 169.
37 Klay, *Redeployment*, 169.
38 Klay, *Redeployment*, 170.
39 Klay, *Redeployment*, 171.
40 Klay, *Redeployment*, 171.
41 Jacques Rancière, *The Lost Thread: The Democracy of Modern Fiction*, ed. and trans. Steven Corcoran (London: Bloomsbury, 2017), 21.
42 Rancière, *The Lost Thread: The Democracy of Modern Fiction*, 21.
43 Mark Danielewski, *Only Revolutions* (New York: Pantheon, 2006), copyright page.
44 Klay, *Redeployment*, 175.
45 Klay, *Redeployment*, 176.
46 Adrian Bonenberger and Brian Castner, "Letter from the Editors," *The Road Ahead*, ed. by Adrian Bonenberger and Brian Castner (New York: Pegasus Books, 2017), xiv.
47 Klay, *Redeployment*, 177.
48 Klay, *Redeployment*, 177.
49 Solmaz Sharif, "Look," *Look* (Minneapolis: Graywolf Press, 2016), 4.
50 Klay, *Redeployment*, 177.
51 Klay, *Redeployment*, 178.
52 Klay, *Redeployment*, 178.
53 Klay, *Redeployment*, 178.
54 Klay, *Redeployment*, 182.
55 Klay, *Redeployment*, 182.
56 Georgiana Banita, *Plotting Justice: Narrative Ethics and Literary Culture after 9/11* (Lincoln: University of Nebraska Books, 2012), 300.
57 Klay, *Redeployment*, 184.
58 Klay, *Redeployment*, 184.
59 Klay, *Redeployment*, 185.
60 Klay, *Redeployment*, 185.
61 Klay, *Redeployment*, 202.
62 Klay, *Redeployment*, 208.

63 Klay, *Redeployment*, 209.
64 Klay, *Redeployment*, 207.
65 Klay, *Redeployment*, 207.
66 Klay, *Redeployment*, 209.
67 Klay, *Redeployment*, 209.
68 Westphal, *Geocriticism*, 163.
69 Klay, *Redeployment*, 210.
70 Klay, *Redeployment*, 212.
71 Klay, *Redeployment*, 212.
72 Klay, *Redeployment*, 212.
73 Klay, *Redeployment*, 212.
74 Jonathan Lethem, "Snowden in the Labyrinth," *The New York Review of Books*, October 24, 2019.
75 Lethem, "Snowden in the Labyrinth."
76 Snowden, *Permanent Record*, 38.
77 Max Kirchner, *Speaking Truth to Power: Theorising Edward Snowden's Whistleblowing through Foucault's Concepts of Parrhesia and the Event* (Bristol: University of Bristol, 2014), 12.
78 Kirchner, *Speaking Truth to Power: Theorising Edward Snowden's Whistleblowing through Foucault's Concepts of Parrhesia and the Event*, 49.
79 Snowden, *Permanent Record*, 66.
80 Snowden, *Permanent Record*, 66.
81 Snowden, *Permanent Record*, 3.
82 Westphal, *Geocriticism*, 97.
83 Snowden, *Permanent Record*, 78.
84 Snowden, *Permanent Record*, 166.
85 Snowden, *Permanent Record*, 215.
86 Snowden, *Permanent Record*, 215.
87 Westphal, *Geocriticism*, 162.
88 Westphal, *Geocriticism*, 162.
89 Snowden, *Permanent Record*, 216.
90 Snowden, *Permanent Record*, 216.
91 Snowden, *Permanent Record*, 216.
92 Snowden, *Permanent Record*, 226.
93 Snowden, *Permanent Record*, 227.
94 Snowden, *Permanent Record*, 227.
95 Snowden, *Permanent Record*, 227.
96 Snowden, *Permanent Record*, 228.
97 Snowden, *Permanent Record*, 228.

98 Nussbaum, *The Boston Review*, 1994.
99 Nussbaum, *The Boston Review*, 1994.
100 Nussbaum, *The Boston Review*, 1994.
101 Snowden, *Permanent Record*, 238.
102 Snowden, *Permanent Record*, 240.
103 Snowden, *Permanent Record*, 239.
104 Snowden, *Permanent Record*, 240.

Chapter III

1 Christian Bauman, "Odd Men Out," *The New York Times*, September 28, 2012.
2 Paul Crenshaw, "Names," *Hobart*, November 2, 2015.
3 Erik Edstrom, *Un-American* (New York: Bloomsbury, 2020), 66.
4 Edstrom, *Un-American*, 42.
5 Crenshaw, "Names."
6 Crenshaw, "Names."
7 Rancière, *Dissensus: On Politics and Aesthetics*, 53.
8 Rancière, *Dissensus: On Politics and Aesthetics*, 53.
9 Rancière, *Dissensus: On Politics and Aesthetics*, 53.
10 Rancière, *Dissensus: On Politics and Aesthetics*, 58.
11 Rancière, *Dissensus: On Politics and Aesthetics*, 61.
12 Grace Paley, "Grace Paley, the Art of Fiction, No. 131," *The Paris Review*, no. 124 (Fall 1992). https://www.theparisreview.org/interviews/2028/the-art-of-fiction-no-131-grace-paley.
13 Elliot Ackerman, "The Fourth War," *Names and Places* (New York: Penguin Press, 2019), 18.
14 Ackerman, "The Fourth War," *Names and Places*, 18.
15 Nussbaum, *The Boston Review*, 1994.
16 Ackerman, "The Fourth War," *Names and Places*, 35.
17 Westphal, *Geocriticism*, 16.
18 Ackerman, "The Fourth War," *Names and Places*, 19.
19 Ackerman, "The Fourth War," *Names and Places*, 19.
20 Ackerman, "The Fourth War," *Names and Places*, 19.
21 Ackerman, "The Fourth War," *Names and Places*, 20.
22 Ackerman, "The Fourth War," *Names and Places*, 27.
23 Ackerman, "The Fourth War," *Names and Places*, 27.
24 Westphal, *Geocriticism*, 16.
25 Ackerman, "The Fourth War," *Names and Places*, 27.

26 David Chandler, "Response to Robbins." http://www.davidchandler.org/wp-content/uploads/2014/10/Radical-Philosophy-cosmopolitan-paradox.pdf.
27 Ackerman, "The Fourth War," *Names and Places*, 33.
28 Ackerman, "The Fourth War," *Names and Places*, 33.
29 Ackerman, "The Fourth War," *Names and Places*, 33.
30 Ackerman, "The Fourth War," *Names and Places*, 36.
31 Snowden, *Permanent Record*, 66.
32 Ackerman, *Green on Blue*.
33 James Baumlin, "Ethos," *Encyclopedia of Rhetoric*, ed. Thomas O. Sloane (Oxford: Oxford University Press, 2001), 263.
34 Baumlin, "Ethos," *Encyclopedia of Rhetoric*, 264.
35 Samuel Hynes, *On War and Writing* (Chicago: University of Chicago Press, 2018), 35–59.
36 Jameson, *Postmodernism, or the Cultural Logic of Late Capitalism*, 6.
37 Jameson, *Postmodernism, or the Cultural Logic of Late Capitalism*, 365.
38 Ackerman, *Green on Blue*, 25.
39 Ackerman, *Green on Blue*, 25.
40 Michiko Kakutani, "Elliot Ackerman's Green on Blue," *The New York Times*, February 28, 2015.
41 Rancière, *Dissensus: On Politics and Aesthetics*, 147.
42 Foucault, *Fearless Speech*, 111–13.
43 Daniel O'Gorman, *Fiction of the War on Terror: Difference and the Transnational 9/11 Novel* (New York: Palgrave Macmillan, 2015), 78.
44 O'Gorman, *Fiction of the War on Terror*, 78.
45 Ackerman, *Green on Blue*, 100.
46 Ackerman, *Green on Blue*, 221.
47 Ackerman, *Green on Blue*, 223.
48 Ackerman, *Green on Blue*, 226.
49 Kristin Beck and Anne Speckhard, *Warrior Princess: A U.S. Navy SEAL's Journey to Coming Out Transgender* (McLean, VA: Advances Press, 2013), 218.
50 Beck and Speckhard, *Warrior Princess: A U.S. Navy SEAL's Journey to Coming Out Transgender*, 219.
51 Beck and Speckhard, *Warrior Princess: A U.S. Navy SEAL's Journey to Coming Out Transgender*, iii.
52 Beck and Speckhard, *Warrior Princess: A U.S. Navy SEAL's Journey to Coming Out Transgender*, iii.
53 Beck and Speckhard, *Warrior Princess: A U.S. Navy SEAL's Journey to Coming Out Transgender*.
54 Daniela Valdes and Kinnon MacKinnon, *Take Detransitioners Seriously*, The Atlantic, January 18, 2023.

55 Beck and Speckhard, *Warrior Princess: A U.S. Navy SEAL's Journey to Coming Out Transgender*.
56 Beck and Speckhard, *Warrior Princess: A U.S. Navy SEAL's Journey to Coming Out Transgender*.
57 Beck and Speckhard, *Warrior Princess: A U.S. Navy SEAL's Journey to Coming Out Transgender*, 7.
58 Beck and Speckhard, *Warrior Princess: A U.S. Navy SEAL's Journey to Coming Out Transgender*, 7.
59 Chelsea Manning, *README.txt* (New York: Farrar, Straus and Giroux, 2022), 55.
60 Beck and Speckhard, *Warrior Princess: A U.S. Navy SEAL's Journey to Coming Out Transgender*, 10.
61 Beck and Speckhard, *Warrior Princess: A U.S. Navy SEAL's Journey to Coming Out Transgender*, 15.
62 Beck and Speckhard, *Warrior Princess: A U.S. Navy SEAL's Journey to Coming Out Transgender*, 15.
63 Beck and Speckhard, *Warrior Princess: A U.S. Navy SEAL's Journey to Coming Out Transgender*, 30.
64 Beck and Speckhard, *Warrior Princess: A U.S. Navy SEAL's Journey to Coming Out Transgender*, 35.
65 Beck and Speckhard, *Warrior Princess: A U.S. Navy SEAL's Journey to Coming Out Transgender*, 39.
66 Rancière, *The Lost Thread: The Democracy of Modern Fiction*, 12.
67 Rancière, *The Lost Thread: The Democracy of Modern Fiction*, 13.
68 Beck and Speckhard, *Warrior Princess: A U.S. Navy SEAL's Journey to Coming Out Transgender*, 51.
69 Foucault, *Fearless Speech*, 73.
70 Beck and Speckhard, *Warrior Princess: A U.S. Navy SEAL's Journey to Coming Out Transgender*, 176.
71 Beck and Speckhard, *Warrior Princess: A U.S. Navy SEAL's Journey to Coming Out Transgender*, 177.
72 Beck and Speckhard, *Warrior Princess: A U.S. Navy SEAL's Journey to Coming Out Transgender*, 177.
73 @mchooyah, April 10, 2019.
74 @valorforus, April 10, 2019.
75 @valorforus, April 11, 2019.
76 @zeroblog30, April 5, 2019.
77 @valorforus, April 11, 2019.
78 @nowthisnews, August 2, 2017.

Chapter IV

1. Giorgio Agamben, *State of Exception*, trans. Kevin Attel (Chicago: University of Chicago Press, 2005), 40.
2. Mohamedou Ould Slahi, *Guantánamo Diary* (New York: Little, Brown), 155.
3. Slahi, *Guantánamo Diary*, 158.
4. Slahi, *Guantánamo Diary*, 158.
5. Slahi, *Guantánamo Diary*, 163.
6. Alexandra Schultheis Moore, "Teaching Mohamedou Ould Slahi's *Guantánamo Diary* in the Human Rights and Literature Classroom," *The Radical Teacher*, vol. 104, no. 27 (2016), 27–36.
7. Slahi, *Guantánamo Diary*, 171.
8. Slahi, *Guantánamo Diary*, 171.
9. Slahi, *Guantánamo Diary*, 171.
10. Slahi, *Guantánamo Diary*, 181.
11. Slahi, *Guantánamo Diary*, 184.
12. Slahi, *Guantánamo Diary*, 337.
13. Slahi, *Guantánamo Diary*, 339.
14. Slahi, *Guantánamo Diary*, 339.
15. Slahi, *Guantánamo Diary*, 312.
16. Slahi, *Guantánamo Diary*, 339.
17. Slahi, *Guantánamo Diary*, 340.
18. Slahi, *Guantánamo Diary*, 341.
19. Moore, "Teaching Mohamedou Ould Slahi's *Guantánamo Diary* in the Human Rights and Literature Classroom," 33.
20. Foucault, *Fearless Speech*, 50.
21. Moore, "Teaching Mohamedou Ould Slahi's *Guantánamo Diary* in the Human Rights and Literature Classroom," 35.
22. Moore, "Teaching Mohamedou Ould Slahi's *Guantánamo Diary* in the Human Rights and Literature Classroom," 35.
23. Benjamin Percy, "On the Ground," *The New York Times*, October 4, 2012.
24. Rancière, *Dissensus: On Politics and Aesthetics*, 192–3.
25. Kevin Powers, *The Yellow Birds* (New York: Little, Brown), 78.
26. O'Gorman, *Fiction of the War on Terror: Difference and the Transnational 9/11 Novel*, 105.
27. Powers, *The Yellow Birds*, 78.
28. Powers, *The Yellow Birds*, 156.
29. Westphal, *Geocriticism*, 88.
30. Hickman, *Murder at Camp Delta*, 14.

31 David Petraeus, *Counterinsurgency: FM 3-24* (Boulder: Paladin Press, 2007).
32 Westphal, *Geocriticism*, 5.
33 Powers, *The Yellow Birds*, 215.
34 Powers, *The Yellow Birds*, 216.
35 Powers, *The Yellow Birds*, 217.
36 Powers, *The Yellow Birds*, 224.
37 Powers, *The Yellow Birds*, 224.
38 Powers, *The Yellow Birds*, 225.
39 Powers, *The Yellow Birds*, 225.
40 Powers, *The Yellow Birds*, 226.
41 Powers, *The Yellow Birds*, 226.
42 Powers, *The Yellow Birds*, 226.
43 Powers, *The Yellow Birds*, 226.
44 Powers, *The Yellow Birds*, 226.
45 Agamben, *State of Exception*, 3.
46 Tim Dirven, "To Live and Die in Gitmo," *Newsweek*, January 15, 2015.
47 Lloyd Bitzer, "The Rhetorical Situation," *Philosophy & Rhetoric*, vol. 1, no. 1 (1968), 3.
48 Bitzer, "The Rhetorical Situation," 6.
49 Redfield, *The Rhetoric of Terror*, 51.
50 Joseph Hickman, *Murder at Camp Delta* (New York: Simon and Schuster, 2014), 10–11.
51 Hickman, *Murder at Camp Delta*, 11.
52 Hickman, *Murder at Camp Delta*, 14.
53 Hickman, *Murder at Camp Delta*, 34.
54 Hickman, *Murder at Camp Delta*, 109–10.
55 Hickman, *Murder at Camp Delta*, 61.
56 Hickman, *Murder at Camp Delta*, 63.
57 Hickman, *Murder at Camp Delta*, 63.
58 Hickman, *Murder at Camp Delta*, 63.
59 Hickman, *Murder at Camp Delta*, 66.
60 Hickman, *Murder at Camp Delta*, 74.
61 Hickman, *Murder at Camp Delta*, 76.
62 Hickman, *Murder at Camp Delta*, 73.
63 Hickman, *Murder at Camp Delta*, 76.
64 Hickman, *Murder at Camp Delta*, 76.
65 Hickman, *Murder at Camp Delta*, 76.
66 Hickman, *Murder at Camp Delta*, 86.
67 Hickman, *Murder at Camp Delta*, 87.

68 Hickman, *Murder at Camp Delta*, 44.
69 Hickman, *Murder at Camp Delta*, 44.
70 Hickman, *Murder at Camp Delta*, 45.
71 Hickman, *Murder at Camp Delta*, 89.
72 Hickman, *Murder at Camp Delta*, 90.
73 Hickman, *Murder at Camp Delta*, 90.
74 Hickman, *Murder at Camp Delta*, 91.
75 Hickman, *Murder at Camp Delta*, 94.
76 Hickman, *Murder at Camp Delta*, 96.
77 Hickman, *Murder at Camp Delta*, 96.
78 Hickman, *Murder at Camp Delta*, 96.
79 Hickman, *Murder at Camp Delta*, 131.
80 Hickman, *Murder at Camp Delta*, 144.
81 Hickman, *Murder at Camp Delta*, 146.
82 Hickman, *Murder at Camp Delta*, 146.
83 Hickman, *Murder at Camp Delta*, 183.
84 Like Denbeaux, I could not quite believe America was this capable of atrocity and deception, this hideous embrace of censorship and torture. Even though I had traveled to Iraq as a journalist, the story of America's gulag, Guantánamo Bay, continued to haunt me after reading Hickman's book. Like Hickman, I scouted the Internet and developed an identity there. I began investigating the stories of soldier-writers to see how many had similar experiences to Hickman's. I published a review of Hickman's book. Then I decided to bring Hickman's story into the classroom at Duke University. While team-teaching a course called Revolution and Terror with Dr. Eric Oakley, I visited Seton Hall's Center for Policy and Research website. I printed up the NCIS documents pertinent to the case. Inspired by Oakley's emphasis on simulation/game as an engaging tool in the history classroom, I decided to create a simulation of my own as a way of vetting Hickman's claims. Thus, we turned the students of a Duke TIP (Talent Identification Program) class into a simulated Crime Scene Investigation unit. They participated in a fiction in which they were soldiers investigating the deaths of Ahmed, al-Utaybi, and al-Zahrani. We provided the students with the redacted primary documents provided by the military. We broke the students into groups, providing each cohort with the same documents and the same task of assessing the official narrative. This process and the attendant reflection on ethics, academic freedom, and narrative that followed addressed the basic goals Nussbaum outlined in her defense of a "cosmopolitan education": Firstly, a cosmopolitan education teaches students more about themselves. Secondly, a cosmopolitan education helps students solve problems that require international cooperation. Thirdly, such

a pedagogy recognizes moral obligations to the rest of the world that are real, and that otherwise would go unrecognized. Finally, through these pedagogical practices encourage a "consistent and coherent argument based on distinctions we are really prepared to defend." Thus, just as these soldier-writers repurpose the ethos of American ideals, so do they also map a territory for students to do the same. Fundamental to the simulation of Denbeaux's simulation is the study of a complex problem and an analysis of American principles tested on an international stage. At the conclusion of the simulation, the Duke students arrived at the same decision as the Seton Hall students. The Camp Delta suicides were not suicides. The students allowed that these "murders" might have been accidental, and they could not quite understand the motive, but they simply refused to ignore the contradictions and redactions they observed in the government documents. Allowing that it is possible that Hickman, Denbeaux, and the teams at Seton Hall and Duke are all wrong and that the military's official narrative is right, the thrust of this study remains focused on the risks Hickman took to speak out against the state. Hickman's parrhesia now exists in the public record, part of a growing collective testament from his generation of veterans. Hickman, like Ackerman, Beck, Klay, Powers, and Snowden, spoke up about what he saw on the "vaporous" global frontiers of the Forever War. He abandoned his career in the US military to tell the story of what he believed happened to Ahmed, al-Utaybi, and al-Zahrani. Additionally, through the tools of the Internet, Hickman reached out to the scholarly community to help him tell his story. Not only did he vet his account through Seton Hall and the editors of Simon and Schuster, but Hickman also Skyped into our Duke classroom after we had completed our simulation and allowed himself to be interrogated by the students. I documented that day and managed to capture a decent image of a Guantánamo Bay guard projected above a roomful of students who, earlier that morning, had pretended to be crime scene investigators. Like Eliot's artist and all reputable scientists, Hickman and these Duke students had all participated in "self-sacrifice" in order to shine a light on the deaths of three individuals whom a good portion of the United States would just assume forget. These students forgot themselves in order to properly remember others. They set nation aside in order to study and think critically about the state and a population of people who do not belong to their state. They took part in the fundamentally artistic program of performance and play in order to scientifically investigate an institutional process of document gathering and document drafting. Dissensus does not just take place on the public pages of a published book. True dissensus can happen in any public space anywhere around the world. This aesthetic of dissent, which marks the soldier-writers of this book, sometime involves these soldiers becoming novelists who stage dissensus by performing the voices of those who have survived America's wars. Sometimes, however, this parrhesiac, dissensual, and cosmopolitan aesthetic transports the writer beyond fiction and into not just the performance of scholarship but also the dynamic digital-material zones of the twenty-first-century classroom where performer transforms into the witness, the scholar, and the witness to scholarly practice, the discursive stage now recursive, now played back as the young writer performs the voice of the soldier in a mutual play of disidentification that reconciles the binary of soldier and writer into a unified performative identity: the soldier-writer.

85 Hickman, *Murder at Camp Delta*, 220.
86 Agamben, *State of Exception*, trans. Kevin Attel, 3.

Chapter V

1   Elliot Ackerman, "Why the Capitol Riot Reminded Me of War," *The New York Times*, January 13, 2021.
2   Dick Hebdige, *Subculture: The Meaning of Style* (New York: Routledge, 1979), 132.
3   Hebdige, *Subculture: The Meaning of Style*, 120.
4   Hebdige, *Subculture: The Meaning of Style*, 117.
5   For further research into the "canon" of soldier-writing, see Molin's excellent "Time Now" blog and its reading list of literature emerging from the Iraq and Afghanistan Wars: https://acolytesofwar.com/.
6   Peter Molin, "Interview," *Twitter*, April 2, 2019.
7   Molin, "Interview."
8   Hebdige, *Subculture: The Meaning of Style*, 119.
9   Rancière, *Dissensus: On Politics and Aesthetics*, 209.
10 Rancière, *Dissensus: On Politics and Aesthetics*, 210.
11 Elliot Ackerman, "After Our Nation Grieves, It Can Grow," *The New York Times*, May 6, 2020.
12 Edstrom, *Un-American*, 246.
13 Foucault, *Fearless Speech*, 112.
14 Foucault, *Fearless Speech*, 114.
15 Foucault, *Fearless Speech*, 114.

Bibliography

Primary Texts

Ackerman, Elliot. *Green on Blue*. New York: Scribner, 2015.
Ackerman, Elliot. "The Fourth War." *Names and Places*. New York: Penguin, 2019.
Beck, Kristin and Anne Speckhard. *Warrior Princess: A U.S. Navy SEAL's Journey to Coming Out Transgender*. McLean, VA: Advances Press, 2013.
Bonenberger, Adrian. "About." *Wrath-bearingTree.com*. March 2018.
Crenshaw, Paul. "Names." *The Best American Essays: 2016*. New York: Mariner, 2016.
Edstrom, Erik. *Un-American*. New York: Bloomsbury, 2020.
Euripedes. "Ion." *Ten Plays*. London: Penguin, 1998.
Hemingway, Ernest. *For Whom the Bell Tolls*. New York: Scribner, 1940.
Hickman, Joseph. *Murder at Camp Delta*. New York: Simon and Schuster, 2015.
House, 1991.
Junger, Sebastian. *Tribe: On Homecoming and Belonging*. New York: Twelve Books, 2016.
Klay, Phil. *Redeployment*. New York: Penguin, 2014.
Klay, Phil. "The Warrior at the Mall." *The New York Times*. April 14, 2018.
Melville, Herman. *Moby Dick*. New York: Norton, 1967.
Powers, Kevin. *The Yellow Birds*. New York: Back Bay Books, 2013.
Snowden, Edward. *Permanent Record*. New York: Metropolitan Books, 2019.
Snowden, Edward and John Perry Barlow. "A Conversation across Cyberspace." *YouTube*. Uploaded by PDF Forum. June 11, 2014. https://www.youtube.com/watch?v=3QrZlHFgxA0.

Secondary Texts

Aristotle. *Rhetoric*. Translated by W. Rhys Roberts. New York: Dover, 2004.
Barlow, John Perry. "Interview." *The American Spectator* 34.3 (April 2001): 24–30.
Baudrillard, Jean. *The Spirit of Terrorism*. New York: Verso, 2002.
Bitzer, Lloyd. "The Rhetorical Situation." *Philosophy & Rhetoric* 1.1 (1968): 1–14.
Brown, Andrew. "Whole Earth Visionary." *The Guardian*. August 4, 2001.
Brown, B. Kevin. "To Announce the Good News Boldly: Pope Francis Calls for Parrhesia." *Catholic Courier*, September 25, 2019.

Cage, Caleb. *War Narratives: Shaping Beliefs, Blurring Truths in the Middle East.* College Station: Texas A&M University Press, 2019.

Carroll, Peter. "The Spanish Civil War in the 21st Century: From Guernica to Human Rights." *The Antioch Review* 70.4 (Fall 2012): 641–56.

Casanova, Pascale. "Principles of a World History of Literature." *The World Republic of Letters.* Cambridge: Harvard University Press, 2004.

De Lagasnerie, Geoffroy. *The Art of Revolt: Snowden, Assange, Manning.* Stanford, CA: Stanford University Press, 2017.

Deleuze, Gilles and Felix Guattari. "Savages, Barbarians, Civilized Men." *Anti-Oedipus.* New York: Penguin, 2009.

Dimock, Wai Chee. "Genre as World System: Epic and Novel on Four Continents." *Narrative* 14.1 (2006): 85–101.

Doherty, Brian. "John Perry Barlow 2.0." *Reason* 36.4 (August/September 2004): 42–9.

Elias, Amy. "The Commons ... and Digital Planetarity." *The Planetary Turn: Relationality and Geoaesthetics in the Twenty-first Century.* Eds. Amy Elias and Christian Moraru. Evanston, IL: Northwestern University Press, 2015.

Foucault, Michel. *Fearless Speech.* Los Angeles: Semiotext(e), 2001.

Friedrich, Hugo. *The Structure of Modern Poetry.* Evanston: Northwestern University Press, 1974.

Giles, Paul. "Suburb, Network, Homeland: National Space and the Rhetoric of Broadcasting." *The Global Remapping of American Literature.* Princeton: Princeton University Press, 2011.

Gramsci, Antonio. *Selections from the Prison Notebooks.* New York: International Publishers, 1971.

Greenberg, Andy. "An NSA Co-worker Remembers the Real Edward Snowden: 'A Genius among Geniuses.'" *Forbes.* December 16, 2013.

Hebdige, Dick. *Subculture: The Meaning of Style.* New York: Routledge, 1979.

Hynes, Samuel. *On War and Writing.* Chicago: The University of Chicago Press, 2018.

Jameson, Fredric. *Postmodernism: Or the Cultural Logic of Late Capitalism.* Durham: Duke University Press, 1991.

Jameson, Fredric. "An American Utopia." *An American Utopia: Dual Power and the Universal Army.* New York: Verso, 2016.

Kaplan, E. Ann. *Trauma Culture: The Politics of Terror and Loss in Media and Literature.* New Brunswick: Rutgers University Press, 2005.

Ketchum, Richard. *Saratoga: Turning Point of America's Revolutionary War.* New York: Macmillan, 1999.

Lynskey, Dorian. *The Ministry of Truth.* New York: Doubleday, 2019.

Marx, Leo. *The Machine in the Garden: Technology and the Pastoral Ideal in America.* Oxford: Oxford University Press, 2000.

McElroy, Wendy. "Individual Rights vs. Identity Politics." *Ifeminists.com.* October 6, 2004.

McHale, Brian. "Introduction." *The Cambridge Introduction to Postmodernism*. New York: Cambridge University Press, 2015.

Moraru, Christian. "Metabolics." *Cosmodernism: American Narrative, Late Globalization, and the New Cultural Imaginary*. Ann Arbor: The University of Michigan Press, 2014.

Moraru, Christian. "Geomethodology." *Reading for the Planet: Toward a Geomethodology*. Ann Arbor: The University of Michigan Press, 2016.

Muñoz, José Esteban. *Disidentifications: Queers of Color and the Performance of Politics*. Minneapolis: The University of Minnesota Press, 1999.

Nussbaum, Martha. "Patriotism and Cosmopolitanism." *The Boston Review*. October 1, 1994.

Nussbaum, Martha and Joshua Cohen. *For Love of Country*. Boston: Beacon Press, 2002.

O'Gorman, Daniel. *Fiction of the War on Terror: Difference and the Transnational 9/11 Novel*. New York: Palgrave Macmillan, 2015.

O'Keefe, Daniel. "Two Concepts of Argument." *The Journal of American Forensic Association* 13.3 (1977): 121–8.

Poster, Mark. "Postcolonial Theory in the Age of Planetary Communications." *Quarterly Review of Film and Video* 24 (2007): 379–93.

Rancière, Jacques. *Dissensus: On Politics and Aesthetics*. Edited and Translated by Steven Corcoran. New York: Bloomsbury, 2015.

Rancière, Jacques. *The Lost Thread: The Democracy of Modern Fiction*. Edited and Translated by Steven Corcoran. New York: Bloomsbury, 2017.

Rawls, John. *Political Liberalism*. New York: Columbia University Press, 2005.

Redfield, Marc. *The Rhetoric of Terror*. New York: Fordham University Press, 2009.

Said, Edward. *Covering Islam: How the Media and the Experts Determine How We See the Rest of the World*. New York: Vintage, 1997.

Simon, Jonathan. "Parrhesiastic Accountability: Investigatory Commissions and Executive Power in an Age of Terror." *The Yale Law Journal* 114.6 (April 2005): 1419–57.

Turner, Fred. *From Counterculture to Cyberculture: Stewart Brand, the Whole Earth Network, and the Rise of Digital Utopianism*. Chicago: University of Chicago Press, 2006.

Turner, Frederick Jackson. *The Frontier in American History*. New York: Henry Holt And Company, 1958.

Valdes, Daniela and Kinnon MacKinnon. "Take Detransitioners Seriously." *The Atlantic*. January 18, 2023.

Walkowitz, Rebecca L. "The Location of Literature: The Transnational Book and the Migrant Writer." Lane, *Global Literary Theory*, 918–29. London: Routledge, 2013.

Walton, Douglas. *Media Argumentation: Dialectic Persuasion, and Rhetoric*. Cambridge: Cambridge University Press, 2007.

Westphal, Bertrand. *Geocriticism: Real and Fictional Spaces*. Edited and Translated by Robert Tally, Jr. New York: Palgrave Macmillan, 2011.

Index

Abrams, David, *Fobbit* 77–8
Abu Hussar 83–91
Ackerman, Elliot 15, 26, 28, 32–3, 77–80, 83, 85–8, 92–5, 97, 100, 104–5, 107, 153–4, 158, 162
    on Abu Hussar 90
    "collective insanity" 155
    "The Fourth War" 27, 77, 82–92
    Green on Blue 27, 77, 81, 91–103
    and Klay 93
    narrative diplomacy 83, 89
    Places and Names 112
    "politicization" 155
Adams, Samuel 5
Adorno, Theodor 161
aesthetic(s) 6–8, 10, 13, 15, 19, 21, 23–4, 32, 39, 48, 50–1, 55, 67, 77, 88, 101–2, 105, 109–10, 124, 126, 128–30, 133, 136, 146, 149, 156, 158, 160–1, 163
Afghanistan 32–4, 78, 91–2, 95, 97–8, 100, 104, 107–10, 119, 121, 126, 132, 154–6, 158, 161–2
Afghanistan Papers, leak of 7
Agamben, Giorgio, "state of exception" 118, 139–40, 150
Ahmed, Ali Abdullah, murder of 5, 139, 142, 147, 149–50, 174–5 n.84
Allaga-Kelly, Maggie 115
allegiances 1, 3, 5, 14, 38, 63–4, 70, 77, 87, 121, 126
American Revolution 5, 23, 43, 47, 62, 89, 134, 158
Amis, Martin, "The Last Days of Muhammad Atta" 100
Aristotle 9, 93–4
Armstrong, M. C., *The Mysteries of Haditha* 133
Assange, Julian 21, 23, 158
Athens/Athenians 3–4, 35, 81, 88, 94, 123, 125
authoritarianism 7

Baldwin, James 2
Banita, Georgiana 55, 69
Barlow, John Perry 35, 42–8
    "A Declaration of the Independence of Cyberspace" 42, 44, 71
    interview with 43–5
    liminal territory 46
Barnes, Jake, *The Sun Also Rises* 98
Beats and the Lost Generation 52, 93
Beck, Kristin (Chris Beck) 15, 26–8, 33, 77–80, 88, 92, 105–6, 110–13, 126, 149, 153, 158–9
    honour for service of 104
    "Operation Iraqi Freedom" 104
    "Second Life-Navy SEALS 1991–2011" 110
    transgender 15, 77, 79, 88, 91–2, 103–15, 161
    Warrior Princess: A U.S. Navy SEAL'S Journey to Coming Out Transgender 27, 77, 81, 91, 103–15, 158–9
Bergdahl, Bo 132–3
Biden, Joe 22, 154–5, 158–9, 162
Bitzer, Lloyd 140
Blasim, Hassan 11–12
Bonenberger, Adrian, *The Road Ahead* 52
Brand, Stewart 39–43, 105
    The Whole Earth Catalog 40
Brown, George 108, 113
Bumgarner, Mike 147
Bush, George W. 8, 17, 69, 126, 159

Cage, Caleb, *War Narratives: Shaping Beliefs, Blurring Truths in the Middle East* 33
capitalism 10, 12, 84, 109–10
cartography 28, 35, 61, 64, 83, 86–7, 96, 107, 113, 131, 136, 139, 145, 151, 158
Castner, Brian, *The Road Ahead* 52
Castro, Carl 104
censorship 114, 120, 125, 127, 148, 174 n.84

Index

China 121, 145
Christianity 14, 16–17, 50–1, 54, 60, 109, 157
citizenship 2, 8, 10, 14, 36–7, 71, 94, 123, 125–6
Civil War in Syria 84
Cohen, Joshua 71, 154
Conrad, Joseph 9
consensus 7–8, 23
Corcoran, Steven 9
cosmopolitan/cosmopolitanism 3, 10–14, 16, 21, 24–5, 28, 32, 35, 37, 41, 50, 53, 57, 69, 71–2, 83–5, 87, 91–2, 102, 110, 117–18, 122, 124, 127, 135, 141–2, 155–6
    combat cosmopolitanism/cosmopolites 12, 14, 156, 161
    cosmopolitan education 83–5, 174 n.84
    martial cosmopolitanism 12, 14, 17, 27–8, 31, 69, 72
counterinsurgency (COIN) 133–4
Counterinsurgency: FM 3-24 133
Crenshaw, Paul 78, 89–90, 105, 145
    "Names" 77–81, 83, 92, 130, 135
Crime Scene Investigation 149, 174 n.84
Cuba 6, 119–20, 123–4, 126, 139–40, 142, 154
cyberculture 10
cyberspace 42–3, 47, 63

Danielewski, Mark 52
dehumanization 12, 98–9
Deleuze, Gilles 63
democracy 3–5, 7–10, 12–13, 16, 21–2, 37, 42, 44, 47, 50, 52, 56, 66, 68, 77, 81–3, 85, 88–9, 99, 139, 150
Denbeaux, Mark 147–9, 174–5 n.84
detention facility 28, 32, 127, 129, 132
digital revolution 1–2, 9, 13–14, 32–3, 35, 41–2, 45, 52, 54, 59–75, 77, 81, 106, 114, 121–2, 142, 154–6
Diogenes the Cynic 10, 28, 55, 71, 94
Dirven, Tim 139
discrete spaces 32
disidentity/disidentification 4–7, 16–17, 23–4, 29, 33, 37, 41, 54, 56–7, 60, 62–3, 70, 73–5, 77, 79, 85, 87, 90–3, 98, 101–4, 110, 118, 128, 132, 135, 153, 155, 176 n.84

dissensus/dissensual 3, 7–9, 16–18, 20–1, 23–4, 26–8, 32, 35, 37, 47–8, 55–6, 62, 64, 69–70, 73–4, 81–2, 84, 87, 91, 94–5, 99, 101–2, 105–6, 109–10, 117–30, 132, 141–2, 149–50, 156, 161, 163, 174 n.84
dissent 1–2, 5–8, 15, 17, 19, 21, 23, 73–5, 80–1, 102, 114, 117–18, 128, 146, 149–50, 154, 156, 159–60, 175 n.84
dissidents 146
dissonance 78, 95, 99–101, 103, 111, 130
diversity 10, 13, 15, 18, 51, 58, 62, 79
Doherty, Brian 45
Don DeLillo, *Falling Man* 100
Dorothy (character in *The Wizard of Oz*) 61
Dorsey, Jack 155
Drake, William 141, 143
Dubois, W. E. B. 2
Duke TIP (Talent Identification Program) class 174 n.84
DUSTWUN (Duty Status Unknown) 133

Edstrom, Erik, *Un-American* 80, 162
Einstein, Albert 84
electronic frontier 10, 15, 41, 44–5, 48, 62, 72
Electronic Frontier Foundation (EFF) 2, 10, 15, 43–4, 46
Ellsberg, Daniel 15
enhanced interrogation 122, 144, 150–1
Enlightenment, principles of 14
ethical identification 7, 79, 86
ethical remapping 31, 54, 57, 61, 68, 77–9, 90, 92, 100, 118, 128, 136, 149
ethical subversion 95, 128, 131
Euripides, *Ion* 3–4
    Apollo 4, 125
    Athens 3–5
    Creusa 3–4
    Delphi 125
    Ion 4–5, 123, 125

fascism 10, 24, 132
Filkins, Dexter 49
First World War 10, 55, 85–7, 89, 95, 112. *See also* Second World War
Fitzgerald, F. Scott, "The Crack-Up" 90

Flaubert, Gustave 9
    Un Coeur Simple (*see Un Coeur Simple* (Flaubert))
foreign truths 33
forward operating base (FOB) 26–7, 77–8, 81, 83, 88, 91, 94, 99, 156
Foucault, Michel 5, 27, 52, 63, 99, 111, 123, 125, 162
    "analytics of truth" 28–9
    Fearless Speech 3–4
    locations 4–5
    on parrhesia 3
"The Fourth War" (Ackerman) 27, 77, 82–92
    Marine 83
free speech/freedom of speech 3, 12–13, 42, 44, 126–7
Friedrich, Hugo 118
frontiers 2–3, 12, 14–15, 24, 26, 38–9, 41–4, 46, 48, 62, 72–3, 78, 93, 97, 103–4, 107–8, 110, 113, 127, 134–6, 138, 150
Fukuyama, Francis 10–12
    The End of History and The Last Man 10

Gallagher, Matt 32–3, 72, 95
Gaza 121, 154–5, 162
geography 26–7, 31, 35–6, 42, 54–5, 61–4, 67, 81–2, 86, 90, 94, 96–7, 99, 104–5, 107–8, 113, 119, 123–4, 128, 134, 136–7, 140, 145, 148, 153, 158–9
geopolitics/geopolitical 3, 7, 14–15, 49, 85, 87, 92, 97, 102, 119–21
George III 5
Giles, Paul 40, 48, 52
    "geographical consciousness" 35
    The Global Remapping of American Literature 32–3
    permeability 32, 38
globalism 11, 24
globalization 9–10, 13, 42
Goodwin, Gene Gabriel 50
Gore, Al 43–4
Gramsci, Antonio, "organic intellectual" 66
Green on Blue (Ackerman) 27, 77, 81, 91–103, 158
    Ali 97, 101
    Atal 101–3
    Aziz 27, 81, 95–8, 100, 158
    Badal 100, 102
    Al-Bukhari, Imam 94–5
    cognitive map of 96, 98–9, 103
    Gazan 97, 101–3
    Mister Jack 97, 101–3
    Pashto words 100–1
    Taqbir 97
Greenwald, Glenn 47, 63
Gregory, Derek, "imaginative geography" 99
Groundhog Day film 124
Guantánamo Bay detention camp 5–6, 13, 22, 27–8, 32, 34, 91, 117–19, 121–6, 136, 139–42, 145, 147–50, 159–60, 174–5 n.84
Guantánamo Diary (Slahi) 140, 159
    dissensual narrative strategy 117–27
    "Echo Special" 118, 126, 151
    "Gitmo" 123
    Mauritanians 118–20, 122, 124, 126

Hebdige, Dick 25, 28–9, 154, 156–7, 160
    Subculture 28, 154, 156
Hemingway, Ernest 53, 55, 98
Hickman, Beck 15, 21, 28, 33, 126, 133, 153, 174 n.84
    Murder at Camp Delta (*see Murder at Camp Delta* (Hickman))
Hickman, Joseph 5–6, 9, 13
Hijazi, Ahmed Abdel Mu'ti 50, 56
humanity 10, 17–18, 26, 31, 39–40, 68, 72, 89, 102, 133
Hynes, Samuel, *On War and Writing* 95
hyperobject 26, 43, 62

identity politics 8, 23, 33–4, 49, 51, 53, 57, 132
identity reconstruction 79–80, 90, 112
indoctrination 79–80
international cooperation 47, 84–5, 174
International Principles on the Application of Human Rights to Communication Surveillance 42
Internet 2–3, 5, 9–10, 14, 23, 26, 31, 38, 40–1, 43–4, 48, 62–3, 71, 80, 104, 108, 134, 142, 174 n.84
Internment Serial Numbers 139

Iraq 8, 16–20, 33–4, 36, 46, 48, 56, 83, 86, 90–2, 104, 108–9, 121, 133, 136–7, 155, 157, 161
Iraq War 8, 11, 18, 28, 138
Isocrates 94
Israel 56, 120

Jameson, Frederic 96, 98–9
   "cultural dominant" 96
Jobs, Steve 40
Junger, Sebastian, "In combat" 29

Kakutani, Michiko 98
Kaplan, E. Ann
   "empty empathy" 34
   Trauma Culture: The Politics of Terror and Loss in Media and Literature 34
Kapor, Mitch 44
Kennedy, Joe 114
Kennedy, John F. 39
Kesey, Ken, *One Flew Over the Cuckoo's Nest* 39
Kirchner, Max 62–3, 68
   paper on Snowden and parrhesia (2014) 63
Klay, Phil 7, 15–17, 21, 26, 28, 32–3, 35–9, 48, 82, 91, 93–5, 105, 107, 153–4, 158
   and Ackerman 93
   The Citizen-Soldier: Moral Risk and the Modern Military 4, 7, 149
   "Money as a Weapons System" 49–50
   "patriotic correctness" 37–8
   "Psychological Operations" (*see* "Psychological Operations", *Redeployment* (Klay))
   "The Warrior at the Mall" 31, 35, 37, 78

LaCapra, Dominick, "empathic unsettlement" 99
Lagasnerie, Geoffroy de 21–3, 62–3, 108, 146
   The Art of Revolt 21–2
Lawrence, D. H. 73
Lethem, Jonathan, review of *Permanent Record* 60–2
Levinas, Emmanuel 21
liberty 12, 14, 42, 106, 114–15

liminal zones/liminality 5, 24, 32, 36, 46, 50, 54, 56, 58, 62, 68, 70, 83, 86, 94, 102, 111, 126, 131, 134, 139–40
literary marketplace 33, 57, 93
literary movement 25, 93

Manning, Chelsea 21, 23, 105, 108
martial cosmopolitanism 12, 14, 17, 27–8, 31, 69, 72
Marxism 24, 110, 156
Marx, Leo 50
The Mauritanian film 124
McClure, John 33
McElroy, Wendy 34
McHale, Brian 131
McLuhan, Marshall
   "Typography" 48
   Understanding Media 47–8
modernism 9–10, 13
Molin, Peter 160
"Money as a Weapons System" (Klay) 49
   Nathan ("the Professor") 49–50
monolithic 6, 27–8, 34, 37, 50–1, 54, 79, 96, 100, 109, 112, 121, 156–9
Moore, Alexandra Schultheis 126
Moraru, Christian 40, 52, 69
   Cosmodernism 13
Muñoz, José Esteban 37
Murder at Camp Delta (Hickman) 159
   Ahmed, Ali Abdullah, murder of 5, 139, 142, 147, 149–50, 174–5 n.84
   Camp America 139, 145–6
   Camp Delta 139, 141, 145–6, 174 n.84
   Camp No 139, 145–6
   Chinese reeducation camps 145
   Jose Vasquez 145–6
   "Keystone Kops" 143–4
   NCIS 149, 174 n.84
   Seton Hall project 147–9, 174–5 n.84
   al-Utaybi, Mani, murder of 5, 142, 149–50, 174–5 n.84
   al-Zahrani, Yasser, murder of 139, 142, 147, 149–50, 174–5 n.84
Musk, Elon 155
Muslim 16–17, 19, 53, 94, 120–1, 157

national identity 1, 10, 26, 41, 49, 81, 90, 91, 119, 121, 135, 147
nationalism 11, 24, 41, 99–100, 120, 141, 148

nation-state 2, 5, 7, 15, 25, 31, 45, 67, 73, 89, 93, 118, 132, 155, 161
neogeography 52, 128
new fiction 9
Nussbaum, Martha 10, 12–13, 62, 71–2, 81–3, 87, 104
  on cosmopolitanism/cosmopolitan education 84–5, 87, 174 n.84
  For Love of Country: Debating the Limits of Patriotism 11–13
  "nestling feeling of patriotism" 71
  "Patriotism and Cosmopolitanism" 12

Oakley, Eric 174 n.84
Obama, Barack 22, 36, 89, 159
O'Brien, Tim 55
  The Things They Carried 49
O'Gorman, Daniel 99, 129–30, 132
  "connective dissonance" 99–101, 130
Oliver, John 47
O'Neill, Robert 113
outspokenness 2–3, 8, 13, 16, 20, 35, 79, 94, 110, 113, 124, 127, 142, 153

Pakistan 83, 91, 104
Palestine/Palestinian 88, 120–1
Paley, Grace 32, 72, 82, 161
parrhesia/parrhesiac 3–8, 14–16, 21, 24–5, 27–8, 32, 35, 47–8, 63, 72, 74, 84, 99, 101, 103, 105, 110–11, 117, 123–5, 132, 141, 147, 156, 162, 175 n.84
patriarchy 112
patriotic/patriotism 2, 7, 10, 12–13, 27–8, 31, 38, 71–2, 77, 81, 83, 88, 90, 104, 106, 113, 117, 132, 140, 142, 150, 153–5, 157–8, 161
Percy, Benjamin 128
Permanent Record (Snowden) 25, 31, 60–75, 92, 119, 157
  9/11 terrorist attack 65, 71
  Bill of Rights 74
  cartography 61, 64
  contemporary common sense 70
  geography and parrhesia 63–5, 72
  Hawaii 60–2, 64–73, 157–8
  holidays (religious holidays) 69–71
  human encryption 64, 66, 73–4

  Intelligence Community (IC) 69–70, 92
  Lethem's review of 60–2
  Northern Virginia 26, 32, 61, 65
  patriotism 71–2
  "The Tunnel" 68, 75
  whistleblowers 11, 21, 60, 63, 70–3
  "Whistleblowing" 68–9, 73–4
Personal Democracy Forum 42–3, 46
Phelan, James 64
Philodemus 162
Plutarch 111
Poitras, Laura 63
polysemy 157
postmodern/postmodernism 13, 67, 74, 135, 156
Powers, Kevin 15, 28, 33, 126, 140, 151, 153, 160
  The Yellow Birds (see *The Yellow Birds* (Powers))
"Psychological Operations", *Redeployment* (Klay) 16–21, 25–6, 31, 49–60, 79
  Hijazi's epigraph 50
  Laith al-Tawhid, murder of 19–20, 57–60, 122
  "Lalafallujah" 19–20, 56–8, 60
  language 51–3, 56
  linguistic violence 54
  monolithic identity 50–1, 54
  PsyOps specialist in 52–3, 55–6
  sensory state 9, 17–18, 20
  "Special Assistant" 53–4
  Waguih 16–20, 51–60, 157
  Zara 16–18, 20, 51–60, 157
  Zarqawi 17
Pynchon, Thomas 157

Al Qaeda 86–8, 91, 97, 100, 125

Rancière, Jacques 7, 19, 23, 34, 40, 56, 63, 66, 81–3, 85, 99, 109, 128, 139, 162
  "Consensus" 8
  "consensus of fear" 103, 109, 139
  democracy in literature 17
  Dissensus: Politics and Aesthetics 7–8
  language 51
  The Lost Thread: The Democracy of Modern Fiction 7–9
  "way of life," politics 8

RAND corporation 11
Redeployment (Klay) 49–50, 157
   "Money as a Weapons System" 49–50
   "Psychological Operations" (*see*
     "Psychological Operations",
     Redeployment (Klay))
   "Unless It's A Sucking Chest Wound"
     49
resistance 5, 9, 31, 51–6, 73, 75, 77, 80,
   128, 133, 143, 146, 151, 158
respatialization 23
Revolution and Terror course 174 n.84
rhetoric 1–3, 5, 7, 9, 12–14, 16–17, 21,
   23–5, 27, 31, 33–4, 36–8, 41–3, 45,
   47–8, 64–5, 69, 72, 77, 81, 86, 98,
   104–5, 113–14, 118, 127, 135, 140,
   142, 150, 163
Rogan, Joe 47
Russell, Matheson 24
Russia 1–2, 5, 13, 32–3, 41–3, 46, 61, 72–3,
   121, 158, 162

S.139 bill 2
sacred identity category 51–2, 54, 60, 128
Second World War 66–7, 95. *See also* First
   World War
self-identification 6, 77, 80
*The Senate Intelligence Committee Report
   on CIA Torture* 7
Sharif, Solmaz, "Look" 53
Sheckley, Robert, "Is That What People
   Do?" 61
Shelley, Mary, *Frankenstein* 71
Siems, Larry 119
Simon, Jonathan 35
Slahi, Mohamedou Ould 28, 150
   Guantánamo Diary (*see Guantánamo
     Diary* (Slahi))
Snowden, Edward 1–6, 9, 11, 13, 15, 21–3,
   26, 32–3, 35, 41–8, 80, 82, 94, 105,
   108, 112, 114, 126, 153, 158
   "brave speech" 5
   Permanent Record (*see Permanent
     Record* (Snowden))
   social media (*see* Internet)
social media platforms 1–3, 15, 29, 32,
   41–3, 71, 93, 105–6, 113–15, 155,
   160

Sons of Liberty 5
sovereign/sovereignty 6, 15, 24, 35, 96,
   137, 139, 141
Speckhard, Anne 77, 81, 105–8, 110–13,
   119, 149, 159
Stockholm syndrome 133, 141
subjectivity 3, 16, 21, 38, 47, 53, 61–2, 64,
   66, 99, 106, 108, 111, 140, 146, 153,
   156
Syria 46, 83–6, 88–92, 112

Taylor, Paul 148
territorialized nation 7, 41, 94
Titus, Dina 106
transcendent 36, 42, 102, 141, 153, 162
transgender 15, 77, 79, 88, 91–2, 103–15,
   161
transgression/transgressive 22, 37, 43, 59,
   65, 72, 91, 96, 104–5, 108, 112–13,
   127
transnational/transnationalism 10–12,
   15, 23, 39, 41–4, 47, 83, 88, 90, 112,
   127, 129–30, 141, 159
transtextual 93
Trump, Donald 1, 36, 41, 114–15, 154–5,
   158
truth-tellers 3, 14, 21–2, 29, 47, 63, 75,
   111, 146
truth-telling 3–4, 12, 25, 27–9, 31, 61, 63,
   75, 90, 119, 123, 128, 145, 162
Turkey 83–5, 90–1
Turner, Fred 10
   *From Counterculture to Cyberculture:
     Stewart Brand, the Whole Earth
     Network, and the Rise of Digital
     Utopianism* 40
Turner, Frederick Jackson 43–4
   The Frontier in American History 14

Ukraine 11, 28, 32–3, 121, 154–5, 158
Un Coeur Simple (Flaubert) 109
   Felicity 109–10
The United States 1–2, 4, 8, 32–3, 47,
   62, 64, 79, 84, 88, 91, 104, 119–23,
   126, 132, 134–5, 139–40, 157,
   175 n.84
unsettled territory 99
Updike, John 41

US Patriot Act 139
al-Utaybi, Mani, murder of 5, 139, 142, 147

Veteran Writing Workshop, New York University 154

Walkowitz, Rebecca 13
Walton, Douglas 48
  "simulative reasoning" 63
Walton, Kendall 65, 69, 72
Washington, George 5, 15, 36, 38
Westphal, Bertrand 26, 40, 44, 52, 59, 62, 66–7, 69, 85, 135
  "fictional pragmatics" 65
  "geocriticism" 67
white supremacy 34, 132
Williams, William Carlos 19

Woolf, Virginia 9, 21
working-class 11–12

The Yellow Birds (Powers) 27, 117–18, 127–38
  Bartle, John 128–38, 159
  "flickering effect" 131–2, 134, 137
  Fort Knox, Kentucky 135
  "heterocosm" 131, 135
  Murph 129, 132–4, 136–8, 159
  paratactic language 130–2, 135
  "Regional Confinement Facility" 135
  Sergeant Sterling 130, 133

al-Zahrani, Yasser, murder of 5, 139, 142, 147
Zappa, Frank 157

www.ingramcontent.com/pod-product-compliance
Lightning Source LLC
Chambersburg PA
CBHW052046300426
44117CB00012B/1994